Marietta Holley

## Samantha Among the Colored Folks

My ideas about the race problem

Marietta Holley

**Samantha Among the Colored Folks**
*My ideas about the race problem*

ISBN/EAN: 9783743335974

Manufactured in Europe, USA, Canada, Australia, Japa

Cover: Foto ©Suzi / pixelio.de

Manufactured and distributed by brebook publishing software (www.brebook.com)

Marietta Holley

**Samantha Among the Colored Folks**

# Samantha Among the Colored Folks

"My Ideas on the Race Problem"

By

JOSIAH ALLEN'S WIFE
(MARIETTA HOLLEY)

Illustrated by E. W. KEMBLE

New York
Dodd, Mead and Company
Publishers

COPYRIGHT, 1892, 1894,
BY
DODD, MEAD & COMPANY.

*All rights reserved.*

## PUBLISHER'S NOTE.

SAMANTHA ON THE RACE PROBLEM was the title adopted for the editions of this book that were issued exclusively for the subscription market.

In preparing the new edition for popular sale it has been deemed advisable to change its title to SAMANTHA AMONG THE COLORED FOLKS as one more in keeping with its character. Otherwise its contents remain the same.

# LIST OF ILLUSTRATIONS.

|  | PAGE |
|---|---|
| "They wuz Tracts and Bibles" | 7 |
| Uncle Nate Gowdey | 12 |
| "The dumb Fools!" | 18 |
| A Black | 21 |
| "The old and feeble Ones" | 30 |
| "I sot demute" | 34 |
| "The dark Faces of these Apostles" | 40 |
| "With Philury's Help" | 46 |
| Character Sketch | 51 |
| "When Ury had that Fight with Sam" | 56 |
| Melinda | 61 |
| Melinda has a Fit | 63 |
| "It wuz 'Hold the Fort' he belched out in" | 69 |
| "I ketched her by her Limb" | 73 |
| Peter and Melinda Ann | 77 |
| Deacon Henzy | 83 |
| "Josiah's bald Head and Mine" | 86 |
| The Colored Children | 93 |
| Old Dr. Cork | 99 |
| The Slave Woman who poisoned the Child | 104 |
| Madeline | 110 |
| Colonel Seybert | 122 |
| "Low, brutal, envious Mind" | 128 |
| Defending his Home | 133 |
| The Leader | 138 |
| Felix and the Teacher | 143 |

| | PAGE |
|---|---|
| "The Old, the Feeble" | 149 |
| "His Overseer" | 153 |
| "A little tumble-down Cottage" | 155 |
| Cleopatra | 156 |
| Rosy | 161 |
| "He wuz glad to set down" | 167 |
| The old Negro | 172 |
| "Gawge Perkins am Daid" | 176 |
| One of the Mourners | 179 |
| "You can repair your Dwellin' House | 185 |
| "And I have got the Pans" | 189 |
| "I am needed there" | 192 |
| "The Butter-Maker up in Zoar" | 194 |
| "Josiah give up" | 196 |
| Deacon Huffer | 208 |
| "Under the white Cross" | 211 |
| The Jonesvillians | 215 |
| "Boy laughed" | 220 |
| Raymond Fairfax Coleman | 223 |
| "With a jumpin' Toothache" | 225 |
| "The Relation on Maggie's Side" | 230 |
| Babe | 237 |
| "My Tone riz up" | 239 |
| "I had been out a walkin'" | 242 |
| A Poor White | 244 |
| Rosy's Baby | 254 |
| Ury | 256 |
| Some Neighbors | 258 |
| Aunt Mela | 264 |
| "Despatched to get Buttermilk" | 271 |
| "The big Piazza" | 277 |
| "A perfect Dagon" | 279 |
| A Ku-Kluxer | 291 |
| "Pilot a helpless Unionist" | 296 |

## LIST OF ILLUSTRATIONS.

|  | PAGE |
|---|---|
| "Set down in our Swamp" | 301 |
| "He hastened off" | 305 |
| "To kiss Snow and Boy good-night" | 308 |
| "And killed her Hens" | 312 |
| "Onexpected Company" | 316 |
| "Misery" | 320 |
| "Wherefoah, Bredren, let us pray" | 322 |
| Abe | 326 |
| "He wuz a walkin' up and down" | 331 |
| "This dark Earth Valley" | 334 |
| Hiram Wiggins's two Daughters | 338 |
| "A clear River running through" | 343 |
| "Everything wuz ready" | 347 |
| "In the Chair of the Ruler" | 353 |
| "Faced the Gang of masked Men" | 360 |
| "When the Moon had risen" | 363 |
| "Exiled Birds" | 369 |
| Victor | 373 |
| "Makin' Speeches" | 375 |
| Father Gasperin | 378 |
| "Felix, his Wife and Little Ned" | 380 |
| "I sot out on the Stoop" | 384 |

"THEY WUZ TRACTS AND BIBLES."

## CHAPTER 1.

IT was entirely onexpected and onlooked for. But I took it as a Decree, and done as well as I could, which is jest as well as anybody ought to be expected to do under any circumstances, either on my side or on hisen.

It was one of the relations on his side that come on to us entirely onexpected and on the evenin' stage that runs from Jonesville to Loontown. He was a passin' through this part of the country on business, so he stopped off at Jonesville to see us.

He come with his portmanty and a satchel, and I mistrusted, after consultin' them signs in the privacy of my own mind, that he had come to stay for quite a spell.

But I found in the fulness of time that my worst apprehensions wuz not realized.

I found instead of pantaloons and vests and things which I suspected wuz in the big satchel, I found out they wuz tracts and Bibles.

Why, I wuz fairly took aback when I discovered this fact, and felt guilty to think I had been cast down, and spozed things that wuzn't so.

But whether they are on his side or on your own, visitors that come when you are deep in house-cleanin', and most all your carpets took up, and your beds oncorded, and your buttery shelves dry and arid, can't be welcomed with quite the cordiality you would show one in more different and prosperous times.

But we found out after a little conversation that Cousin John Richard Allen wuz a colporter, and didn't lay out to stay only one night. So, as I say, I done the best I could with him, and felt my conscience justified.

He had a dretful good look to his face, for all mebby he wouldn't be called beautiful. His eyes wuz deep and brilliant and clear, with a meanin' in 'em that comes from a pure life and a high endeavor —a generous, lovin' soul.

Yes, though it wuz one on his side instid of mine, justice makes me say he seemed to be a good feller, and smart as a whip, too. And he seemed to feel real friendly and cousinly towards us, though I had never laid eyes on him more than once or twice before. Josiah had known him when they wuz boys.

He had lived in Vermont, and had been educated high, been through college, and preachin' schools of the best kind, and had sot out in life as a minister, but bein' broke up with quinsy, and havin' a desire to be in some Christian work, he took to colporterin', and had been down in the Southern States to work amongst the freedmen for years.

He went not long after the war closed. I guess he hated to give up preachin', for I believe my soul that he wanted to do good, and bein' so awful smart it wuz a cross, I know—and once in a while he would kind o' forget himself, and fall into a sort o' preachin', eloquent style of talkin', even when he wuz conversin' on such subjects as butter, and hens, and farmin', and such. But I know he did it entirely onbeknown to himself.

And to the table—the blessin' he asked wuz as likely a one as I ever see run at anybody's table, but it wuz middlin' lengthy, as long about as a small-sized sermon.

Josiah squirmed—I see he did, he squirmed hard, though he is a good Christian man. He wuz afraid the cream biscuit would be spilte by the delay; they are his favorites, and though I am fur from bein' the one that ought to speak of it, my biscuit are called delicious.

And though I hate to say it, hate to show any onwillingness to be blessed to any length by so good a man and so smart a one—yet I must say them biscuit wuzn't the biscuit they would have been had the blessin' been more briefer, and they had been eat earlier.

Howsomever, they wuz pretty good ones after all, and Cousin John Richard partook of five right along one after the other, and seemed to enjoy the fifth one jest as well as he did the earlier editions. They wuzn't very large, but light, and tender.

Wall, after supper, he and my pardner sot down in the settin'-room, while I wuz a washin' up the dishes, and a settin' the sponge for my griddle-cakes for breakfast.

And I hearn 'em a talkin' about Uncle Noah, and Uncle Darius, and Cousin Melinda, and Sophronia Ann, and Aunt Marrier and her children—and lots more that I had never hearn of, or had forgot if I had.

They seemed to be a takin' solid comfort, though I see that Cousin John Richard every time he got a chance would kinder preach on 'em.

If there wuz a death amongst 'em that they talked over, John Richard would, I see, instinctively and onbeknown to himself preach a little funeral sermon on 'em, a first-rate one, too, though flowery, and draw quite a lot of morals. Wall, I thought to myself, they are a takin' sights of comfort together, and I am glad on it. I dearly love to see my pardner happy.

When all of a sudden, jest as I had got my sponge all wet up, and everything slick, and I wuz a washin' my hands to the sink, I see there wuz a more excited, voyalent axent a ringin' out in my pardner's voice, I see he wuz a gettin' het up in some argument or other, and I hurried and changed my gingham bib apron for a white one, and took my knittin' work and hastened into the room, bein' anxious to avert horstilities, and work for peace.

And I see I wuz only jest in time; for my companion wuz a gettin' agitated and excited to a high degree, and Cousin John Richard all rousted up.

And the very first words I hearn after I went in wuz these offensive and quarrelsome words that do so much to stir up strife and dessensions—

They have madded me time and agin. They proceeded out of my companion's mouth, and the words wuz:

"Oh shaw!"

I see in a minute that John Richard couldn't brook 'em. And I wunk to Josiah Allen to stop, and let Cousin John Richard go on and say what he wuz a minter, both as a visiter, who wuz goin' to remain with us but a short period, and also a relation, and a ex-minister.

My wink said all of this, and more. And my companion wuz affected by it. But like a child a cryin' hard after bein' spanked, he couldn't stop short off all to once.

So he went on, but in fur mellerer axents, and more long-sufferin'er ones:

"Wall, I say there is more talk than there is any need of. I don't believe things are to such a pass in the South. I don't take much stock in this Race Problem anyway. The Government whipped the South and freed the niggers. And there it is, all finished and done with. And everything seems quiet so fur as I can hear on.

"I hain't heard nuthin' about any difficulty to speak on, nor I don't believe Uncle Nate Gowdey has, or Sime Bently. And if there wuz much of anything wrong goin' on, one of us three would have been apt to have hearn on it.

"For we are, some of us, down to the corners about every night, and get all the news there is a stirrin'.

"Of course there is some fightin' everywhere. Uncle Nate hearn of a new fight last night, over to Loontown. We get holt of everything. And I don't believe there is any trouble down South, and if there is, they will get along well enough if they are left alone, if there hain't too much said."

**UNCLE NATE GOWDEY.**

Sez John Richard, "I have lived in the South for years, and I know what I am talking about. And I say that you Northern people, and in fact all the nation, are like folks sitting on the outside of a volcano, laughing and talking in your gay indifference, and thinking the whole nation is in safety, when the flames and the lava torrents of destruction are liable to burst out at any time and overwhelm this land in ruin."

And then agin, though I hate to set it down—then agin did my pardner give vent to them dangerous and quarrelsome sentiments before I could reach him with a wink or any other precautionary measures. That rash man said agin:

"Oh shaw!"

And I see, devoted Christian as John Richard wuz, the words gaulded him almost more than he could endure, and he broke out in almost heated axents, and his keen dark eye a flashin', and says he:

"I tell you the storm is brewing! I have watched it coming up and spreading over the land, and unless it is averted, destruction awaits this people."

His tone wuz a very preachin' one, very, and I felt considerable impressed by it; but Josiah Allen spoke up pert as a peacock, and sez he:

"Why don't the Southern folks behave themselves, then?"

And sez John Richard:

"Do you blame the Southern white folks exclusively?"

"Yes," sez Josiah, in them same pert axents; "yes, of course I do."

"Then that shows how short-sighted you are, how blind!"

"I can see as well as you can!" sez Josiah, all wrought up—"I don't have to wear goggles."

Oh, how mortified, how mortified I felt! John Richard did wear blue goggles when he wuz travellin'. But what a breach of manners to twit a visiter of such a thing! Twit 'em of goggles, blue ones too! I felt as if I should sink.

But I didn't know Cousin John Richard Allen. He hadn't give up ease and comfort and the joys of a fireside, for principle's sake, for nuthin'. No personal allusions could touch him. The goggles fell onto him harmlessly, and fell off agin. He didn't notice 'em no more'n if they hadn't been throwed.

And he went on growin' more and more sort o' lifted up and inspired-lookin', and a not mindin' what or who wuz round him. And sez he:

"I tell you again the storm is rising; I hear its mutterings in the distance, and it is coming nearer and nearer all the time."

Josiah kinder craned his neck and looked out of the winder in a sort of a brisk way. He misunderstood him a purpose, and acted as if John Richard meant a common thunder-storm.

But Cousin John Richard never minded him, bein' took up and intent on what his own mind wuz a lookin' at onbeknown to us—

"I have been amongst this people night and day for years; I have been in the mansions of the rich, the ruins of the beautiful homes ruined by the war, and in the cabins of the poor. I have been in their schools and their churches, and the halls where the law is misadministered—I have been through the Southern land from one end to the other—and I know what I am talking about.

"I went there to try to help the freedmen. I knew these people so lately enslaved were poor and ignorant, and I thought I could help them.

"But I was almost as ignorant as you are of the

real state of affairs in the South. But I have been there and seen for myself, and I tell you, and I tell this nation, that we are on the eve of another war if something is not done to avert it."

My pardner wuz jest a openin' his mouth in a derisive remark, but I hitched my chair along and trod on his foot, and onbeknown to me it wuz the foot on which he wuz raisin' a large corn, and his derisive remark wuz changed to a low groan, and Cousin John Richard went on onhendered.

"I went South with good motives, God knows. I knew this newly enfranchised race was sorely in want of knowledge, Christian knowledge most of all.

"I thought, as so many others do, that Christianity and education would solve this problem. I never stopped to think that the white race, of whose cruelty the negroes complained, had enjoyed the benefits of Christianity for hundreds of years, and those whose minds were enriched by choicest culture had hearts encased in bitterest prejudices, and it was from the efforts of their avarice and selfishness that I was trying to rescue the freedmen. We accomplished much, but I expected, as so many others have, choicer Christian fruits to spring from this barren soil, that has grown in the rich garden cultivated for centuries.

"Education has done and will do much—Christianity more; but neither can sound a soundless deep, nor turn black night into day.

"But I never thought of this. I worked hard and meant well, Heaven knows. I thought at first I could do marvellous things; later, when many failures had made me more humble, I thought if I could help only one soul my labor would not be in vain. For who knows," sez John Richard dreamily, "who knows the tremendous train of influences one sets in motion when he is under God enabled to turn one life about from the path of destruction towards the good and the right?

"Who knows but he is helping to kindle a light that shall yet lighten the pathway of a Toussaint L'Ouverture or a Fred Douglass on to victory, and a world be helped by the means?

"And if only one soul is helped, does not the Lord of the harvest say, 'He that turns one man from the error of his ways has saved a soul from death'?"

Cousin John Richard's eye looked now as if he wuz a gazin' deep into the past—the past of eager and earnest endeavor, and way beyend it into the past that held a happy home, and the light from that forsaken fireside seemed to be a shinin' up into his face, divinely sad, bitter sweet, as he went on:

"I loved my wife and children as well as another man, but I left them and my happy, happy home to go where duty called.

"My wife could not endure that hot climate, and she lay dying when I was so far South that I could not get to her till she had got so far down in the Valley that she could not hear my voice when I spoke to her."

Ah! the waves of memory wuz a dashin' hard aginst Cousin John Richard then, as we could see. It splashed some of the spray up into his bright eyes.

But he kept on: "I was rich enough then to put

my children to school, which I did, and then returned to my labors.

"I loved my work—I felt for it that enthusiasm and devotion that nerves the heart to endure any trials—and I don't speak of the persecutions I underwent in that work as being harder than what many others endured.

"You know what they passed through who preached the higher truth in Jerusalem. The Book says, 'They were persecuted, afflicted, tormented, had cruel buffetings and scourgings, were burned, were tortured, not accepting deliverance.'

"In the early days after the war, in some parts of the South there were hardly any indignities that could be inflicted upon us that we were not called upon to endure. We had our poor houses burned down over our heads, our Bible and spelling-books thrown into the flames; we have had rifles pointed at our breasts, and were ordered to leave on peril of death.

"And many, many more than you Northerners have any idea of met their death in the dark cypress forests and in the dreary, sandy by-ways of the Southern States.

"They died, 'not accepting deliverance' by cowardly flight. How many of them thus laid down their lives for conscience' sake will never be known till that hour when *He* comes to make up His jewels.

"I bear the marks upon me to-day, and shall carry them to my grave, of the tortures inflicted upon me to make me give up my work of trying to help the weak and seek and save them that were lost."

"The dumb fools!" hollered out Josiah. "What

did they act so like idiots for—and villains? The Southerners always did act like the Old Harry anyway."

My dear companion is fervid and impassioned in his feelin's and easily wrought on, and he felt what

"THE DUMB FOOLS!"

he said. John Richard wuz a relation on his own side, and he could not calmly brook the idee of his sufferin's.

But Cousin John didn't look mad, nor excited, nor anything. He had a sort of a patient look onto his face, and as if he had tried to reason things out for some time.

"Such a state of affairs was inevitable," sez he.

"Then you don't blame the cussed fools, do you?" yelled out Josiah, fearfully wrought up and agitated.

Oh, what a word to use, and to a minister too—"cussed"! I felt as if I should sink right down into the suller—I wuz about over the potato ben—and I didn't much care if I did sink, I felt so worked up.

But Cousin John Richard didn't seem to mind it at all. He had got up into a higher region than my soul wuz a sailin' round in—he had got up so high that little buzzin', stingin' insects that worried me didn't touch him; he had got up into a calm, pure atmosphire where they couldn't fly round.

He went on calm as a full moon on a clear night, and sez he:

"It is difficult to put the blame for this state of affairs on any one class, the evil is so far spread. The evil root was planted centuries ago, and we are partaking of its poison fruit to-day.

"In looking on such a gigantic wrong we must look on it on other sides than the one whose jagged edges have struck and bruised us—we must look on it on every side in order to be just.

"After years and years of haughty supremacy, ambition and pride growing rankly, as they must in such a soil, fostered, it would seem, by Northern indolence and indifference, the South was conquered by armed force—brought down to the humiliation of defeat by a successful, if generous foe.

"And then, what was far harder for them to endure, a race of people that they had looked upon much as you look upon your herd of cattle was suddenly raised from a condition of servitude to one of legal equality, and in many cases of supremacy.

"It was hard for this hot-blooded, misguided, warm-hearted Southern people to lose at once all their brilliant dreams of an independent, aristocratic Confederacy—it was hard for them to lose home, and country, and wealth, and ambition at one blow.

"It was hard for their proud, ambitious leader to have his beautiful old country home, full of aristocratic associations and sweet memories, turned into the national graveyard.

"And this one tragedy that changed this sweet home into a mausoleum is not a bad illustration of what the Southern people endured.

"No matter what brought this thing about—no matter where the blame rested—it was *hard* for them to stand by the graves of their loved ones, who fell fighting for the lost cause—to stand amongst the ruins of their dismantled homes, and know that their proud, ambitious dreams were all ended.

"But this they could endure—it was the fortune of war, and they had to submit. But to this other indignity, as they called it, they would *not* submit.

"Through centuries of hereditary influences and teachings this belief was ingrained, born in them, bone of their bone, flesh of their flesh, soul of their soul, implanted first by nature, then hardened and made invulnerable by centuries of habits, beliefs, and influences—this instinctive, hereditary contempt and aversion for the black race only as servants.

"And they *would not* endure to have them made their equals.

"Now, no preaching, be it with the tongue of men

or angels, could vanquish this ingrained, inexorable foe, this silent, overmastering force that rose up on every side to set at naught our preaching.

A BLACK.

"After twenty-five years of Christian effort it remains the same, and at the end of a century of Gospel work it will still be there just the same.

"And those who do not take into consideration

this overwhelming power of antagonism between the races when they are considering the Southern question are fools.

"The whites *will* not look upon the negroes as their equals, and you cannot make them—"

"Wall, they be!" hollered out Josiah. "The Proclamation made 'em free and equal, jest as we wuz made in the War of 1812."

"But oh, what a difference!" sez Cousin John Richard sadly.

"The American colonies were the peers of the mother country. It was only a quarrel between children and mother. The same blood ran in their veins, they had the same traits, the same minds, the same looks, they were truly equal.

"But in this case it was an entirely different race, necessarily inferior by their long years of degradation, brought up at one bound from the depths of ignorance and servitude to take at once the full rights awarded to intellect and character.

"It was a great blunder; it was a sad thing for the white race and for the black race!"

Josiah wuz jest a openin' his mouth to speak in reply to Cousin John Richard's last words, when all of a sudden we heard a knock at the door, and I went and opened it, and there stood Miss Eben Garlock, and I asked her to come in, and sot her a chair.

I never over and above liked Miss Eben Garlock, though she is a likely woman enough so fur as I know.

But she is one of the kind of wimmen who orniment the outside of their heads more than the inside, and so on with their hearts and souls, etc.

She is a great case for artificial flowers, and ribbin loops, and fringes. And the flowers that wuz a blowin' out on her bunnet that day *would* have gone a good ways towards fillin' a half-bushel basket. And the loops that wuz a hangin' all round her boddist waist would have straightened out into half a mile of ribbin, I do believe.

The ribbin wuz kinder rusty, and she had pinned on a bunch of faded red poppies on to the left side of her boddist waist, pretty nigh, I should judge, over her heart.

Which goes to prove what I said about her trimmin' off the outside of her heart and soul.

Her clothes are always of pretty cheap material, but showy, and made after sort o' foamin' patterns, with streamers, and her favorite loops and such. And they always have a look as if they wuz in danger of fallin' off of her. She uses pins a good deal, and they drop out considerable and leave gaps.

Wall, I always use her well; so, as I say, I sot her a chair and introduced her to Cousin John Richard, and he bowed polite to her, and then leaned back in his chair and seemed restin'. Good land! I should thought he'd wanted to.

Miss Garlock seemed real agitated and excited, and I remembered hearin' that forenoon that they had lost a relation considerable distant to 'em. He lived some fifteen or sixteen miles away.

He and Eben Garlock's folks had never agreed; in fact, they had hated each other the worst kind. But now Miss Garlock, bein' made as she wuz, wuz all nerved up to make a good appearance to the funeral and show off.

She had come to borry my mournin' suit that I had used to mourn for Josiah's mother in; and I am that careful of my clothes that they wuz as good as new, though I had mourned in 'em for a year. Mournin' for some folks hain't half so hard on clothes as mournin' for others; tears spots black crape awful, and sithes are dretful hard on whalebones; my clothes wuz good, good as new.

But I am a eppisodin', and to resoom.

Miss Garlock wanted to borry my hull suit down to shoes and stockin's for Eben's mother, who lived with her. She herself wuz a goin' to borry Miss Slimpsey's dress—she that wuz Betsey Bobbets—it wuz trimmed more and more foamin' lookin'. But she wanted my black fan for herself, and my mournin' handkerchief pin, it bein' a very showy one. Ury had gin it to me, and I never had mourned in it but once, and then not over two hours, at a church social, for I felt it wuz too dressy for me. But Miss Garlock had seen it on that occasion and admired it.

And then, after I had told her she could have all these things in welcome, she kinder took me out to one side and asked me "if I had jest as lives lend her a Bible for a few days. She thought like as not the minister would call to talk with Eben's mother, and she felt that she should be mortified if he should call for a Bible, for they had all run out of Bibles," she said.

"The last one they had by 'em had jest been chawed up by a pup Eben wuz a raisin'; she had ketched him a worryin' it out under the back stoop. She said he had chawed it all up but a part o' the Old

Testament, and he wuz a worryin' and gnawin' Maleky when she got it away from him."

Wall, I told her she could have the Bible, and she asked me to have the things done up by the time they got back from Miss Slimpsey's, and I told her I would, and I did.

Wall, if you'd believe it, I had hardly got them things done up in a bundle and laid 'em on the table ready for Miss Garlock, when that blessed man, John Richard, commenced agin right where he left off, and sez he, a repeatin' his last words as calmly as if there had been no Garlock eppisode

"It was a great blunder, a sad thing for the white race and the black race."

"Wall, what would you have done?" sez Josiah.

"I don't know," sez Cousin John sadly—"I don't know; perhaps mistakes were inevitable. The question was so great and momentous, and the danger and the difficulties seemed so impenetrable on every side."

"Lincoln did the best he could," sez Josiah sturdily; "and I know it."

"And so do I know it," sez Cousin John. "That wise, great heart could not make any other mistake only a mistake of judgment, and he was sorely tried to know what was best to do. The burden weighed down upon him so, I fancy he was glad to lay it down in any way.

"The times were so dark that any measure adopted for safety was only groping towards the light, only catching at the first rope of safety that seemed to lower itself through the heavy clouds of war.

"The heavy eyes and true hearts watching

through those black hours will never be forgotten by this republic.

"And now, in looking back and criticising the errors of that time, it is like the talk of those who are watching a storm at sea, when, in order to save the ship, wrong ropes may be seized, and life-boats cast out into the stormy waves may be swept down and lost. But if the ship is saved, let the survivors of the crew forever bless and praise the brave hands and hearts that dared the storm and the peril.

"But when the sky is clearer you can see more plainly than when the tempest is whirling about you and death and ruin are riding on the gale.

"You can see plainer and you can see farther.

"Now, it was a great and charitable idea, looking at it from one side, to let those who had tried their best to ruin the Union at once take an equal place with those who had perilled life and property to save it—to give them *at once* the same rights in making the laws they had set at defiance.

"It was a generous and charitable idea, looking on it from one side, but from another side it looked risky, very risky, and it looked dangerous to the urther peace and perpetuity of that Union.

"A little delay might not have done any harm—a little delay in giving them the full rights of citizenship.

"And it might, Heaven knows, have been as well if the slaves had had a gradual bringing up of mind and character to meet the needs of legal responsibility, if they had not been *at once* invested with all the rights and responsibilities which well-trained Christian scholars find it so difficult to assume, if they had not been required to solve by the ballot deep questions of statesmanship, the names of which they could not spell out in the newspaper.

"Could such ignorance make them otherwise than a dangerous element in politics, dangerous to themselves and dangerous to the welfare of the Union?

"Tossed back and forth as they were between two conflicting parties, in their helplessness and ignorance becoming the prey of the strongest faction, compelled, at the point of the sword and the muzzle of the revolver, to vote as the white man made them—the law of Might victorious over the Right—it was a terrible thing for the victim, and a still worse one for the victor.

"What could happen in such a state of affairs only trouble and misery, evasions and perversions of the law, uprisings of the oppressed, secret bands of armed men intent on deeds of violence, whose only motives were to set at naught the law, to fight secretly against the power they had been openly forced to yield to.

"What could happen save warfare, bloodshed, burning discontent, and secret nursing of wrongs amongst the blacks; hatred towards the Union amongst the whites, towards the successful foe who had humiliated them so beyond endurance by this last blow of forcing them into a position of equality towards their former slaves, and rousing up in them a more bitter animosity towards the poor blacks who had been the innocent cause of their humiliation."

"Wall, what could have been done?" sez Josiah.

"It is hard to tell," sez John Richard. "It is a hard problem to solve; and perhaps," sez Cousin

John, lookin' some distance off—"perhaps it was God's own way of dealing with this people.

"You know, after the children of Israel had broken the chains of their bondage and passed through the Red Sea, they were encamped in the wilderness for forty years before they reached the Land of Promise.

"Maybe it is God's way of dealing with this people, to make them willing to press forward through the wilderness of their almost unendurable trials and go forward into their own country, from whence their fathers were stolen by these pale faces, and there, in that free, fresh land to found a new republic of their own.

"And with all the education and civilization they have gathered during these long, miserable years of slavery, helped by all they have learned, taught by their losses as well as their gains, found a new republic that shall yet take its place as one of the great nations of the world—yes, perhaps lead the nations, and reveal God's glory in higher, grander forms than colder-blooded races have ever dreamed of. For it has seemed as if this people have been peculiarly under His protection and care.

"All through this long, bloody War of the Rebellion, when it would seem as if the black race must be crushed between either the upper or lower millstone of raging sectional warfare, they simply, as if bidden by a higher power than was seen marching with the armies, 'stood still and saw the salvation of the Lord.'"

"Where would you have 'em set up for themselves?" sez Josiah, a lookin' some sleepy, but holdin', as it were, his eyes open with a effort. "Would you have 'em go to Mexico, or Brazil, or where?"

"To Africa," sez Cousin John Richard, "or that is what is in my own mind. I don't know that it would be better than another place, but I think so."

"But, good land!" sez Josiah, lookin' more wakeful, "think of the cost. Why, it would run the Government in debt to that extent that it never would get over it." He looked skairt at the idee. But Cousin John didn't; he wuz calm and serene as he went on:

"Thousands and thousands would be able and willing to go on their own account. But if this nation took them all back at its own expense, is it not a lawful debt? Who brought them here in the first place? They did not come of their own accord; no, they were stolen, hunted like beasts of prey amongst their own fields and forests, felled like wild animals, and dragged, bleeding from their wounds, into slave ships to be packed into a living cargo of sweltering agony, and brought off from friends and home and native land for our selfishness' sake, to add to our wealth.

"It seems to me we owe them a debt that we should pay for our own conscience' sake as a nation."

"But the Government couldn't afford it; it would cost too much." Josiah is very close.

"As I said," sez Cousin John Richard, "thousands of the more intelligent ones who have property of their own would go at their own expense for the sake of founding free, peaceful homes, where their children could have the advantages of inde-

"THE OLD AND FEEBLE ONES."

pendence, freed from the baleful effects of class antagonism and race prejudices.

"Many of the old and feeble ones, and those who were prosperous and well off, would not go at all. And of those who remained, if the Government should transport them and support them there for a year it would not cost a twentieth part so much as to carry on a civil war.

"And I tell you war will come, Josiah Allen, if something is not done to avert the storm."

And agin John Richard's eyes took on that fur-off look, as if he wuz lookin' at things dretful some distance off.

"Amongst the lower classes you can hear muttered curses and half-veiled threats, and you feel their passion and their burning hatred towards the race that gave them the Indian gift of freedom—gave it, and then snatched it out of their hands, and instead of liberty gave them injustice and worse oppression.

"And the storm is coming up. Evil spirits are in the atmosphere. Over the better feelings of the white race, dominating them, are the black shapes of contempt and repulsion towards the race once their servants, made their equals by a wordy fiction of their enemies, but still under their feet.

"And in their haughty breasts, as of old, only stronger, is the determination to have their own way, to rule this 'ignorant rabble,' to circumvent the cowardly will of their Northern foe, who had brought this thing to pass, to still rule them in one way if not in another—rule or ruin.

"And the storm is coming up the heavens. The lightning is being stored, and the tempest of hail, the burning lightning, and deafening thunder peals are awaiting this day of wrath when the storm shall burst.

"And you sit on in your ease and will not believe it."

His eyes wuz bent on my pardner's form, who wuz leanin' back in a almost luxurious attitude in his soft copper-plate-covered rockin' chair, but I see he didn't mean him in particeler; no, his eyes had in 'em a wide, deep look that took in the hull country, North and South, and he went on in almost eloquent axents:

"The Northern soldier who twenty-five years ago hung up his old rifle and powder-horn with a sigh of content that the war against oppression and slavery had been won still sits under them in content and self-admiration of his prowess, and heeds not at all the signs in the heavens.

"And the wise men in the National Capital sit peacefully in their high places and read over complacently the words they wrote down a quarter of a century ago:

"'All slaves are free.'

"And the bandage that Justice wears, having slipped too far down over their wise eyes, they have not seen the handcuffs and chains that have weighed down the still enslaved.

"And they read these words:

"'We proclaim peace in all your borders.'

"And lost in triumphant thoughts of what they had done, they did not heed this truth, that instead of peace hovering down upon the borders of the fair Southern land, they had blindly and ignorantly, no doubt, let loose the bitter, corroding, wearing curse of animosity and ignorant misrule.

"Yes, those wise men had launched these turbulent spirits instead of peace on the heads of the free and enlightened, if bigoted white people of the South, and upon the black race.

"And never stopped to think, so it would seem, whether three millions strong of an ignorant, superstitious, long-degraded people, the majority of whom could not read nor write, and were ignorant of the first principles of truth and justice, could suddenly be lifted up to become the peers, and in many cases the superiors, of a cultured and refined people who had had long ages of culture and education behind them, and, above all, class prejudices.

"They never paused to ask themselves whether it was in reality just to the white race, or whether this superior class would quietly submit to the legal equality and rule of the inferior.

"The difficulty of this problem did not seem to strike them, whether by any miracle the white race would at once forget its pride and its prejudices.

"Whether by a legal enactment a peacock could be made to change its plumage for the sober habit of a dove, or an eagle develop the humility of a snail.

"The wise men expected to do more than this, and failed.

"And they never seemed to ponder this side of the question : Whether it was not cruelty to the weaker class to thus raise up to a greater strength the prejudice and animosity of the dominant race.

"And whether this premature responsibility they had caused them to assume was not as cruel as to put knives and rifles into the hands of babies, and send them out to fight a battle with giants—fight or die.

"And so these wise men, having done their best,

"I SOT DEMUTE."

it would seem, to rouse the blind passions and intensify the ignorant prejudice and class hatred of the blacks, sit at their ease.

"And so the farce has been played out before a

pitying heaven, and has been for a quarter of a century, growing more pitiful to look at year by year.

"The farce of slave and tyrant masquerading in the robes of liberty and equality, and the poor Northern zealot playing well his part with a fool's cap and bells. The weak crushed and trodden under foot, the strong shot down by secret violence—murder, rapine, and misrule taking the part of law, and both races swept along to their ruin like a vision of the night."

Why, John Richard's talk wuz such, he looked on things so different from what I ever had, he put such new and strange idees into my head that I can truly say that he skairt me most to death. I sot demute; I didn't even think to look to see how my pardner wuz affected by the startlin' views he wuz promulgatin'. I dropped stitches, I seamed where I hadn't ought to seam; I wuz extremely nerved up and agitated, and he went on a talkin' more stranger and startlinger than ever, if possible.

"And still these wise men sit and hardly lift their wise eyes. *But when the storm bursts*," sez Cousin John Richard, in a louder voice than he had used, and more threatenin' like and prophetic—" when the storm bursts, methinks these wise men will look up, will get up if there is enough left of them to stand after the shock and the violence of the tempest has torn and dashed over them. For the clouds *will* fill with vengeance, the storm *will* burst if something is not done soon to avert the fury of its course.

"Now, this nation can solve this great question peacefully if it will."

And I sez in agitated axents:

"How?"

I wuz fearful wrought up. I never had mistrusted there wuz such a state of things anywhere; it come all onbeknown onto me, and sort o' paralyzed my faculties. I had forgot by this time, if you'll believe it, whether I wuz a knittin' or a tattin'. Why, I shouldn't have been surprised if somebody had spoke up and said I wuz a shearin' a sheep or pickin' a goose. I shouldn't have sensed it, as I know of, I wuz so dumbfounded and lost and by the side of myself.

Sez I, "How?"

And sez he, "Let the colored race go into a home and a country of their own. Let them leave the people and the influences that paralyze and hinder their best efforts. Let them leave a race that they burden and hamper and oppress, for injustice reacts worse upon the victor than upon the victim. The two races cannot live together harmoniously; they have tried the experiment for hundreds of years, and failed."

I murmured almost mechanically:

"Won't religion and education make 'em harmoniouser?"

But before John Richard could answer my question, Eben Garlock come in for the mournin' bundle, and I gin it to him.

He said he couldn't set down, but still he didn't seem ready to go

Everybody has such visitors that don't want to go and don't want to stay, and you have to use head work to get 'em started either way.

Eben is different from his wife ; he is more sincere

and open-hearted, and hain't so affected. He speaks out more than she duz, and finally he told us what wuz on his mind.

I see he had on a good new black overcoat, and the case wuz he wanted to swop with Josiah for the day of the funeral, and take his old London brown overcoat.

And I sez, "For the land's sake! Why?"

"Wall," sez he, a lookin' real candid and sincere as he said it, "the fact is, you know the corpse and I never agreed with each other, and everybody knows it; and I don't want to act as if I wuz a mournin' too much. I hate deceit," sez he.

"Wall," sez I, "if that is how you feel you can take the coat in welcome."

And Josiah sez, "Yes, of course you can have it."

And Eben took off his glossy new black overcoat and put on Josiah's old shabby brown one and sot off. And I don't know how he and his wife settled it, and I don't much care.

Wall, if you'll believe it, Eben hadn't much more'n got into his buggy at the gate when Cousin John Richard began agin, took up his remarks jest where he had laid 'em down. I don't spoze he sensed Eben's comin' in hardly any.

I spoze it wuz some as if a fly should light on the nose of a Fourth of July oritor, it would be brushed off without noticin' it, and the oration would go right on.

Sez John Richard, "All the religion and education in the world cannot make the two races unite harmoniously and become one people, with kindred tastes and united hearts and interests."

Sez I agin, speakin' mechanically, "You think the foot is too big for the shoe?"

"Yes, exactly," sez he. "The shoe is a good sound one, but the foot is too big; it won't go into it."

"But," sez I, "as Josiah remarked to you, wouldn't it cost awfully?"

"Will it cost any less ten years from now? The colored population of the South increases at the rate of five hundred every twenty-four hours.

"By the most careful estimates it has been found that in less than twenty years the black race will outnumber the whites to the number of a million. What will be done then? Will the white man leave this country to make room for the negro? It is plain that there will not be room for both."

And I murmured almost entirely onbeknown to myself, "No, I don't spoze he would."

"No, indeed," sez Cousin John Richard. "The Anglo-Saxon will not leave this country, his inheritance, for the sake of peace or to make room for another race; then what will be done? I hear the voice of the Lord," sez John Richard solemnly, "I hear His voice saying, 'Let my people go.'" The silence seemed solemn; it seemed some like the pauses that come in a protracted meetin' between two powerful speakers. I felt queer.

But I did speak up almost entirely onbeknown to myself, and sez I, "Could they take care of themselves in a colony of their own? Do they know enough?"

Sez John Richard, "A race that has accumulated property to the extent of six millions of dollars in one Southern State since the war, under all the well-nigh unendurable drawbacks and persecutions that have beset it, will be able, I believe, to at least do as much, when these hampering and oppressive influences are withdrawn and the colored man has a clear field, in an atmosphere of strength and courage and encouragement—where in this air of liberty he can enjoy the rewards of his labor and behold the upbuilding of his race.

"And what a band of missionaries and teachers will go out from this new republic, upon every side of them, in darkest Africa, to preach the peaceful doctrine of the cross!

"In these same dark forests, where their ancestors were hewn down and shot down like so many wild beasts, and dragged, maimed and bleeding, to become burden bearers and chained slaves to an alien race—

"Under the same dim shadows of these lofty trees will these men stand and reveal to the ignorant tribes the knowledge they learned in the torturing school of slavery.

"The dark baptism wherewith they were baptized will set them apart and fit them for this great work. They will speak with the fellowship of suffering which touches hearts and enkindles holy flames.

"Their teachings will have the supreme consecration of agony and martyrdom. They will speak with the pathos of grief, the earnestness and knowledge born through suffering and 'the constant anguish of patience.'

"It is such agencies as these that God has always blessed to the upbuilding of His kingdom. And will not the dwarfed natures about them gradually be transformed by the teachings of these apostles into a civilized, God-fearing people?

"Methinks the dark faces of these apostles will shine with the glowing image of God's love and providence—the providence that watched over

"THE DARK FACES OF THESE APOSTLES."

them and kept them in a strange land, and then brought them back in safety, fitted to tell the story of God's love and power, and His mercy that had redeemed them and made them free.

"And when the lowest and most unknowing one shall ask, 'Who are these?' methinks the answer will be as it was to St. John : ' These are they who come out of great tribulations.' "

I wuz demute, and didn't say nuthin', and John Richard sez, in a deep axent and a earnest one, " But will this Government be warned by past judgments and past experience and be wise in time ?

" I don't know," sez he, a answerin' himself ; for truly I didn't know what to say nor how to say it.

" You spoke just now of the expense. It will cost less now to avert an evil than it will cost for its overthrow, when time, and national follies, and men's bad passions, and inevitable causes have matured it, and the red cloud has burst in its livid fury over a doomed land. But time will tell.

" But while delays go on, the mills of the gods are grinding on ; time nor tide cannot stop them. And if this nation sits down at its ease for a decade longer, woe to this republic !"

I wuz so thrilled, and skairt, and enthused by Cousin John Richard's eloquence and strange and fiery words and flowery language that when I sort o' come to myself I looked up, a expectin' to see Josiah bathed in tears, for he weeps easy.

But even as I looked, I heard a low, peaceful snore. And I see that Josiah Allen had so fur forgot good manners and what wuz due to high principles and horspitality as to set there fast asleep. Yes, sleepin' as sweet as a babe in its mother's arms.

I looked mortified, I know.

But Cousin John Richard took it all historically— nuthin' personal could touch him, so it seemed.

And sez he to me. " There is a fair instance of what I have told you, cousin—a plain illustration of the indifference and unbelief of the North as to the state of affairs in the Southern States."

"Wall," sez I, "Josiah has been broke of his rest some durin' the year with newraligy, and you must overlook it in him."

And, wantin' to change the subject, I asked him if he wouldn't like a glass of new milk before retirin' and goin' to bed.

And he said he would; and I brung it in to him with a little plate of crackers on a tray. And as I come by Josiah Allen I made calculation ahead to hit him axidentally on his bald head with my elbow.

And he started up, with his face nearly covered with smiles and mortification, and sez he:

"That last remark of yours, Cousin John Richard, wuz very convincin' and eloquent."

The remark wuz, "I like new milk very much."

But I wouldn't throw that milk into his face. And Cousin John received the milk and the remark with composure.

And I kep' them two men down on to relations, and sheep, and such like subjects till I got 'em off to bed.

I give John Richard a good dose of spignut syrup, for he complained of a sore throat, and he wuz hoarse as a frog. Good land! I should have thought he would be, talkin' as much as he had, and eloquent too.

Eloquence is dretful tuckerin'; I know well its effects on the system, though mebby I hadn't ort to be the one to say it.

Wall, in the mornin' Cousin John Richard wuz

weak as a cat. All tired out. He couldn't hardly get round. And I made him lay down on the lounge in the settin' room, and I give him spignut syrup once a hour most all day, and kep' him warm, and lumps of maple sugar for his cough.

And by night he seemed like a new man—that spignut syrup is wonderful; few people know the properties of it.

Wall, Josiah and I both took such a likin' to that good onselfish eloquent creeter that we prevailed on him to stay a week with us right along.

And we took him to see the children, and Josiah took him up to Uncle Thomas'es, and Cousin Sophronia's on his own side, and we done well by him.

And I fixed up his clothes with Philury's help—they wuz good ones, but they needed a woman. But we mended 'em and rubbed 'em up with ammonia where it wuz needed, and they wuz in good condition when he went back to his work.

Good land! wild oxen, nor camels, nor nuthin' couldn't have kep' him from that "field" of hisen.

But when it come the mornin' for him to leave, he hated to go—hated to like a dog.

And we hated to have him go, we liked him the best that ever wuz. And we tried to make him promise to come to see us agin. But he seemed to feel dubersome about it; he said he would have to go where his work called him.

His bizness now up North wuz to see about some money that had been subscribed for a freedmen's school and meetin' house. But he promised to write to us now and then, and he spoke with deep feelin' about the "sweet rest he had had there," and how he never should forget it; he talked real eloquent about it, and flowery, but he meant every word, we could see he did.

It happened curius about the chapter Josiah read that mornin'—he most always reads the first one he opens to. And it wuz the one where Paul tells about his hard work and trials, and how the Lord had brought him out of 'em all.

How he wuz beaten with rods, and stuned, and wuz in perils of waters, and perils by his own countrymen, and perils by the heathen, and in the wilderness, and amongst false brethren, in weariness, and painfulness, and hunger and thirst, and cold and nakedness.

And how he gloried in his weakness and infirmities, if so God's strength should be made perfect and His will be accomplished.

I declare for it, I couldn't help thinkin' of Cousin John Richard, though mebby it hain't right to compare one of our relations to Paul, and then agin I didn't spoze Paul would care. I knew they both on 'em wuz good, faithful, earnest creeters anyway.

Then Cousin John Richard prayed a prayer that almost caught us up to the gates of Paradise, it wuz so full of heavenly love, and tenderness, and affection for us, and devotion to his work, and everything good, and half saintly.

And then most imegiatly he went away on the mornin' stage.

And at the very last, when most every other man would be a thinkin' of umberells or shawl straps, he took our hands in hisen and sez:

"Stand fast in the faith! be strong!" And then he bid us "good-bye, and God bless us!" and wuz gone.

Good, faithful, hard-workin' creeter. The views he had promulgated to us wuz new and startlin', and Josiah and he couldn't agree on 'em; but where is there two folks who think alike on every subject?

But whether they wuz true or false, I knew that John Richard believed every word he had said about the state of affairs in the South.

"WITH PHILURY'S HELP."

## CHAPTER II.

JOSIAH had to go to Shackville with a hemlock saw log that day, so he went off most imegiatly after Cousin John Richard departed.

And I resoomed the occupation I had laid down for the last week, and did a big day's work, with Philury's help, a cleanin' house.

But I had a good warm supper when my companion returned. I always will, work or no work, have meals on time, and good ones too—though I oughtn't to boast over such doin's.

We had cleaned the kitchen that day, papered it all over new and bright, and put down three breadths of a new rag carpet, acrost the west end.

And I had put up some pretty new curtains of cream-colored and red cheese cloth, one breadth of each to a winder, and looped 'em back with some red lute-string ribbon.

And I had hung my canary-cage in between the two south winders, over the stand of house plants ; and the plants had done dretful well, they wuz in full blow.

And then I brung in the two big easy-chairs covered with handsome new copper plate—one for Josiah and one for me.

And when I had set the supper-table, covered with a snowy cloth, in front of the south winders, the place looked well. We had took the carpet up in the dinin' room and had to set the table there. But it looked well enough for anybody.

And havin' had Philury to do the heaviest of the work, I didn't feel so very beat out, and I changed my dress and sot quiet and peaceful and very calm in my frame a waitin' for my companion, while the grateful odor of broiled chicken, and cream biscuit, and the rich coffee riz up and permeated the room.

Josiah duz love a cup of hot, fragrant coffee with cream into it when he has been to work in the cold all day. And it wuz quite cold for the time of year.

Wall, I had put on a good new gingham dress and a white apron, and I had a lace ruffle round my neck ; and though I hain't vain, nor never wuz called so, only by the envious, still I knew I looked well.

And I could read this truth in my companion's eyes as he come home cold and cross and hungry—come into that warm, pleasant room and into the presence of his devoted pardner.

At once and imegiatly his cares, his crossness,

and his troubled mean dropped from him like a garment he wuz tired of, and he felt well.

And his appetite was good—excellent.

And it wuzn't till after the dishes wuz all washed up, and we wuz a settin' on each side of the stand, which had a bright cloth and a clean lamp on it, I with my knittin' work and he with his *World*, that he resoomed and took up the conversation about Cousin John Richard's beliefs.

And I see, jest what I had seen, that as well as he liked John Richard, that worthy creeter had not convinced him; and he even felt inclined, now the magnetism of his presence wuz withdrawn, to pow at his earnest beliefs and sentiments.

I waved off Josiah's talk; I tried to evade his eloquence (or what he called eloquence). For somehow John Richard's talk had made more impression onto me than it had onto Josiah, and I could not bear to hear the cherished beliefs of that good man set all to naut.

So I tried to turn off Josiah's attention by allusions to the tariff, the calves, the national debt, to Ury's new suit of clothes, to the washboard, to Tirzah Ann's married life, and to the excellencies and beauties of our two little granddaughters Babe and Snow —Tirzah Ann's and Thomas Jefferson's little girls.

But though this last subject wuz like a shinin' bait, and he ketched on it and hung there for some time, a descantin' on the rare excellencies of them two wonderful children, yet anon, or nearly so, he wriggled away from that glitterin' bait and swung back to the subject that he had heard descanted on so powerfully the night John Richard come.

And in spite of all my nearly frenzied but peaceful efforts—for when he wuz so tired and beat out I wouldn't use voyalence—he would resoom the subject.

And sez he for the third or fourth time:

"John Richard is a crackin' good feller—they most all of 'em are that are on my side—but for all that I don't believe a word of what he said about the South."

I kep' demute, and wouldn't say what I did believe or what I didn't, for I felt tired some myself; and I felt if he insisted and went on, I should be led into arguin' with him.

For Cousin John Richard's talk had fell into meller ground in my brain, and I more than mistrusted it wuz a springin' up there onbeknown to me.

Josiah Allen and I never did, and I spoze never will, think alike about things, and I am fur more mejum than he is.

And then he sort o' satisfies himself by lookin' at one side of a idee, while I always want to walk round it and see what is on the other side on it, and turn it over and see what is under it, etc., etc.

But anon he bust out agin, and his axent was one that must be replied to; I felt it wouldn't do to ignore it any longer.

Sez he, "I am dead sick of all this talk about the Race Problem."

"Then why," sez I, mildly but firmly, "why do you insist on talkin' on it?"

"I want to tell you my feelin's," sez he.

Sez I, "I know 'em, Josiah Allen."

And then I sot demute, and hoped I had averte

the storm—or, ruther, I would call it the squall, for I didn't expect a hard tempest, more of a drizzle.

So I knit fast, and sot in hope.

But anon he begun agin:

"I am sick on't. I believe more'n half the talk is for effect. I don't believe the South is a bleedin'; I hain't seen no blood. I don't believe the niggers are a rizen, I hain't seen 'em a gettin' up. I believe it is all folderol."

And then I sez, a lookin' up from my knittin' work:

"Be mejum, Josiah Allen; you don't live there. You hain't so good a judge as if you lived in the South; you hain't so good a judge as John Richard is, for he has lived right there."

And he snapped out real snappish:

"Wall, there is lots of places I never lived in, hain't there? But anybody can know sunthin', whether they live anywhere or not."

But I kep' on real mejum and a talkin' deep reason, I know well.

"When anybody is a passin' through deep waters, Josiah Allen, they can feel the cold waves and the chill as nobody can who is on dry land."

And then Josiah said them inflammatory words agin that he had hurled at the head of John Richard, and that had gaulded him so. He sez in a loud, defiant axent, "Oh shaw!"

And I sez, "You hain't there, Josiah Allen, and you hain't so well qualified to shaw, and shaw accordin' to principle, as if you wuz there."

"Wall, I say, and contend for it," sez he, almost hotly, "that there is too much dumb talk. Why don't the niggers behave themselves, and why don't the Southerners treat 'em as I treat Ury?

"Ury has worked for me upwards of seven years, and he hain't riz, has he? And I hain't been a howlin' at him, and a whippin' him, and a shootin' at him, and a ridin' him out on a rail, and a burnin' him to the stake if he wouldn't vote me in President; and he hain't been a massecrecin' us, not that I have ever hearn on, or a rapinin' round, and I hain't rapined Philury, have I?

"If there is any truth in these stories, why don't the South foller on and do as I do? That would end their troubles to once.

"Let the Southerners act as I do, and the niggers act like Ury, and that would end up the Race Problem pretty sudden."

Sez I, in pretty lofty axents, for I begun to feel eloquent and by the side of myself, "How many generations has it took to make you honest and considerate, and Ury faithful and patient? How long has it took, Josiah Allen?"

"Why, about seven years or thereabouts. He come in the middle of winter, and now it is spring."

Sez I, "It has took hundreds and hundreds of years, Josiah Allen."

And I went on more noble and deep:

"Ury's parents and grandparents, and back as fur as he knows, wuz good, hard-workin', honest men—so wuz yours. You are both the children of freedom and liberty. You haven't been saddled with a burden of ignorance and moral and physical helplessness and want. He has no lurid background of abuse and wrongs and arrogance to inflame his fevered fancies.

"You might as well say that you could gather as good grain down in your old swamp that has never been tilled sence the memory of man, as you can in your best wheat field, that has been ploughed, and harrowed, and enriched for year after year.

"The old swamp can be made to yield good grain, Josiah Allen, but it has got to be burned over, and drained, and ploughed, and sown with good grain.

"There is a Hand that is able to do this, Josiah Allen. And," sez I, lookin' off some distance beyend him and Jonesville, "there is a Hand that I believe is a dealin' with that precious soil in which saints and heroes are made, and where the beauteous flower of freedom blows out.

"Has not the South been ploughed with the deep plough of God's purpose—burned with the lightnin' of His own meanin', enriched with the blood of martyrs and heroes? Has not the cries of His afflicted ones rose to the heavens while onbeknown to 'em the chariot of Freedom wuz marchin' down towards the Red Sea, to go ahead on 'em through the dretful sea of bloodshed and tribulations, while the black clouds of battle riz up and hid the armies of Slavery and Freedom, hid the oppressors and the oppressed?

"But the sea opened before 'em, and they passed through on dry land.

"Now they are encamped in the wilderness, and the tall, dark shapes of Ignorance and Hereditary Weakness and Vice are a stalkin' along by their sides, and coverin' 'em with their black shadows. The stumps are thick in their way. The old trees of Custom and Habit, though their haughty tops may have been cut off a little by the lightnin' of war, yet the black, solid, onbroken stumps stand thick in their way—so thick they can't force their way through 'em—and the black mud of Open Enmity, and Arrogance, and Prejudice is on one side of 'em, and on the other the shiftin', treacherous quicksands of Mistaken Counsel.

"Their way is blocked up, and the light is dim over their heads. Religion and Education is the light that is goin' ahead on 'em; but that piller of fire is some ways ahead of 'em, and its rays are hindered by the branchin' shadows over their heads. And who will be the Moses to lead 'em out of this wilderness into their own land?"

I wuz almost entirely by the side of myself with deep emotions of pity and sympathy and a desire to help 'em, and I felt riz up, too, in my mind—awful riz up—and I spoke out agin, entirely onbeknown to myself:

"Who will be the Moses to lead 'em into the Promised Land?"

"Wall, it won't be me," sez Josiah. "I am goin' out to bed down the horses."

I wuz took aback, and brung down too sudden from the Mount of Eloquence I had been standin' on.

And I put on my nightcap and went to bed.

Now, I don't spoze you would believe it—most anybody wouldn't—but the very next mornin' Josiah Allen resoomed and took up that conversation agin, that I fondly hoped he had thrown down for good when he so suddenly departed to the horse barn.

But if you can believe it, before I got breakfast ready, while he was a wipin' his hands to the sink on the roller towel, he broke out agin as fresh seemingly in debate as ever.

If I had mistrusted it ahead I should have made extra preparation for breakfast, for the purpose of quellin' him down, but I hadn't dreamed of his resoomin' it agin; and I only got my common run of brekfasses, though it wuz very good and appetizin'.

I had some potatoes warmed up in cream, and some lamb-chops broiled brown and yet juicy, some hot muffins light as a feather, and some delicious coffee—it wuz good enough for a King or a Zar—but then it wuzn't one of my choice efforts, for principle's sake, which I often have to make in the cookin' line, and—good land!—which every other human woman has to make who has a man to deal with.

We can't vote, and we have to do sunthin' or other to get our own way.

Wall, as I wuz a sayin'. he broke out anew, and sez he:

"I am sick as a dog of all this talk about the Race Problem."

And then agin I uttered them wise words I had spoken the night before; they wuz jest heavy with wisdom if he had only known it; and sez I:

"What makes you keep a bringin' it up, then and a talkin' about it?"

And agin he sez, "He done it to let me know how he felt about it."

And agin I sez, "I knew it before."

And I silently but smoothly poured my sweet cream over my sliced potatoes, and turned my lamb-chops and drawed my coffee forwards so it would come to a bile.

And he repeated, "I believe in lettin' things alone that don't consarn us; it hain't none of our bizness."

And seein' he wuz bound on talkin' on it, why, I felt a feelin' that I must roust up and set him right where I see he wuz wrong; I see it was my duty as a devoted pardner. And so, after we had got down to the table, and he sez agin in more powerful and even high-headed axents, "that it wuz none of our bizness," then I spunked up and sez, "It seems to me, Josiah Allen, that the cause of eternal truth is *always* our bizness."

"Oh, wall! it hain't best to meddle; that is my idee, and that is my practice. Don't you know that when Ury had that fight with Sam Shelmadine, I said I wouldn't either make nor break? I said I won't meddle, and I didn't meddle. It wuzn't my bizness."

"But you found it wuz your bizness before you got through with it—you lost Ury's help six weeks in your hurryenst time, when he wuz away to the lawsuit, etc., etc. And it made Philury sick, and you and I had to be up with her more or less, and you took cold there one night, and had a sickness that

"WHEN URY HAD THAT FIGHT WITH SAM."

lasted you for weeks and almost killed you; and if you *had* died," sez I in deep tones of affection and pathos, "if you *had* left your devoted pardner forever, could you have looked me in the face and said that this trouble of theirs wuzn't nuthin' that affected us? No; when a black cloud comes up the sky you can't tell where the lightnin' is a goin' to hit— whether it will strike saint or sinner." I see he wuz affected by my tender and eloquent allusion to his passin' away; for a moment he looked softened and almost as if he wuz a goin' to lay down the argument somewhere and leave it there. But anon his linement clouded up, and he assumed the expression of doggy obstinacy his sect knows so well how to assume, and sez he:

"But this is sunthin' entirely different. There hain't no earthly possibility that this nigger question can affect us one way or another; there hain't no way for it to," sez he.

Sez I, "Hain't you got a heart, Josiah Allen, to help others who are in trouble and jeopardy, and don't know which way to turn to get the right help?"

"I have got a heart to help Number One—to help Josiah Allen—and I have got a heart to mind my own bizness, and I am a goin' to."

And he passed over his cup agin for the third cup of coffee. That man drinks too much coffee—it hain't good for him; but I can't help it; and my coffee *is* delicious anyway, and the cream is thick and sweet, and he loves it *too* well, as I say; but as good as it wuz, it couldn't draw his mind from his own idees.

Sez he agin, in louder axents and more decideder ones:

"There hain't no possible way that we can be affected by the Race Problem one way or another."

And I begun to feel myself a growin' real eloquent. I don't love to get so eloquent that time of the day, but mebby it wuz the effect of that gauldin' tone of hisen. Anyway, I sez:

"It is impossible to guard one's self aginst the effects of a mighty wrong.

"The links that weld humanity together are such curius ones, wove out of so many strands, visible and invisible, strong as steel and relentless as death, and that reach out so fur, so fur on every side, how can any one tell whether a great strain and voyalence inflicted on the lowest link of that chain may not shatter and corrode and destroy the very highest and brightest one?

"The hull chain of humanity is held in one hand, and we are bein' pulled along by that mighty, inexorable hand into we know not what.

"The link that shines the brightest to-day may be rusty to-morrow, the strongest one may be torn in pieces by some sudden and voyalent wrench, or some slow, wearin' strain comin' from beneath.

"How can we tell, and how dast we say that a evil that affects one class of humanity can never reach us—how do we know it won't?"

"Because we do know it!" hollered Josiah. "I know it is jest as I tell you, that that dumb nigger question can't never touch us anyway. I've said it, and I'll stick to it."

But I still felt real eloquent, and I went right on

and drew some metafors, as I most always do when I get to goin', I can't seem to help it.

Sez I, "The temperate man may say the liquor question will never affect him, but some day he gathers his sober children about him, and finds one is missin'—the pet of them all driven down in the street to death by a drunken driver.

"A Christian woman sez, 'This question of Social Purity cannot affect me, for I am pure and come from a pure ancestry.' But there comes a day when she finds the lamb of her flock overtaken and slain by this evil she thought could never touch her.

"The rich capitalist sets back in his luxurious chair and reads of the grim want that is howlin' about the hovels of the poor laborers, the deaths by exposure and starvation. The graves of these starved victims seem fur off to him. They can never affect him, he thinks, so fur is he removed in his luxurious surroundin's from all sights of woe and squalor.

"But even as he sets there thinkin' this, in his curtained ease, a bullet aimed by the gaunt, frenzied hand of some starvin' child of labor strikes his heart, and he finds in death the same level that the victims of want found by starvation.

"The mighty chain of humanity has drawn 'em on together, the high and the low, down to the equality of the grave.

"The hull chain of humanity is held in one hand anyway, and is beyond our control in its consequences.

"And how dast we to say with blind confidence that we know thus and so; that the evils that affect our brothers will not some time come to us; that the shadows that lay so heavy on their heads will not some time fall on us?"

"They hain't our brothers," hollered out Josiah in fearful axents. He wuzn't melted down at all by my eloquent remarks; no, fur from it.

"They hain't my brothers, and I know these dumb doin's in the South won't affect us, nor can't, and you can't make it," sez he.

The idee of my wantin' to! But that is the nater of men—wantin' to say sunthin' to kinder blame a female. And truly he acted mad as a hen to think I should venter to talk back, or even speak on the subject.

Oh, short-sighted man that he wuz—when the darkness wuz even then gatherin' in the distance onbeknown to us, to take the shape of the big shadow that wuz to fall on his poor old heart and mine—the shadow reachin' from the Southern sky even unto the North, and that would blot out all the sunshine for us for many and many a weary day, and that we must set down under for all the rest of our lives!

But I am a eppisodin'.

MELINDA.

## CHAPTER III.

WALL, it never rains but it pours, duz it? And it has been my experience durin' quite a middlin' long life (jest how long, hain't no matter, as I know on, to anybody but the man who takes our senses).

But as I wuz sayin', it has always been my experience that if company gets to comin' either on my side or hisen, they keep a comin'.

And it wuz only a short time after John Richard's departure and exodus that I got a letter from a aunt on my side kinder askin' and proposin' to have her daughter Melinda Ann come to Jonesville to make us a long visit.

And only a little while after this, one of hisen writ to the same effect.

And we had 'em both here to one time.

It wuz hard, but it seemed providential, and couldn't be helped, and it worked out a onexpected good in the end that paid us some for it. But I wouldn't go through it agin for a dollar bill.

You see the way on't is, I sot out in married life determined to do as well or better by the relations on his side than I did by them on my own side. I wuz bound to do well by the hull on 'em, jest bound to.

But I made up my mind like iron that I would stand more, take more sass, be more obleegin', and suffer and be calm more from hisen than from mine, and I would do awful, awful well by both sides.

And it wuz these beliefs carried out and spread out into practice that caused my agonies and my sufferin's that I went through for weeks.

The way on't wuz, I had a letter from the city from my great-aunt Melinda Lyons, a tellin' me that ner oldest girl, Melinda Ann (a old maiden), wuz all run down with nervous prostration, nervous fits and things, and she asked me if I would be willin' to have her come down into the country and stay a few weeks with me.

Wall, Aunt Melinda had done a good many good turns by me when I wuz a girl, and then I set quite a good deal of store by Melinda Ann, she and I wuz jest about of a age, and I talked it over with Josiah, and we give our consents and writ the letter, and the next week Melinda Ann come on, bag and baggage. A leather trunk and a bag for baggage.

Wall, we found Melinda Ann wuz very good dispositioned and a Christian, but hard to get along with.

MELINDA HAS A FIT.

The least thing we could do or say that wuz not jest so would throw her into a fit—a nervous fit you know—she would have spazzums, and all sally away, and faint like, and act.

And then I would have to soothe her with catnip, and bring her up with mustard poultices, and apply a soap-stone to her.

Why, one night Josiah happened to throw he bootjack down kinder hard (he had a corn and hit it, bein' the cause).

Wall, I stood over Melinda more'n two hours after that, three poultices bein' applied in vain for relief, till arneky softened the blow to her.

And one night the slats came out of the hired man's bed, jest acrost the hall from hern, and it took more'n a quart of catnip to make her hull agin.

And the cat fell through the suller winder—we have got a blind cat that acts like fury, always a fallin' round and a prowlin'—wall, I thought Melinda Ann would never come to.

She thought it wuz Injuns; and the cat did scream awful, I'll admit; it fell onto some tin ware piled up onto a table under the winder, and it skairt even the cat almost to death, so you can imagine the condition it throwed Melinda into. I thought it wuz ghosts, and so did Josiah, and felt riz up in my mind and full of or.

But I am a eppisodin', and to resoom.

Wall, I guess Melinda Ann had been there about a week, and as well as I liked Aunt Melinda, and as well as I loved duty, I wuz a beginnin' to feel perfectly beat out and fearfully run down in my mind and depressted, for fits is depresstin', no matter how much duty and nobility of soul you may bring to bear onto 'em, or catnip.

Wall, I wuz a beginnin' to look bad, and so wuz Josiah, although Josiah, though I am fur from approvin' of his course, yet it is the truth that he seemed to find some relief in givin' vent to his feelin's out on one side, and blowin' round and groanin' out to the barn and in the woodhouse, more than I did, who took it calm, and considered it a dispensation from the first, and took it as such.

Wall, if you'll believe it, right on the top of these sufferin's come a letter from a relation of Josiah's, a widowed man by the name of Peter Tweedle.

He wuz a distant relation of Josiah Allen—lived about two hundred miles away.

He writ that he wuz lonesome—he had lost his companion for the third time, and it wore on him. He felt that the country air would do him good. (We found out afterwards that he had rented his house sence his bereavement and had lived in a boarding-house, and had been warned out by the crazed landlady and the infuriated boarders, owing to reasons which will appear hereafter, and *had* to move on).

Wall, he wanted to come and visit round to our house first, and then to the other relations.

And I sez to myself, it is one of 'em on his side, and not one word will I say agin the idee, not if I fall down in my tracks.

And Josiah was so kinder beat out with Melinda, and depressted and wore out by havin' to go round in his stockin' feet so <u>much</u> and whisperin', that he said, "That any change would be a agreeable one, and he should write for Peter to come."

And I, buoyed up by my principle, never said a word agin the idee, only jest this:

"Think well on it, Josiah Allen, before you make the move."

And sez Josiah, "It will be a comfort to make a move of any kind."

He had been kep' awful still, I'll admit. But I couldn't see how it wuz goin' to make it any better to have another relation let in, on whomsoever's side they wuz.

Howsomever, I see that Josiah wuz determined, and I felt a delicacy about interferin', knowin' well that I had one of the relations on my own side in the house. Who wuz I, I sez to myself—who be I, to set up agin hisen? No, I never will. So the letter of acceptance wuz writ, and in less than a week's time Peter Tweedle come.

We spozed he would bring a satchel bag with him; mebby a big one, but—good land! Josiah had to go after his baggage with the Democrat wagon. We see he had come to stay; it wuzn't a evenescent visit, but a long campane.

We didn't know at the time that they wuz most all musical instruments; we thought they wuz clothes.

I see a black shadder come over my companion's face as he shouldered the fifth trunk and took it up two flights of stairs into the attick.

He had filled the bedroom and hall.

Wall, I guess Peter Tweedle hadn't been in the house over half an hour before he walked up to the organ and asked me if it wuz in good repair.

I sez, " I guess so."

Sez he, " How many banks of reeds is in it ?"

I sez, " I don't know."

Sez he, " Have you any objections to my tryin' it ?"

I sez, " No."

Sez he, " Sence my last affliction I have turned my mind agin towards music, I find it soothes." Sez he, " After my first bereavement I took up the pickelo—I still play on it at intervals; I learned that and the snare drum durin' them dark hours," sez he. " And I still play on 'em in lonesome moments. I have 'em both with me," sez he.

" Durin' my next affliction I learned the clarinet, the fife, and the base violin. Now," sez he, " I am turnin' my mind onto the brass horn in various keys. But I have brought all my instruments with me," sez he, in a encouragin' axent. " I frequently turn from one to another. When I get lonesome in the night," sez he, " I frequently run from one to another till I have exhausted the capabilities of each, so to speak."

I sithed and couldn't help it, but I held firm on the outside, and he turned to the organ.

" I love the organ," sez he ; and with that he sot down on the music-stool, opened up all the loud bases, the double octave coupler, blowed hard, and bust out in song.

Wall, it all come jest as sudden onto Melinda as a thunder-clap out of a parlor ceilin', or a tornado out of a teacup, it wuz as perfectly onexpected and onlooked for as they would be, and jest as skairful.

For this wuz one of her bad days, and bein' a old

maid, we thought mebby it would excite her too much to know a widower wuz in the house, so we had kep' it from her.

And the first intimation she had of Peter'ses presence wuz this awful loud blast of sound.

His voice wuz loud in the extreme, and it wuz "Coronation" he bust out in.

He is pious, there hain't a doubt on't, but still "Coronation" is the loudest him in the him-book.

Wall, the very first time he blasted forth I knew jest as well as I knew afterwards what the result would be.

I hastened upstairs, and there she wuz, there sot Melinda Ann in a fit; she hadn't had time to get onto the bed, and there she sot bolt upright in her rockin' chair in a historical fit. We had better let her known he wuz there.

Wall, I histed her onto the bed as quick as I could, and hollered down the back stairs for catnip.

And as soon as I had brung her to a little, she would clench right into me, and groan and choke, and sort o' froth to the mouth.

And I'll be hanged if I didn't feel like it myself, for right down under our feet I heard that loud, thunderin' organ, for his legs wuz strong, and he blowed hard.

But yet so curius is human nater, specially wimmen's human nater—right there in my agony I couldn't help bein' proud o' that instrument. I had no idee, I said to myself, not a idee, that it had such a volume of sound.

But loud as it wuz, Peter'ses clarion voice rung out loud and high above it.

It wuz a fearful time, very. But even at that moment I sez to myself agin:

"He is a relation on *his* side—be calm!" and I wuz calm.

"IT WUZ 'HOLD THE FORT' HE BELCHED OUT IN."

Wall, I rubbed Melinda Ann and explained it her, and poulticed her, and got her kinder sett. down.

And I see it took up her mind some. She didn't seem to dislike it now, after the first shock wuz over.

And I left her propped up on her piller a listenin', and went down and got supper.

Wall, it wuz all I could do to get that man away from the instrument long enough to eat.

He seemed to be kinder absent-minded and lost like till he got back to it agin.

Wall, it had been still for some time; you couldn't hear a thing from the dinin' room up in Melinda's room. And when he bust out agin imegiatly after supper, it wuz too much, too much, for I spoze she had been in a drowze.

It wuz "Hold the Fort" he belched out in, with all the steam on. He had a way, Peter had, of bustin' out loudest when he begun, and then kinder dwindle down towards the last of the piece. (But it wuz one of 'em on *his* side, and I didn't murmur, not out loud, I didn't.)

Wall, I knew what wuz before me at the first volley of sound. I sez to myself:

"Melinda Ann! Melinda Ann!" and hurried upstairs.

And there she wuz layin' back on her piller with her eyes rolled up in her head and fixed, and her nuckels clenched.

Wall, I brung her to agin after a long and tejus process, and then agin I see that she sort o' enjoyed it; and I left her propped up and went down and helped do up the work.

Wall, Peter never stopped playin' till a late bedtime.

And then I might have slept some at first, only Josiah begun a noise where he left off, a scoldin' and a jawin'.

And oh! my sufferin's that I suffered with that man. I reminded him that Peter wuz a relation on *his* side—no avail.

I brung up his lonesome state.

Josiah said, "He'd ought to be lonesome! He'd ought to be fur away in the middle of the desert or on a island in the depths of the seas. Alone! alone!"

He raved, he swore, he said, "Dumb him!" repeatedly.

You see Josiah hated music anyway, only the very softest, lowest kind; and Peter'ses wuz powerful —powerful and continuous.

But I reminded Josiah Allen in the cause of duty that he had complained that the house wuz too still sence Melinda Ann had come, and he wanted a noise.

"I never wanted to be in a Lunatick Asylum," sez he; "I didn't hanker for Bedlam," he yelled.

Wall, suffice it to say that I never got a wink of sleep till past midnight. And mebby it wuz about one o'clock, when all of a sudden we wuz all waked up by a low, rumblin' noise, strange and weird.

My first thought was a earthquake, and then a cyclone.

But Josiah Allen had waked up first and got his senses before I did, and sez he:

"It is that dumb fool a playin' on a base viol."

And that wuz what it proved to be. He had got lonesome in the night, and got up and onpacked the base viol, and wuz playin' a low, mournful piece on it, so's not to wake us up.

He said in the mornin' that he held it in for that purpose.

He is a good-natured creeter, and a mourner, there hain't no doubt on't, and so I told Josiah.

And he snapped out enough to take my head off :

"He'd ought to mourn! I mourn," sez he, "Heaven knows I do. But I shan't mourn after the first ray of daylight, for I'll take his trunks and throw 'em out doors, and him on top of 'em. And I'll cast out Melinda Ann like a viper," sez he. "I'll empty the house of the hull crew of fools and lunaticks! I'll do it," sez he, "if I have a breath left in my body."

When he sez this I thought of Melinda Ann. Had she got a breath left? Wuz she alive? Or wuz she not?

I jest sprung over Josiah Allen, I trompled on him, I won't deny it, in my haste to get up, and I left him groanin' and a sayin' in a low, mournful axent :

"That foot could never be stepped on agin by him."

But I didn't stop to comfort him ; no, my mind wuz too much took up with the relation on my side.

I hastened upstairs, and there wuz my worst fears realized.

Melinda Ann wuz wild as a hen hawk.

She had got the winder up and wuz jest a springin' out. I ketched her by her limb and hollered for Josiah. Before he got there she had got her hands clenched into my hair and wuz a tryin' to choke me.

But, good land! she didn't know what she wuz a doin'.

Wall, Josiah Allen by main strength got her into the house agin, and after a tussle we got her onto the bed. And then I begun to doctor her up.

But I never tried to go to bed agin that night, for it wuz daylight before I got her quieted down.

Wall, Josiah had to go off that mornin' early on bizness, to be gone all day. And I wuz glad on't, for I wuz afraid, in spite of all I could do, he would

"I KETCHED HER BY HER LIMB."

do sunthin' to disgrace himself in the eyes of both sides. His last words to me wuz:

"If I find either of them cussed fools in the house

when I get back, I'll burn the house down over their heads."

But I knew he wouldn't, I knew he would quiet down while he wuz gone, and he did.

But my sufferin's through that day can't never be told or sung. And the martyrs that I called on, and the groans and sithes that I smothered in my breast waist, couldn't be told.

But jest as I expected, when Peter first blasted out on the clarinet loud and strong, not bein' afraid of wakin' anybody up, I had to drop everything and go right up to Melinda Ann. But the attack wuz light, and, as usual, after she got over the first shock she enjoyed it.

And I happened to mention—havin' that pride I have spoke of, of havin' the relations on his side stand on their best foot before mine—I happened to mention that Peter got up and played in the night because he wuz lonesome, and that he said he would give half his property (he wuz well off) if he had somebody to play the organ while he played the clarinet.

I see she grew more meller-lookin' and brightened up, and she sez:

"I used to be a good player."

And if you'll believe it—I don't spoze you will, for Josiah wouldn't when I told him that night—

But when Josiah Allen came home that night they wuz a playin' together like a pair of turkle doves, she a playin' the organ, and he a settin' by her a tootin', both as happy as kings.

And from that time out she never got skairt agin when he bust out sudden in song or begun gradual.

And her fits grew lighter and lighter and fur seldomer.

And though our sufferin's wuz heavy and severe to hear that organ and clarinet, or base viol, or pickelo, or brass horn a goin' day and night, yet I seemed to see what wuz a comin' on't, and I held Josiah by main force to stand still and let providential circumstances have a straight path to move on in.

Wall, after two weeks of sufferin' on our part almost onexampled in history, ancient or modern, the end come.

Peter Tweedle took Josiah out one side and told him, as bein' the only male relation Melinda Ann had handy to get at, "that he had it in his mind to marry her quietly and take her at once to his home in the city," and he asked Josiah "if he had any objections."

And Josiah told me that he spoke out fervently and earnestly, and sez, "No! Heaven knows I hain't."

And he urged Peter warm to have the weddin' sudden and to once, that very day and hour, and offered to get the minister there inside of twenty minutes.

But I wuz bound to have things carried on decent. So I sot the day most a week off, and I sent for Aunt Melinda and his children that wuz married, and the single one, and we had a quiet little weddin', or it would have been, only the last thing that they done in the house before they left wuz to get the hull crew on 'em to bust out in a weddin' song loud enough almost to raise the ruff.

Wall, Peter writ to Josiah that he hadn't been lonesome sence it took place, not a minute.

And Melinda Ann writ to me that she hadn't had a fit sence, nor a spazzum.

So, as I told Josiah Allen, our sufferin's brung about good to two lonesome and onhappy and fitty creeters, and we ort to be thankful when we look back on our troubles and afflictions with 'em.

And he looked at me enough to take my head off, if a look could guletine, and sez he:

"Thankful! Oh, my gracious Heaven! hear her! Thankful!"

And his tone wuz such that I hain't dasted to bring up the subject sence. No, I don't dast to, but I do inside of me feel paid for all I went through.

PETER AND MELINDA ANN.

## CHAPTER IV.

WALL, it wuzn't more than a few days after the marriage and departure of Peter and Melinda Ann, when I got a letter from Cousin John Richard —he wuz then in South Carolina, hard at work agin, literally follerin' the example of Him who went about doin' good.

The letter wuz writ in pure friendship, and 'then he wanted to find out the ingredients of that spignut syrup I had give him when he wuz at Jonesville, his throat wuz a botherin' him agin, and he said that had helped him.

That is a good syrup, very, though mebby I hadn't ort to say it. It is one that I made up out of my own head, and is a success.

Yeller dock, and dandelion roots, and spignut, steeped up strong, and sweetened with honey.

I sent it to him to once, with some spignut roots by mail; I wuz afraid he couldn't get 'em in the South.

And in my letter I asked him out of politeness, as it were, how he wuz a gettin' along colporterin', and if things looked any brighter to him in the South.

And such a answer as I got—*such* a letter! why, it wuz a sermon almost. Jest as skairful, jest as earnest, and jest as flowery as the talk he had talked to us when he wuz with us.

Why, it fairly sent the cold chills over me as I read it.

But it madded Josiah. He wuz mad as a hen to hear it, and he said agin that he believed Cousin John Richard (Josiah knew he wuz jest as good as gold, and he wouldn't brook a word from anybody else agin him), but he said he believed he wuz a losin' his faculties.

He didn't believe a word on't. He didn't believe there wuz any danger nor any trouble; if folks would only let the South alone and mind their own bizness, it would get along well enough. But some folks had always got to be a putterin' around, and a meddlin', and he shouldn't wonder a mite if John Richard wuz a doin' jest such a work as that.

And I sez mildly, "Sometimes things *have* to be meddled with in order to get ahead any."

"Wall," sez he, "don't you know how, if there is any trouble in a family, the meddlers and interferers are the ones that do the most mischief?"

"But," sez I, "teachin' religion and distributin' tracts and spellin' books hadn't ort to do any hurt."

"Wall, I d'no," sez Josiah. "I d'no what kind of tracts he is a circulatin', mebby they are inflamitory. If they are offen a piece with some of his talk here, I should think the South would ride him out."

And so Josiah went on a runnin' John Richard's work and belief down to the lowest notch; and I wuz glad enough when Deacon Henzy come in on a errant, for I wuz indeed in hopes that this would change the subject.

But my hopes, as all earthly expectations are liable to be, wuz blasted. For Josiah went right on with his inflamed speeches and his unbelief about any danger a threatenin' the nation from the South.

And I truly found myself in the condition of the one mentioned in Scripture (only different sex and circumstances), where it sez the last state of that man wuz worse than the first. For while my pardner's talk had consisted mostly of the sin of unbelief, Deacon Henzy's remarks wuz full of a bitter hatred and horstility towards the ex-slaveholders of the Southern States.

He truly had no bowels of compassion for 'em, not one.

He come from radical abolitionist stock on both sides, and wuz brung up under the constant throwin' of stuns, throwed by parents and grandparents at them they considered greater sinners than themselves.

And Deacon Henzy had gathered up them stuns and set 'em in a settin' of personal obstinacy and bigotry, and wore 'em for a breastplate.

And hard it wuz to hit any soft place under them rocky layers of prejudices inherited and acquired.

And he and his folks before him didn't know what the word mejum wuz, not by personal experience.

It needed only a word to set him off. Josiah

spoke that word, and the wheel begun to turn and grind out denunciations of the Southerners as a class and as a people.

Oh, how he rolled out big-soundin' terms of scathin' reproaches and burnin' rebukes, and the horrible wickedness of one human bein' enslavin' another one and enrichin' himself on the unpaid labor of a brother man!

Why, it wuz fairly skairful to hear him go on, fur skairfuller than Josiah's talk.

He had always talked rampant on the subject I knew, but as rampant as he had always been he wuz now fur rampanter than I had ever known him to be.

But as I found out most imegiatly, he wuz agitated and excited on this occasion almost more than he could bear, when he first come in.

For he soon went on and told us all about it.

A boy he had took—Zekiel Place by name—had run away and left him; or, that is, he had made all his preparations to go when the Deacon found it out, and the boy give him the chance of lettin' him go or keepin' him and payin' him wages for his work.

Now, Deacon Henzy, like so many other human creeters, wuz so intent on findin' out and stunin' other folks'es faults, that he didn't have time to set down and find out about his own sins and stun himself, so to speak.

He never had thought, so I spoze, what a hard master he wuz, and how he had treated Zekiel Place.

But I knew it; and all the while he went on a talkin' about "the ignorance and wastefulness and shiftlessness of this class of boys, and how impossible it wuz to manage 'em and keep 'em down in their places; how you had to set down on 'em and set heavy if you didn't want to be bairded to your face and run over by 'em; how if you give 'em an inch they would take a ell, and destroy and waste more than their necks wuz worth," etc., etc., etc.—

All the while he wuz a goin' on and a sayin' all this I kep' up a thinkin', for I knew that Zekiel was a middlin' good boy, and had been misused by the Deacon, so I had hearn—had been worked beyend his strength, and whipped, and didn't get enough to eat, so the boy said.

The Deacon had took him for his board and clothes; but his board wuz hard indeed, and very knotty, and his clothes wuz very light, very.

And so, bein', as I spoze, sort o' drove to it, he riz. And as I say, the Deacon was madder than any hen I ever see, wet or dry

"The idee," sez he, "of that boy, that I have took care on ever sence he wuz a child, took care on him in health, and nussed him, and doctored him when he wuz sick" (lobelia and a little catnip wuz every mite of medicine he ever give him, and a little paregoric, so I have been *told*)—"the idee of that boy a leavin' me—a rizin' up and a sayin' as pert as a piper, 'If you don't want to hire me, let me go.'"

"Wall, which did you do, Deacon?" sez I.

"Why, I hired the dumb upstart! I couldn't get along without his work, and he knew it."

"'The laborer,' Deacon Henzy," sez I, solemn, "' is worthy of his hire.'"

"Wall, didn't I lay out to pay him? I laid out

this very fall to get him a pair of pantaloons and a vest and a cravat. I laid out to pay him richly. And he had better a trusted to me, who have been a perfect father and gardeen to him, than to have riz up and demanded his pay. But," sez he, "there is no use of talkin' about it now, it only excites me and onmans me, and I come in merely to borry a augur and have a little neighborly visit.

And then wantin', I spoze, to take his mind offen his own troubles, he sort o' launched off agin onto his favorite theme of runnin' down the Southerners.

"The Southern people," sez he, "are a mass of overbearin', tyrannical slave-drivers, selfish, without principles or consciences, crackin' their whips over the blacks, drivin' 'em to work, refusin' 'em any justice."

"Why," sez I, "the slaves are liberated, Deacon Henzy."

"Wall, why be they?" sez he. "It wuzn't from any good will on the part of the bloated aristocracy of the South. They liberated 'em because they *had* to. Why didn't they free 'em because it wuz right to free 'em? because it wuz right and just to the slaves? because it wuz a wicked sin that cried up to the heavens to make 'em labor, and not pay 'em for it?"

Why, he went on in fearful axents of wrath and skorn about it, and finally bein' so wrought up, he said, "that them that upholded 'em wuz as bad as they wuz."

Why, we had never dreamed of upholdin' 'em, nor thought on't; but he felt so.

He threw stuns fearful at the South, and at Josiah

and me because we didn't jine in with him and rip and tear as he did.

And them stuns kinder hurt me after a while; and so, when he asked me for the seventh time:

DEACON HENZY.

"Why didn't they free their slaves before they wuz obleeged to?"

Then I sez, "It wuz probable for the same reason that you didn't liberate Zekiel—mostly selfishness!"

"What! what did you say?" He could not believe his ear; he craned his neck, he turned the other ear. He wuz browbeat and stunted; and agin he sez: "*What* did you say?"

And I sez agin, calm as cream, but sharp and keen as a simiter, "I said it wuz selfishness, Deacon, and the power of old custom—jest the reasons why you didn't free Zekiel."

His linement fell more'n a inch. Like the Queen of Sheba before Solomon (only different sex) he had no spirit left in him.

He never had mistrusted; it made him feel so awful good to run the South further down than anything or anybody wuz ever run—he never mistrusted that he had ever done anything onjust, or mean, or selfish.

He loved to deplore Southern sins, but never looked to see if Northerners wuzn't committin' jest as ojeus ones.

I mean good, well-meanin' Christian men, not to say anything about our white slaves in the cities who make shirts for five cents apiece, and sign their contracts with their blood.

Nor the old young children who are shut away from God's sunshine and air in Northern manufactories and mines, and who are never free to be out under the beautiful sky till the sun has gone down or the grass is growin' between it and their hollow, pitiful faces.

Nor the droves of street ruffians and beggars whose souls and bodies suffer and hunger jest as much under the Northern Star as under the Southern Cross.

No, I didn't mean any of these, but jest respectable church-goers like Deacon Henzy.

And he, like so many others, wuz jest as blind to the idee as if he had been born with leather spectacles on and had wore 'em ever sence.

It is a good thing for folks North or South to have their blinders tilted up a little now and then, and get a glimpse of daylight into their orbs. I had tilted up hisen, and wuzn't sorry a mite, not a mite. He had been a throwin' stuns powerful, and he had got hit from one.

And pretty soon, after settin' demute for quite a spell, he got up and left for home, feelin' and actin' quite meek and humble-sperited for him.

And I have hearn sence, and it comes straight to me—Zekiel's mother told Miss Biddlecom's Liza, and Liza's sister-in-law told it to the Editor of the *Augur'ses* wife's mother-in-law, and she told it to she that wuz Celestine Gowdey, and she that wuz Celestine told old Miss Minkley, and she told me—it come straight—that Deacon Henzy give Zekiel that very night a dollar bill, and from what I hear he has mellered up and used him first rate ever sence.

Yes, that man wuz blind as a bat and blinder. He had been for years a hackin' at the beams that riz up on the Southern brethren's eyes, and there he wuz a growin' a hull crop of motes, and payin' no attention to 'em.

But selfishness and injustice grows up jest as rank under Northern skies as Southern ones, and motes and beams flourish equally rank in both sections.

And Christians North and Christians South have to tussle with that same old man the Bible speaks of, and anon or oftener they get throwed by him.

"JOSIAH'S BALD HEAD AND MINE."

## CHAPTER V.

I wuz a strange thing to come most imegiatly after Cousin John Richard's visit, and our almost excited interview with Deacon Henzy—that Thomas J. should make the dicker he did make, and havin' made it, to think that before a very long time had passed over Josiah Allen's bald head and mine (it wuz *his* head that wuz bald, not mine) that we two, Josiah Allen and me, should be started for where we wuz started for, to come back we knew not when.

Yes, it happened curius, curius as anything I ever see—that is, as some folks count curosity. As for me, I feel that our ways are ordered and our paths marked out ahead on us.

You know when the country is new, somebody will go ahead through the forests and "blaze" the trees, so the settlers can foller on the path and not get lost.

Wall, I always feel that we poor mortals are sot down here in a new country—and a strange one, God knows—and the wilderness stretches out round us on every side, and we are likely to get lost, dretful likely.

But there is Somebody who goes ahead on us and marks out our pathway. He makes marks that His true children can see if they only look sharp enough, if they put on the specks of Faith and the blinders of Onworldliness, and look keen. And, above all, reach out their hands through the shadows, and keep close hold of the hand that guides 'em.

And all along the way, though dark shadows may be hoverin' nigh, there is light, and glory, and peace, and pretty soon, bimeby they will come out into a large place, the fair open ground of Beauty and Desire, into all that they had hoped and longed for.

But I am a eppisodin' fearful, and to resoom.

As I say, to the outside observer it seemed queer, queer as a dog, that after all our talk on the subject (and it seemed as if Providence had jest been a preparin' us for what wuz to come), that I myself, Josiah Allen's wife, should go with my faithful pardner down South to stay for we knew not how long.

Wall, the way on't wuz, our son Thomas Jefferson, who is doin' a powerful big bizness, made a dicker with a man from the South for a big piece of land of hisen, a old plantation that used to be splendid and prosperous before the war, but wuz now run down. The name of the place—for as near as I can make out they have a practice of namin' them old plantations—wuz Belle Fanchon, a sort of a French name, I wuz told.

Wall, Thomas J., in the way of bizness, had got in his hands a summer hotel at a fashionable resort, and this man wanted to trade with him. He hadn't owned this plantation long—it had come into his hands on a mortgage.

Wall, Thomas Jefferson was offered good terms, and he made the trad

And early in the fall Maggie, our son's wife, got kinder run down (she had a young child), and comin' from a sort of a consumptive family on her father's side, the doctor ordered her to go South for the winter.

He said, in her state of health (she had been weak as a cat for months) he wouldn't like to resk the cold of our Northern winter.

Wall, of course when the doctor said this (Thomas Jefferson jest worships Maggie anyway) he thought at once of that old plantation of hisen, for he had made the bargain and took the place, a calculatin' to sell it agin or rent it out.

And the upshot of the matter wuz that along the last of October, when Nater seemed all rigged out in her holiday colors of red and orange to bid 'em good-bye, our son Thomas Jefferson and Maggie, and little Snow, and the baby boy that had come to 'em a few months before, all set sail for Belle Fanchon, their plantation in Georgia.

Yes, the old girl (Nater) seemed to be a standin' up on every hill-top a wavin' her gorgeous bandana handkerchief to 'em in good-bye; and her blue gauze veil that floated from her forwerd looked some as if it had tears on it, it looked sort o' dim like and hazy.

Josiah and I went to the depot with 'em, and on our way home Nater didn't look very gay and festive to us neither, though she wuz dressed up in pretty bright colors—no, indeed !

Her gorgeous robes looked very misty and droopin' to me. I didn't weep, I wouldn't be so simple as that. The tears sort o' run down my face some, but I wouldn't weep—I wouldn't be so foolish when I knew that they wuz comin' home in the spring, God willin'.

But the kisses they had all left on my face seemed to kinder draw me after 'em. And I felt that quite a number of things might happen between that time and the time when Nater and I would dress up agin to meet 'em—she in her pale green mantilly, and I in my good old London brown, and we would both sally out to welcome 'em home.

But I didn't say much, I jest kep' calm and demute on the outside, and got my pardner jest as good a dinner as if my heart wuzn't a achin'.

I felt that I *had* to be serene anyway, for Josiah Allen was fearfully onstrung, and I knew that my influence (and vittles) wuz about the only things that could string him up agin.

So I biled my potatoes and briled my steak with a almost marble brow, and got a good, a extra good dinner for him as I say, and the vittles seemed to comfort him considerable.

Wall, time rolled along, as it has a way of doin'.

Good land! no skein of yarn, no matter how smooth it is, and no matter how neat the swifts run, nor how fast the winder is—nuthin' of that kind can compare with the skein of life hung onto the swifts of time—how fast they run, how the threads fly, how impossible it is to stop 'em or make 'em go slower, or faster, or anything!

They jest turn, and turn, and turn, and the day's reel offen the swifts, and the months and the years.

Why, if you jest stopped still in your tracks and meditated on it, it would be enough to make you half crazy with the idee—of that noiseless skein of life that Somebody somewhere is a windin'—Somebody a settin' back in the shadows out of sight, a payin' no attention to you if you try to find out who it is, and why he is a windin', and how long he calculates to keep the skein a goin', and what the yarn is a goin' to be used for anyway, and why, and how, and what.

No answer can you get, no matter how hard you may holler, or how out of breath you may get a tryin' to run round and find out.

You have got to jest set down and let it go on. And all the time you know the threads are a runnin' without stoppin', and a bein' wound up by Somebody—Somebody who is able to hold all the innumerable threads and not get 'em mixed up any, and knows the meanin' of every one of 'em, till bimeby the thread breaks, and the swifts stop.

But I am a eppisodin'. Wall, as I said, time rolled along till they had been down South most two months, and Thomas Jefferson wrote me that Maggie seemed a good deal better, and he wuz encouraged by the change in her.

When all of a sudden on a cold December evenin' we got a letter from Maggie. Thomas Jefferson wuz took down sick, and the little girl.

And there wuz Maggie, that little delicate thing, there alone amongst strangers in a strange land.

And sez she, "Mother, what *shall* I do?"

That wuz about all she said in the way of complaint or agony. She wuzn't one to pile up words, our daughter Maggie wuzn't. But that wuz enough.

"Mother, what *shall* I do? what *can* I do?"

I illustrated the text, as artists say, while I wuz a readin'. I see her pale and patient face a bendin' over the cradle of the infant, and little Snow, and over *my boy*, my Thomas Jefferson, who laid on my heart in his childhood till his image wuz engraved there for all time, and for eternity too, *I* think.

Wall, my mind wuz made up before I read the last words: "Your loving and sorrowful daughter, Maggie."

Yes, my mind wuz all made up firm as a rock; and to give Josiah Allen credit, where credit is due, so wuz hisen—his mind wuz made up too.

He blowed his nose hard, and used his bandana on that, and his two eyes, and he said, "Them specks of hisen wuz jest a spilin' his eyes."

And I took up my gingham apron and wiped my eyes.

My spectacles sort o' hurt my eyes, or sunthin', and my first words wuz, "How soon can we start?"

And Josiah's first words wuz, "I'll go and talk it over with Ury. I guess to-morrow or next day."

Wall, Ury and Philury moved right in and took charge of things and helped us off, and in less than a week's time we wuz on our way down through the snow-drifts and icickles of the North to the greenness and bloom of the orange-trees and magnolias. Down from the ice-bound rivers of the North to the merry, leapin' rivulets of Belle Fanchon. Down from the cold peace and calm of our Jonesville farm, down to the beauty and bloom of our boy's home in the South land, the sorrow and pathos of his love-watched sick-bed, and our little Snow's white-faced gladness.

We got there jest as the sun set. The country through which we had been a passin' all day and for some time past wuz a hard and forbidden-lookin' country—sand, sand, sand, on every side on us, and piled up in sand-heaps, and stretched out white and smooth and dreary-lookin'.

Anon, or mebby oftener, we would go by some places sort o' sot out with orange-trees, so I spozed, and some other green trees. And once in a while we would see a house set back from the highway with a piazza a runnin' round it, and mebby two on 'em.

And the children a playin' round 'em, and the children a wanderin' along the railroad-track and hangin' about the depots wuz more than half on 'em black as a coal.

A contrast, I can tell you, to our own little Jonesvillians, with their freckled white faces and their tow locks a hangin' over their forwerds.

The hair of these little boys and girls wuzn't hair, it wuz wool, and it curled tight round their black forwerds. And their clothes wuz airy and unpretentious in the extreme; some on 'em had only jest enough on to hide their nakedness, and some on 'em hadn't enough.

THE COLORED CHILDREN.

But our boy's place wuz beautiful. It looked like a picture of fairy land, as we see it bathed in the red western light. And though we felt that we might on closter inspection see some faults in it, we couldn't seem to see any then.

It wuz a big house, sort o' light grey in color, with a piazza a runnin' clear round it, and up on the next story another piazza jest as big, reared up and runnin' all round—a verandy they called it.

And both stories of the piazza wuz almost covered with beautiful blossomin' vines, great big sweet roses, and lots of other fragrant posies that I didn't know the name of, but liked their looks first rate.

There wuz a little rivulet a runnin' along at one side of the front yard, and its pleasant gurglin' sound seemed dretful sort o' friendly and pleasant to us.

The yard—the lawn they called it—wuz awful big. It wuz as big as from our house over to Deacon Gowdey's, and acrost over to Submit Danker'ses, and I don't know but bigger, and all sorts of gay tropical plants wuz sot out in bunches on the green grass, and there wuz lots of big beautiful trees a standin' alone and in clusters, and a wide path led up from the gate to the front door, bordered with beautiful trees with shinin' leaves, and there in the front door stood our daughter Maggie, white-faced, and gladder-lookin' than I ever see her before.

How she did kiss me and her Pa too! She couldn't seem to tell us enough, how glad she wuz to see us and to have us there.

And my boy, Thomas Jefferson, cried, he wuz so glad to see us.

He didn't boohoo right out, but the tears come into

his eyes fast—he wuz very weak yet; and I kissed them tears right offen his cheeks, and his Pa kissed him too. Thomas Jefferson wuz very weak, he wuz a sick boy. And I tell you, seein' him lay there so white and thin put us both in mind, his Pa and me, what Jonesville and the world would be to us if our boy had slipped out of it.

We knew it would be like a playhouse with the lights all put out, and the best performer dumb and silent.

It would be like the world with the sun darkened, and the moon a refusin' to give its light. We think enough of Thomas Jefferson—yes, indeed.

Oh, how glad little Snow wuz to see us! And right here, while I am a talkin' about her, I may as well tell sunthin' about her, for it has got to be told.

Snow is a beautiful child; she becomes her name well, though she wuzn't named for real snow, but for her mother's sirname. I say it without a mite of partiality. Some grandparents are so partial to their own offsprings that it is fairly sickenin'.

But if this child wuz the born granddaughter of the Zar of Russia or a French surf, I should say jest what I do say, that she is a wonderful child, both in beauty and demeanor.

She has got big violet blue eyes—not jest the color of her Pa's, but jest the expression, soft and bright, and very deep-lookin'. Their gaze is so deep that no line has ever been found to measure its deepness.

When you meet their calm, direct look you see fur into 'em, and through 'em into another realm than ourn, a more beautiful and peaceful one, and one more riz up like, and inspired.

I often used to wonder what the child wuz a lookin' for, her eyes seemed to be a lookin' so fur, fur away, and always as if in search of sunthin'. I didn't know what it wuz, but I knew it wuzn't nuthin' light and triflin', from her looks.

Some picture of holiness and beauty, and yet sort o' grand like, seemed before her rapt vision. But I couldn't see what it wuz, nor Josiah, nor her Pa, nor her Ma.

Her hair is a light golden color, not yeller, nor yet orbun, but the color of the pure pale shiny gold you sometimes see in the western heavens when the sky is bright and glowin'.

It looked luminous, as if a light from some other land wuz a shinin' on it onbeknown to us, and a lightin' it up. You know how the sun sometimes, when it gets where we can't see it, will shine out onto some pink and white cloud, and look as if the color wuz almost alive—so her hair looked round the rose pink and white of her pretty face.

Her little soft mouth seemed always jest on the pint of speakin' some wonderful words of heavenly wisdom, the look on it wuz such, made in jest that way.

Not that she ever give utterance to any remark of national importance or anything of that kind.

But the expression wuz such you seemed to sort o' look for it; and I always knew she had it in her to talk like a minister if she only sot out to.

And she did, in my opinion, make some very wise remarks, very. Josiah spoke to me about 'em several times, and said she went ahead of any minister or politician he ever see in the deepness of her mind.

And I told him he must be very careful and not show that he wuz partial to her on account of relationship.  And I sez:

"Look at me; I never do.  I always look at her with perfectly impartial and onprejudiced eyes, and therefore, therefore, Josiah, I can feel free to say that there never wuz such a child on earth before, and probable never will be agin;" and sez I, "if I wuz partial to her at all I shouldn't dast to say that."

"Wall," sez he, "I dast to say what I am a minter; and I know that for deep argument and hard horse sense she will go ahead of any man on earth, no matter where he is or who he is, President, or Bishop, or anything."

Josiah Allen has excellent judgment in such things; I feel that he has, and I knew he wuz simply statin' the facts of the case.

Ever. sence she wuz a very young infant, little Snow has made a practice of settin' for hours and hours at a time a talkin' to somebody that wuzn't there; or, to state the truth plainer and truthfuller, somebody that we couldn't see.

And she would smile up at 'em and seem to enjoy their company first rate before she could talk even, and when she begun to talk she would talk to 'em.

And I used to wonder if there wuz angels encamped round about her and neighborin' with her; and I thought to myself I shouldn't wonder a mite if there wuz.

Why, when she wuzn't more than several months old she would jest lay in her little crib, with her short golden hair makin' a sort of a halo round her white forwerd, and them wonderful heavenly eyes of hern lookin' up, up—fur off—fur off—and a smilin' at somebody or other, and a reachin' out her little hands to somebody, a wavin' 'em a greetin' or a good-bye.

Curius! Who it wuz I'd gin a dollar bill any time, and more too, to have ketched a glimpse of the Form she see, and hearn the whispers or the music that fell on her ears, too fine and pure for our more earthly senses.

And most probable I never wuz any madder in my hull life than I wuz when old Dr. Cork, who wuz doctorin' her Ma at that time, told me "It wuz wind."

Wind! That is jest as much as he knew. But he wuz an old man, and I never laid it up aginst him, and I never said a word back, only jest this little triflin' remark. I sez, sez I:

"The divine breath of Eden blowin' down into pure souls below, inspirin' 'em and makin' 'em talk with tongues and see visions and dream dreams, has always been called ' wind ' in the past, and I spoze it will be in the future, by fools."

This little remark wuz everything that I said, and for all the world he looked and acted real meachin', and meached off with his saddle-bags.

But now little Snow's golden hair wuz a shinin' out from the piller of sickness, the big prophetic eyes wuz shot up, and the forwerd wuz pale and wan.

But when she heard my voice she opened her eyes and tried to lift up her little snowflake of a hand—a little pretty gesture of greetin' she always had—and her smile wuz sweet with all the sweetness of the love she had for me.

OLD DR. CORK.

And she sez, as I took her into my arms gently and kissed her poor little pale face time and agin, she sez:

"My own Grandma!" Now jest see the deepness and pure wisdom of that remark!

Now, fools might say that because I wuz her father's stepmother that I wuzn't her own Grandmother.

But she see further down; she see into the eternal truth of things. She knew that by all the divine rights of a pure unselfish love and the kinship of congenial souls, that her Pa wuz my own boy, and she wuz my own, heart of my heart, soul of my soul.

Yes, there it wuz, jest as she had always done, goin' right down into any deep subject or conundrum and gettin' the right answer to it imegiatly and to once.

Curius, hain't it? and she not more'n four and a half—exceedingly curius and beautiful.

And as I bent there over her, she put up her little thin hand to my cheek and touched it with a soft caress, then brushed my hair back with the lily soft fingers, and then touched my cheek agin lightly but lovingly.

It wuz as good as a kiss, or several of 'em, I don't know which I would ruther have, if I had been told to chuse between 'em at the pint of the bayonet—some kisses, or these caressin' little fingers on my face.

They wuz both sweet as sweet could be, and tender and lovin'. And she wuz "my own sweet little baby," as I told her morn'n a dozen times.

I loved her and she loved me ; and when you have said that you have said a good deal ; you have said about all there is to say.

And I felt that I wuz glad enough that I could take holt and help take care on her, and win her back to health and strength agin, if it lay in human power.

There wuz a tall, handsome girl in the room when I went in, and I spozed, from her ladylike mean, that she wuz one of the neighbors, and she wuz there a neighborin' with my daughter Maggie, for she seemed to be a doin' everything she could to help.

And I spozed, and kep' on a spozin' for more than a hour, that she wuz a neighborin', till after she went out of the room for a few minutes, Maggie said she wuz a young colored girl, a "quadroon" she called her, that she had hired to help take care of Snow.

Sez I in deep amaze :

"That girl colored ?"

"Yes," sez Maggie.

"Wall," sez I, "she is handsomer than any girl I ever sot eyes on that wuz oncolored."

"Yes," sez Maggie, "Genny is a beautiful girl, and jest as good as she is pretty."

"Wall," sez I, "that is sayin' a good deal."

Maggie told me her name was Genieve, but they called her Genny.

Wall, my daughter Maggie had spells all that evenin' and the next day of comin' and puttin' her arms round me, and sort o' leanin' up aginst me, as if she wuz so glad to lean up aginst sunthin' that wouldn't break down under her head. I see she had been dretful skairt and nervous about Thomas

Jefferson and Snow, and I don't blame her, for they wuz very sick children, very. And there she (in her own enjoyment of poor health too) had had all the care and responsibility on her own self.

But I tell you she seemed real contented when her head sort o' rested and lay up aginst my shoulder, or breast-bone, or arm, or wherever it happened to lay.

And she sez, and kep' a sayin', with a voice that come from her heart, I knew:

"Oh, Mother! how glad, how thankful I am you have come!"

And Thomas Jefferson felt jest so, only more so. He would reach out his weak white hand towards me, and I would take it in both of my warm strong ones, and then he would shet up his eyes and look real peaceful, as if he wuz safe and could rest.

And he sez more than once, "Mother, I am goin' to get well now you have come."

And I sez, cheerful and chirk as could be, "Of course you be."

I'd say it, happy actin' as could be on the outside, but on the inside my heart kep' a sinkin' several inches, for he looked dretful sick, dretful.

Maggie, the weak one when they left Jonesville, wuz the strongest one now except the young babe, that wuz flourishin' and as rosy as the roses that grew round the balcony where he used to lay in his little crib durin' the hot days.

As soon as I got rested enough I took sights of comfort a walkin' round the grounds and a smellin' the sweet breath of the posies on every side of me.

And watchin' the gay birds a flutterin' back and forth like big livin' blossoms on wing.

And a listenin' to the song of the little rivulet as it wound its way round amongst the pretty shrubs and flowers, as if it wuz loath to leave so beautiful a place.

Yes, I see that our son Thomas Jefferson had done well to make the dicker he had made and get this place for his own.

There wuz several little hills or rises of ground on the lawn, and you could see from them the roofs and chimneys of two little villages a layin' on each side of Belle Fanchon, and back of the house some distance riz up a low mountain, with trees a growin' up clear to the top. It wuz over that mountain that we used to see the sun come up (when we *did* see it; there wuzn't many of us that see that act of hisen, but it paid us when we did—paid us well).

First, there would be a faint pink tinge behind the tall green branches of the trees, then golden rays would shoot up like a flight of gold arrows out over the tree-tops, and then pink and yellow and pinkish white big fleecy clouds of light would roll up and tinge the hull east, and then the sun would slowly come in sight, and the world would be lit up agin.

Down the western side of Belle Fanchon stretched the fair country for a long ways—trees and green fields, and anon, or oftener, a handsome house, and fur off the silvery glimpse of a river, where I spoze our little rivulet wuz a hurryin' away to jine in with it and journey to the sea.

Yes, it wuz a fair seen, a fair seen. I never see a prettier place than Belle Fanchon, and don't expect to agin.

The way it come to be named Belle Fanchon wuz as follows—Maggie told me about it the very next day after I arrived and got there:

She said the man that used to own it had one little girl, the very apple of his eye, who wuz killed by poison give to her by a slave woman, out of re-

THE SLAVE WOMAN WHO POISONED THE CHILD.

venge for her own child bein' sold away from her. But it wuz done by the overseer; her Pa wuz innocent as a babe, but his heart was broke all the same.

The little girl's name wuz Fannie—named after the girlish wife he lost at her birth. And he bein' a foreigner, so they say, he called her all sorts of pretty names in different languages, but most of all he called her Belle Fanchon.

And when the little girl died in this terrible way, though he had a housefull of boys—her half brothers—yet they said her Pa's head wuz always bowed in grief after that. He jest shet himself up in the big old house, or wandered through the shadowy gardens, a dreamin' of the little one he had loved and lost.

And he give her name to the place, and clung to it as long as he stayed there for her sake.

It is a kind of a pretty name, I thought when I first heard it, and I think so still.

The little girl lay buried on a low hill at one side of the grounds, amongst some evergreens, and tall rose bushes clasping round the little white cross over her pretty head, and the rivulet made a bend here and lay round one side of the hill where the little grave wuz, like a livin', lovin' arm claspin' it round to keep it safe. And its song wuz dretful low and sweet and sort o' sad too, as it swept along here through the green shadows and then out into the sunshine agin.

It wuz a place where the little girl used to play and think a sight of, so they said. And it wuz spozed that her Pa meant to be laid by her side.

But the fortunes of war swept him out of the beautiful old place and his shadowy, peaceful garden, him and his boys too, and they fill soldiers' graves in the places where the fortune of war took 'em, and her Pa couldn't get back to his little girl. And Belle Fanchon slept on alone under the whisperin' pines—slept on in sunlight and moonlight, in peace and war.

Sleepin' jest as sweet at one time as the other—when the roar of cannon swept along through the pines that wuz above her, as when the birds' song made music in their rustlin' tops.

And jest as calm and onafraid as if her kindred lay by her side.

Though it seemed kinder pitiful to me, when I looked at the small white headstone and thought how the darlin' of the household, who had been so tenderly loved and protected, should lay there all alone under dark skies and tempests.

Nobody nigh her, poor little thing! and an alien people ownin' the very land where her grave wuz made.

Poor little creeter! But that is how the place come to be named.

Snow loved to play there in that corner when she wuz well; she seemed to like it as well as the little one that used to play there.

As for Boy, he wuz too young to know what he did want or what he didn't.

He used to spend a good deal of his time a layin' in his little cradle out in the veranda, and Genieve used to set there by him when she wuzn't needed in the sick-rooms.

And I declare for it if it wuzn't a picture worth lookin' at, after comin', as I had, from the bareness and icy whiteness of a Jonesville winter and the prim humblyness of most of the Jonesville females, especially when they wuz arrayed in their woollen shawls and grey hoods and mittens. To be jest transplanted from scenes like them, and such females a shinin' out from a background of icickles and bare apple-trees and snow-drifts.

And then to shet your eyes in Jonesville, as it were, and open 'em on a balcony all wreathed round with clamberin' roses, and set up aginst a background of orange-trees hangin' full of oranges and orange blossoms too, and in front of that balcony to see a little white crib with some soft lace over the top, and a perfectly beautiful male child a layin' on it, and by the side of him a girl with a slender figure as graceful as any of the tall white flowers that wuz a swayin' and bendin' beneath the balmy South wind, under the warm blue sky.

A face of a fair oval, with full, sweet lips, and an expression heavenly sweet and yet sort o' sad in it, and in the big dark eyes.

They wuz as beautiful eyes as I ever had seen, and I have seen some dretful pretty eyes in my time, but none more beautiful than these.

And there wuz a look into 'em as if she had been a studyin' on things for some time that wuz sort o' pitiful and kind o' strange.

As if she had been a tryin' to get the answer to some momentous question and deep conundrum, and hadn't got it yet, and didn't seem to know when she would get it.

Dretful sad eyes, and yet sort o' prophetic and hopeful eyes too, once in a while.

Them eyes fairly drawed my attention offen the young babe, and I found that I wuz, in spite of myself, a payin' more attention to the nurse than I did to the child, though he is a beautiful boy, beautiful and very forward.

Wall, I entered into conversation with Genieve, and I found that she had lived in that neighborhood ever sence she wuz a small child, her mother havin' owned a small place not fur from Belle Fanchon.

Her mother had gone out nursin' the sick, and Genieve had learnt the trade of her; and then she had, poor child, plenty of time to practice it in her own home, for her mother wuz sick a long time, and sence her death Genieve had gone out to take care of little children and sick people, and she still lived on at the little cottage where her mother died, an old colored woman and her boy livin' with her.

There wuz a few acres of land round the cottage that had fruit trees and berry bushes and vines on it, and a good garden. And the sale of the fruit and berries and Genieve's earnin's give 'em all a good livin'.

Old Mammy and Cato the boy took care of the garden, with an occasional day's work hired, when horses wuz required.

The fruit and vegetables Cato carried to a neighborin' plantation, where they wuz carried away to market with the farmer's own big loads.

And there Genieve had lived, and lived still, a goin' out deeply respected, and at seventy-five cents to a dollar a day.

I felt dretfully interested in her from the very first; and though it is hitchin' several wagons before the horses' heads, I may as well tell sunthin' of her mother's history now as to keep it along till bimeby. As long as it has got to be told I may as well tell it now as any time, as fur as I know.

Maggie told it to me, and it wuz told to her by a woman that knew what she wuz a sayin'.

Genieve's mother wuz a very beautiful quadroon who had been brought up well by an indulgent and good-natured mistress, and a religious one too. There are as good wimmen in the South as in the North, and men too. She had educated Madeline and made a sort of a companion of her. She wuz rich, she could do as she wuz a mind to ; and bein' a widder, she had no one to say to her " Why do ye do so ?"

So she had brought up Madeline as a sort of a pet, and thought her eyes of her.

Wall, this mistress had some rich and high-born French relatives, and one of 'em—a young man— come over here on a visit, and fell in love the first thing with Madeline, the beautiful quadroon companion of his aunt.

And she loved him so well that in the end her love wuz stronger than the principles of religion that the old lady had instilled into her, for she ran away with this Monseur De Chasseny, and, forgettin' its wickedness, they lived an ideally happy life for years in a shootin' lodge of hisen in the heart of a fragrant pine forest in South Carolina. They lived this happy life till his father found him, and by means of family pride, and ambition, and the love of keepin' his own word and his father's pledges, he got him to leave his idyllic life and go back to the duties of his rank and his family in the old country.

MADELINE.

He had pledged his word to marry a rich heiress, and great trouble to both sides of their noble families wuz goin' to take place and ensue if he did not go, and his own family wuz goin' to be disgraced and dishonored if he did not keep his word.

Wall, men are often led to do things that at first they shrink from in mortal horror—yes, and wimmen are too.

De Chasseny vowed that he would not leave the woman he loved and the little girl they both worshipped, not for any reason—not for father, nor pride, nor for honor.

But he did. He left her, with plenty of money though, as it wuz spozed, and a broken heart, a ruined life, and a hoard of bitter-sweet and agonizin' memories to haunt her for the rest of her days.

She wuz a lovin'-hearted woman bound up in the man she loved—the man she had forsaken honor and peace of mind for.

There wuz no marriage—there could be none between a white man and a woman with any colored blood in her veins.

So in the eyes of the world and the law he wuz not guilty when he left her and married a pure young girl.

Whether he wuz found guilty at that other bar where the naked souls of men and wimmen stand to be judged, I don't spoze his rich and titled friends ever thought to ask themselves.

Anyway, he left Madeline and little Genieve—for so he had named the child after an old friend of his—he left them and sailed off for France and the new life to be lived out in the eyes of the world, where Happiness and gratified Ambition seemed to carry the torches to light him on his way.

Whether there wuz any other attendants who waited on him, a holdin' up dim-burnin' lamps to light him as he walked down Memory's aisles, I don't know, but I should dare presume to say there wuz.

I should presume to say that in the still night hours, when the palace lights burned low and the garlands and the feast robes put away for a spell, and his fair young wife wuz sleepin' peacefully at his side—I should presume to say that these black-robed attendants, that are used to lightin' folks down dark pathways, led him back to love—first, true, sweet love—and Madeline, and that under their cold, onsympathizin' eyes he stayed there for some time.

As for Madeline, she wuz stunned and almost senseless by the blow, and wuz for a long time. Then she had a long sickness, and when she come to herself she seemed to be ponderin' some deep thought all to herself.

The nurse who was watchin' with her testified that she dropped to sleep one mornin' before daylight, and when she woke up her patient wuz gone, and the child.

She had some money that her old mistress had give her from time to time, and that she had never had to use; that wuz taken, with some valuable jewelry too that that kind old friend had give her—for she had loved to set off her favorite's dark beauty with the light of precious stones—all these wuz taken; but every article that Monseur De

Chasseny had give her wuz left. And all the money that he left for her not a penny wuz ever called for. She disappeared as if she had never been; lawyers and detectives, hired, it wuz spozed, by De Chasseny, could find no trace of her.

There wuz a good, fatherly old missionary in the little settlement near by who might perhaps have given some information if he had wanted to; but they never thought of askin' him, and they would have been no wiser if they had, most probable.

But about this time a woman in deep mournin', with a beautiful young child, come to the little hamlet near Belle Fanchon.

She said she wuz a colored woman, though no one would have believed it.

The good priest in charge of the Mission—Father Gasperin—he seemed to know sunthin' about her; he had a brother who wuz a priest in South Carolina. He got her employment as a nurse after her health improved a little.

She bought a little cottage and lived greatly respected by all classes, black and white, and nursed 'em both to the best of her abilities—some for nuthin' and some at about a dollar a day.

But her earnest sympathies, her heartfelt affection wuz with the black race. She worked for their good and advancement in every way with a zeal that looked almost as if she wuz tryin' to atone for some awful mistake in the past—as if she wuz tryin' to earn forgiveness for forsakin' her mother's race for the white people, who wuz always faithless to her race, only when selfishness guided them—who would take the service of their whole life and strength, as if it belonged to 'em; who would take them up as a plaything to divert an hour's leisure, and then throw the worthless thing down agin.

Her whole heart wuz bent upon the good of her mother's people. She worked constantly for their advancement and regeneration. She bore their intolerable burdens for 'em, she agonized under their unexampled wrongs. She exhorted 'em to become Christians, to study, to learn to guide themselves aright; she besought 'em to elevate themselves by all means in their power.

She became a very earnest Christian; she went about doin' good; she studied her Bible much. The Book that in her bright days of happiness she had slighted became to her now the lamp of her life.

Most of all did this heart-broken soul, who had bid good-bye to all earthly happiness, love the weird prophecies of St. John the Evangelist.

She loved to read of the Belovéd City, and the sights that he saw, to her become realities. She said she saw visions in the night as she looked up from dyin' faces into the high heavens—she foretold events. Her prophetic sayin's became almost as inspired revelations to them about her.

She said she heard voices talkin' to her out of the skies and the darkness, and I don't know but she did—I don't feel like disputin' it either way; besides, I wuzn't there.

But as I wuz a sayin', from what I wuz told, the little girl, Genieve, inheritin' as she did her mother's imaginative nature and her father's bright mind and wit, and contemplatin' her mother's daily life of duty and self-sacrifice, and bein' brought up as she wuz under the very eaves of the New Jerusalem her mother wuz always readin' about, it is no wonder that she grew up like a posy—that while its roots are in the earth its tall flowers open and wave in the air of Eden.

The other world, the land unseen but near, became more of a reality to her than this. "The voices" her mother said she heard was to her real and true as the voice of good Father Gasperin, who preached in the little chapel every month.

The future of her mother's race wuz to her plain and distinct, lit with light fallin' from the new heavens on the new earth that she felt awaited her people.

The inspired prophecies to her pointed to their redemption and the upbuilding of a New Republic, where this warm-hearted, emotional, beauty lovin' race should come to their own, and, civilized and enlightened, become a great people, a nation truly brought out of great tribulations.

She grew up unlike any other girl, more beautiful than any other—so said every one who saw her. A mind different from any other—impractical perhaps, but prophetic, impassioned, delicate, sorrowful, inspired.

When she became old enough she followed her mother's callin' of nursin' the sick, and it seemed indeed as if her slight hands held the gift of healin' in them, so successful wuz she.

Guarded by her mother as daintily as if she wuz the daughter of a queen, she grew up to womanhood as innocent as Eve wuz when the garden wuz new.

She turned away almost in disgust from the attention of young men, white or colored.

But about a year before I went to Belle Fanchon she had met her king. And to her, truly, Victor wuz a crowned monarch. And the love that sprung up in both their hearts the moment they looked in each other's eyes wuz as high and pure and ideal an attachment as wuz ever felt by man or woman.

Victor wuz the son of a white man and a colored woman, but he showed the trace of his mother's ancestry as little as did Genieve.

His mother wuz a handsome mulatto woman, the nurse and constant attendant of the wife of Col. Seybert, whose handsome place, Seybert Court, could jest be seen from the veranda of Belle Fanchon.

Col. Seybert owned this plantation, but he had been abroad with his family many years, and in the States further South, where he also owned property.

He had come back to Seybert Court only a few months before Thomas J. bought Belle Fanchon.

Mrs. Seybert wuz a good woman, and in a long illness she had soon after her marriage she had been nursed so faithfully by Phyllis, Victor's mother, that she had become greatly attached to her; and Phyllis and her only child, Victor, had attended the Colonel and his wife in all their wanderings. Indeed, Mrs. Seybert often said and felt, Heaven knows, that she could not live if Phyllis left her.

And Victor wuz his mother's idol, and to be near her and give her comfort wuz one of the reasons why he endured his hard life with Col. Seybert.

For his master wuz not a good man. He wuz

hard, haughty, implacable. He wuz attached to Victor much as a manufacturer would be to an extra good piece of machinery by which his gains wuz enhanced.

Victor wuz an exceptionally good servant; he watched over his employer's interests, he wuz honest amongst a retinue of dishonest ones. He saved his employer's money when many of his feller-servants seemed to love to throw it away. His keen intelligence and native loyalty and honesty found many ways of advancin' his master's interests, and he helped him in so many ways that Col. Seybert had come to consider his services invaluable to him.

Still, and perhaps he thought it wuz the best way to make Victor feel his place and not consider himself of more consequence than he wuz—and it wuzn't in the nater of Col. Seybert to be anything but mean, mean as pusley, and meaner—

Anyway, he treated Victor with extreme insolence, and cruelty, and brutality. Mebby he thought that if he didn't " hold the lines tight," as he called it, Victor might make disagreeable demands upon his purse, or his time, or in some way seek for a just recognition of his services.

Col. Seybert, too, drank heavily, which might perhaps be some excuse for his brutality, but made it no easier for Victor to endure.

At such times Col. Seybert wuz wont to address Victor as " his noble brother," and order his " noble brother" to take off his boots, or put them on, or carry him upstairs, or perform still more menial services for him, he swearin' at him roundly all the time, and mixin' his oaths with whatever vile and contemptible epithets he could think of—and he could think of a good many.

And perhaps it did not make it easier for Victor to obey him that he told the truth in his drunken babble.  Victor wuz his brother, and they two wuz the only descendants of the gallant old Gen. Seybert, the handsomest, the wittiest, the bravest and the most courtly man of his day.

He went down to the grave the owner of many hundred slaves, the husband of a fair young bride, and the father of two children, one the only son of his pretty Northern bride, the other the son of his mother's maid.

And what made matters still more complicated and hard to understand, to this unowned, despised son had descended all the bright wit and philosophical mind, and suave, gentle, courteous manners of this fine gentleman Gen. Seybert ; and to the son and legal heir of all his wealth, not a bit of his father's sense, bright mind, and good manners.

One of his maternal great-uncles had been a rich, new-made man of low tastes and swaggerin', aggressive manners.  It wuz a sad thing that these inherited traits and tastes should just bound over one gentlemanly generation and swoop down upon the downy, lace-festooned cradle of this only son and heir—but they did.

All the nobility of mind, the grace, the kindly consideration for others, and the manly beauty, all fell as a dower to the little lonely baby smuggled away like an accursed thing, in his maternal grandmother's little whitewashed cabin.

To the young heir, Reginald, fell some hundreds

of thousands of dollars, two or three plantations, and an honored name and place in society, the tastes of a pot-boy, the mind and habits of a clown, the swaggerin', boastin' cruelty of an American Nero.

Col. Seybert drove and swore, and threatened his negroes as his great-uncle Wiggins drove the white operatives in his big Northern factory, kept them at starvation wages, and piled up his money-bags over the prostrate forms of gaunt, overworked men and women, and old young children, who earned his money out of their own hopeless youth; with one hand dropped gold into his coffers, and with the other dug shallow graves that they filled too soon.

Northern cupidity and avarice, Southern avarice and cupidity, equally ugly in God's sight, so we believe.

It wuz indeed strange that to Reginald should descend all the great-uncle's traits and none of his father's, only the passionate impulses that marred an otherwise almost faultless character; and to Victor, the cast-off, ignored son, should descend all the courtly graces inherited from a long line of illustrious ancestors, and all the brilliant qualities of mind too that made old Gen. Seybert's name respected and admired wherever known.

His sin in regard to Victor's mother wuz a sin directly traceable to the influence of Slavery. As the deeds a man commits when in liquor can be followed back to that source, so could this cryin' sin be traced directly back to the Slave regime.

It wuz but one berry off of the poisonous Upas-tree of Slavery that gloomily shadowed the beautiful South land, and darkens it yet, Heaven knows.

The top of this tree may have been lowered a little by the burnin' fires of war, but the deep roots remain ; and as time and a false sense of security relaxes the watch kept over it, the poison shoots spring up and the land is plagued by its thorny branches, its impassable, thick undergrowth.

The tree may be felled to the earth before it springs up agin with a more dangerous, vigorous growth and destroys the hull nation.

So Cousin John Richard said ; but I don't know whether it will or not, and Josiah don't.

But I am a eppisodin', and to resoom and continue on.

Reginald Seybert wuz tolerably good-lookin' in an aggressive, florid style, and he had plenty of boldness and wealth. And some, or all of these qualities, made it possible for him to marry a good woman of an impoverished but aristocratic Southern family.

The marriage wuz a sudden one—he did not give the young lady time to change her mind. He met her at a fashionable watering-place where they wuz both strangers, and, as I said, he give her no time to repent her choice.

After the honeymoon trip and her husband brought her to his home, she heard many strange things she had been kept in ignorance of—amongst them this pitiful story of Victor and his mother—and being what she wuz, a good, tender-hearted woman, with high ideals and pure and charitable impulses—perhaps it wuz this that made her so good to Victor's mother, so thoughtful and considerate of him, and that made her, during her husband's long absences on his wild sprees, give him every benefit of teachers and opportunity to study.

And Victor almost worshipped his gentle mistress, his unhappy mistress, for it could not be otherwise, that after she knew him well, her feelin's for her husband could hardly have been stronger than pity. Perhaps after a time aversion and disgust crept in, and as she had no children or brothers of her own, she grew strongly attached to Phyllis and to Victor, the only relative—for so this strange woman called him in her thoughts—the only relative near her who wuz kind to her.

For as her beauty faded, worn away by the anguished, feverish beatings of a sad heart, Col. Seybert grew cruel and brutal to her also. It was not in his nature to be kind to anything, or to value anything that did not minister to his selfishness. He lived only for the gratification of his appetites and his ambition.

He prized Victor, as we said, as a manufacturer would prize an extra good loom, on which valuable cloth might be woven, and which would bear any amount of extra pressure on occasion.

Victor's loyal affection and gratitude to his mistress, and his determination to shield her all he could from her husband's brutality, and his love for his mother, made him conceal from them all he could the fiendish cruelties his master sometimes inflicted upon him.

Old Gen. Seybert had been noted all his brilliant life for his tender consideration and thoughtful courtesy towards women, and his desire to shield them from all possible annoyance.

His son Victor had this trait also, added to the warm-hearted gratitude of his mother's race towards one who befriends them.

Many a time did he carry a scarred back and a

COLONEL SEYBERT.

smilin' face into the presence of his mother and mistress.

Many a time did he voluntarily absent himself from them for days, or until the bruises had healed that some too skilfully aimed missile had inflicted upon him.

But soon after he came to Belle Fanchon, and

after he had met and loved Genieve, Col. Seybert's treatment became so unendurable that Victor begged of his mother to go away with him, tellin' her he could now earn a good livin' for her; and he had dreams, hardly formulated to himself then, of the future of his mother's race. They lay in his heart as seeds lie in the dark ground, waitin' for the time to spring up—they were germinatin', waitin' for the dawn to waken them to rich luxuriance.

But his mother felt that she could not leave her kind mistress in her lonely troubles, and she entreated him prayerfully that he would not leave her, "and she could not go away and leave Miss Alice with that tyrant and murderer"—for so she called Col. Seybert in her wrath.

And his mistress's anguished entreaties that he would not leave her, for she felt that she had but a little time to live, her health was failin' all the time—

"And the blessed lamb would die without us anyway," his mother would say to Victor—

And all these arguments added to his loyal desire to befriend this gentle mistress who had educated him and done for him all she could have done for son or brother—all these arguments caused him to stay on.

But after comin' to Seybert Court, Victor had given Col. Seybert another opportunity to empty the vials of his wrath upon him.

Victor had a bosom friend, a young man in about the same circumstances that he wuz—only this friend, Felix Ward, had lived with a kind master and mistress durin' his childhood and early youth.

His father and mother wuz both dead; his father

bein' killed in the war, and his mother soon followin' him.

He wuz an intelligent negro, with no white blood in his veins, so far as he knew. Felix, for so he had been named when he looked like a tiny black doll, by his young mistress, to whom the world looked so happy and prosperous that everything assumed a roseate hue to her.

Her faithful servant, his mother, brought the little image in ebony to her room to show it to her, jest after she had read the letter from the man she loved askin' her to be his wife.

She wuz happy; the world looked bright and prosperous to her. She gave the little pickaninny this name for a good omen—Felix: happy, prosperous.

But alas! though the pretty young mistress prospered well in her love and her life while it lasted, the poor little baby she had named had better have been called Infelix, so infelicitous had been his life—or, that is, the latter part of it.

For awhile, while he wuz quite young, it seemed as if his name would stand him in good stead and bring good fortune with it. For being owned till her death by this same gentle young mistress and her husband, both, like so many Southerners, so much better than the system they represented, they helped him, seein' his brightness and intelligence, to an education, and afterwards through their influence he wuz placed at Hampton School, and at their death, which occurred very suddenly in a scourge of yeller fever, they left him a little money.

At Hampton School he got a good education, and

learned the carpenter's trade. And it wuz at Seybert Court, which wuz bein' repaired, and he wuz one of the workmen, that Victor and he become such close friends.

Victor had come on to superintend some of the work that wuz bein' done there to fit the place for the reception of his master's family, who wuz at that time in New Orleans. And these two young men wuz together several months and become close friends. They wuz related on their mother's side, and they wuz joined together in that closer, subtler relationship of kindred tastes, feelings, and aspirations.

He finally bought a little carpenter's shop and settled down to work at his trade in the little hamlet of Eden Centre, where he soon after married a pretty mulatto girl, the particular friend of Genieve.

With the remains of the money his mistress had left him he bought a little cottage—or, that is, this money partly paid for it, and he thought that with his good health and good trade he could soon finish up the payment and own his own home.

It wuz a pretty cottage, but fallen into disorder and ruinous looks, through poor tenants; but his skilful hands and his labor of love soon made it over into a perfect gem of a cottage.

And there he and his pretty young wife Hester had spent two most happy years, when Col. Seybert come into the neighborhood to live, and his roamin' fancy soon singled out Hester for a victim.

She had been lady's maid in a wealthy, refined family, and her ladylike manners and pretty ways wuz as attractive as her face. She loved her husband, and wuz constant to him with all the fidelity of a lovin' woman's heart, and Col. Seybert she detested with all the force of her nature; but Col. Seybert wuz not one to give way to such a slight obstacle as a lawful husband.

He thought if Felix wuz out of the way the course of his untrue love would run comparatively smooth. Why, it seemed to him to be the height of absurdity that a "nigger" should stand in the way of his wishes.

Why, it wuz aginst all the traditions of his race and the entire Southern Aristocracy that so slight things as a husband's honor and wife's loyalty should dare oppose the lawless passions of a white gentleman.

Of course, so reasoned Col. Seybert; the war had made a difference in terms and enactments, but that wuz about all. The white race wuz still unconquered in their passion and their arrogance, and the black race wuz still under their feet; he could testify to the truth of this by his own lawless life full of deeds of unbridled license and cruelty.

So, wantin' Victor out of the way, and bein' exceedingly wroth aginst him, it wuz easy to persuade certain ignorant poor whites, and the dispensers of what they called law, that Felix wuz altogether too successful for a nigger.

He owned a horse, too, an almost capital offence in some parts of the South.

He had worked overhours to buy this pet animal for Hester's use as well as his own. Many a hundred hard hours' labor, when he wuz already tired out, had he given for the purchase money of this little animal.

It wuz a pretty, cream-colored creeter, so gentle that it would come up to the palin' and eat little bits that Hester would carry out to it after every meal, with little Ned toddlin' along by her side; and it wuz one of the baby boy's choicest rewards for good behavior to be lifted up by the side of the kind-faced creeter and pat the glossy skin with his little fat hands.

This horse seemed to Felix and Hester to be endowed with an almost human intelligence, and come next to little Ned, their only child, in their hearts.

And Hester had herself taken in work and helped to pay for the plain buggy in which she rode out with her boy, and carried Felix to and from his work when he wuz employed some distance from his home.

But no matter how honestly he had earned this added comfort, no matter how hard they had both worked for it and how they enjoyed it—

"It wuz puttin' on too much damned style for a nigger!"

This wuz Col. Seybert's decree, echoed by many a low, brutal, envious mind about him, encased in black and white bodies.

And one mornin', when Hester went out in the bright May sunshine to carry Posy its mornin' bit of food from the breakfast-table, with little Ned followin' behind with his bit of sugar for it, the pretty creeter had jest enough strength to drag itself up to its mistress and fix its pitiful eyes on her in helpless appeal, and dropped dead at her feet.

They found the remains of a poisoned cake in the pasture, and on the fence wuz pinned a placard bearin' the inscription—

"LOW, BRUTAL, ENVIOUS MIND."

" No damned niggers can ride wile wit foaks wak afut—so good buy an' take warnin'."

They did not try to keep a horse after this. Felix took his long mornin' and evenin' walks with a sore, indignant heart that dragged down his tired limbs still more.

And Hester wiped away the tears of little Ned, and tried to explain to his bewildered mind why his pretty favorite could not come up to him when he called it so long and patiently, holdin' out the temptin' lump of sugar that had always hastened its fleet step.

And she wiped away her own tears, and tried to find poor comfort in the thought that so many wuz worse off than herself.

She had Felix and Ned left, and her pretty home.

But in the little black settlement of Cedar Hill, not fur away, where her mother's relations lived, destitution wuz reignin'.

For on one pretext or another their crops that they worked so hard for wuz taken from them. The most infamous laws wuz made whereby the white man could take the black man's earnings.

The negro had the name of bein' a freedman, but in reality he wuz a worse slave than ever, for in the old times he had but one master who did in most cases take tolerable care of him, for selfishness' sake, if no other, and protected him from the selfishness of other people.

But now every one who could take advantage of his ignorance of law did so, and on one pretext or another robbed him of his hard-earned savings.

And it wuz not considered lawful and right by these higher powers for a nigger to get much property. It wuz looked upon as an insult to the superior race about him who had nuthin', and it wuz considered dangerous to the old-established law of Might over Right.

It wuz a dangerous precedent, and not to be condoned. So it wuz nuthin' oncommon if a colored man succeeded by hard work and economy in gettin' a better house, and had good crops and stock, for a band of masked men to surround the house at midnight and order its inhabitants, on pain of death, to leave it all and flee out of the country before daylight.

And if they appealed to the law, it wuz a slender reed indeed to lean upon, and would break under the slightest pressure.

Indeed, what good could law do, what would decrees and enactments avail in the face of this terrible armed power, secret but invincible, that closed round this helpless race like the waves of the treacherous whirlpool about a twig that wuz cast into its seethin' waters?

The reign of Terrorism, of Lynch Law, of Might aginst Right wuz rampant, and if they wanted to save even their poor hunted bodies they had learned to submit.

So, poor old men and wimmen would rise up from the ruins of their homes, the homes they had built with so much hard toil. Feeble wimmen and children, as well as youth and strength, would rise up and move on, often with sharp, stingin' lashes to hasten their footsteps.

Move on to another place to have the same scenes enacted over and over agin.

The crops and stock that wuz left fell as a reward to the victors in the fray.

And if there wuz a pretty girl amongst the fugitives she too wuz often and often bound to the conqueror's chariot wheels till the chariot got tired of this added ornament, then she fell down before it and the heavy wheels passed over her. And so exit pretty girl.

But the world wuz full of them; what mattered one more or less? It wuz no more than if a fly should be brushed away by a too heavy hand, and have its wings broken. There are plenty more, and of what account is one poor insect?

Many a poor aged one died broken-hearted in the toilsome exodus from their homes and treasures.

But there wuz plenty more white-headed old negroes—why, one could hardly tell one from another—of what use wuz it to mention the failure of one or two?

Many a young and eager one with white blood throbbin' in his insulted and tortured breast stood up and fought for home, and dear ones, and liberty, all that makes life sweet to prince or peasant.

What became of them? Let the dark forests reveal if they can what took place in their shadows.

Let the calm heavens speak out and tell of the anguished cries that swept up on the midnight air from tortured ones. How the stingin' whip-lash mingled with vain cries for mercy. How frenzied appeals wuz cut short by the sharp crack of a rifle or the swing of a noose let down from some tree-branch.

How often Death come as a friend to hush the lips of intolerable pain and torture!

Sometimes this tyrannical foe felt the vengeance

he had called forth by his cowardly deeds, and a white man or woman fell a victim to the vengeance of the black race.

Then the Associated Press sent the tidings through an appalled and horrified country—

"Terrible deed of a black brute—the justly incensed citizens hung the wretch up to the nearest tree—so perish all the enemies of law and order."

And the hull country applauded the deed.

The black man had no reporters in the daily papers; if he had, their pens would have been worn down to the stump by a tithe of the unrecorded deeds that are yet, we believe, put down on a record that is onbought and as free to the poorest class as to the highest, and is not influenced by political bias.

But these accounts are not open yet, and the full history of these tragedies are as yet unread by the public.

More awful tragedies than ever took place or ever could take place under any other circumstances, only where one alien and hated race wuz pitted aginst the other.

Ignorance on both sides, inherited prejudices, and personal spite, and animosities blossomin' out in its fruit of horror.

"They were burnt at the stake; they were sawed asunder; they were destitute, afflicted, tormented."

Your soul burns within you as you read of these deeds that took place in Jerusalem; your heart aches for them who wandered about tormented, hunted down on every side; you lavish your sympathy upon them; but then you think it wuz a sav-

DEFENDING HIS HOME.

age age, this wuz one of its brutalities, and you congratulate yourself upon livin' in an age of Christian enlightenment.

You think such deeds are impossible in a land over which the Star of Bethlehem has shone for eighteen hundred years.

Down in many a Southern bayou, in the depths of many a cypress swamp, near the remains of a violated home, lies a heap of ashes--all that remains of a man who died fightin' for his home and his loved ones.

That wuz his only crime—he expiated it with his life. But his liberated soul soared upwards jest as joyfully, let us hope, as if his body received the full sacrament of sorrowful respect.

One of the laws enacted of late in the South permits a white man to kill a black man for a crime committed aginst his honor, and if the white man commits the same crime and the black man takes the same revenge, he is killed at once accordin' to law— one man liberated with rejoicings, the other shot down like a dog. Do you say the black man is more ignorant? That is a bad plea.

And wantin' to act dretful lawful, a short time ago a gang of white law-makers dug up the dead body of a dark-complexioned husband they had murdered accordin' to law, and after breakin' its bones, hung it over agin.

He could find in the law no help to defend his home or protect his honor, no refuge in the grave to which the law had sent him.

I wonder if his freed soul has found some little safe corner in space fenced round by justice and compassion, where it can hide itself forever from the laws and civilization of this 19th Century, in this great and glorious country of the free.

To select this one instance of cruel wrong and injustice from the innumerable ones similar to it is like takin' up a grain of sand from the seashore and contemplatin' it—the broad seashore that stretches out on either hand is full of them.

And why should not wrongs, and crimes, and woes be inevitable—why, indeed?

A race but lately slaves, with the responsible gift of freedom dropped too soon into their weak hands—

The race so lately the dominant and all-powerful one through the nation, by the fiction of law dropped down under the legal rule of these so long downtrodden, oppressed, ignorant masses, what could the result be?

And the law-makers who had proclaimed peace and liberty, on paper, sot afar contemplatin' the great work they had done, and left the Reign of Horror to be enacted by the victors and the victims.

Poor colored man! poor white man! both to be pitied with a pity beyond words.

It wuz not their fault, it wuz but the fallin' hail and lightnin' and tempest out of clouds that had been gatherin' for ages.

But after the tempest cometh peace. And the eyes of Faith beholds through the mists and the darkness the sunshine of a calmer time, the peace and the rest of a fair country, and a free one.

God grant more wisdom to the great commonwealth of this nation, those whose wills are spoken out by their ballots, to the makers and the doers of law.

But I am a eppisodin', and to resoom, and continue on.

Felix and Hester, by some good chance, or by the grace of God, had not been obliged yet to leave their pretty home, so they worked on, tryin' to be so peaceable and friendly that no fault could be found with them.

Col. Seybert's attention when he wuz at Seybert Court wuz very annoyin' to Hester, but she dared not tell Felix, fearin' that he would avenge himself on the Colonel, and bloodshed would result.

So she tried to be very careful. She had an old negro woman stay with her; she took in work all she could at home, and when she went out to work she wuz prudent and watchful, and, fortunately for her peace of mind, the Colonel made short stays at his home—he found more potent attractions elsewhere.

So stood matters when Felix wuz appointed Justice of the Peace at Eden Centre.

He wuz honestly appointed and honestly elected.

Victor had always declined any office, and had Felix taken his advice he would also have refused the office.

But perhaps Felix had some ambition. And maybe he had some curiosity to see what honesty and a pure purpose could accomplish in political matters, to see what such a marvellous thing could amount to.

Anyway, he accepted the nomination and received the office.

And the night after he wuz elected he and Hester

talked the matter over with some pardonable pride as they sot in the door of their pretty little parlor in the warm moonlight.

The creepin' vines on the trellis cast pleasant shadows of leaf and blossom down over their heads and on the pretty carpet at their feet.

This carpet Hester had bought with her own money and wuz proud of.

The moonlight lay there warm and bright, weavin' its magic tapestry of rose leaf and swingin' vine tendrils long after they wuz asleep in their little white-draped room near by.

Baby Ned lay fast asleep, with a smile on his moist, flushed face, in his love-guarded cradle near them.

The little boy did not dream of anything less sweet and peaceful than his mother's good-night kiss that had been his last wakin' remembrance.

But about midnight other shadows, black and terrible ones, trod out and defaced the swayin', tremblin' rose images and silvery moonlight on the floor.

Tall men in black masks, a rough, brutal gang, surrounded the place and crashed in the door of the little cottage.

Amongst the foremost wuz Nick Burley, a low, brutal fellow, one of Col. Seybert's overseers and boon companions.

He had wanted the office, and his friends greatly desired it for him, thinkin' no doubt it would prove many times a great convenience to them.

But Felix won it honorably. He got the majority of votes and wuz honestly elected.

But Burley and his choice crew of secret Regulators could not brook such an insult as to have one of a race of slaves preferred to him, so they proceeded to mete out the punishment to him fit for such offenders.

They tore Felix from his bed, leavin' Hester in a faintin' fit, and the little child screamin' with fright.

THE LEADER.

Took him out in the swamp, bound him to a tree, and whipped him till he had only a breath of life left in him ; then they put him into a crazy old boat, and launched him out on the river, tellin' him "if he ever dared to step his foot into his native State agin they would burn him alive,"

And this happened in our free country, in a country where impassioned oritors, on the day set apart to celebrate our nation's freedom, make their voices heard even above the roar of blatant cannons, so full of eloquence and patriotism are they, as they eulogize our country's liberty, justice, and independence.

"The only clime under God's free sky," they say, "where the law protects all classes alike, and the vote of the poorest man is as potent as the loftiest, in moulding our perfect institutions. Where the lowest and the highest have full and equal civil and political rights."

Oh, it would have been a goodly sight for our American eagle, proud emblem of liberty, to have witnessed this midnight scene we have been describin'; methinks such a spectacle would almost have magnetism to draw him from his lofty lair on Capitol Hill to swoop down into this cypress swamp, and perchin' upon some lofty tree-top, look down and witness this administration of justice and equal rights, to mark how these beneficent free laws enwrap all the people and protect them from foreign invasion and home foes, to see how this nation loves its children, its black children, who dumbly endured generations of unexampled wrongs and indignities at its hands, and then in its peril bared their patient breasts and risked their lives to save it.

How this bird of freedom must laugh in a parrot-like glee, if so grave and dignified a fowl wuz ever known to indulge in unseemly mirth, to see the play go on, the masquerade of Folly and Brutality in the garb of Wisdom and Order, holding such high carnival.

After thus sendin' Felix half dead from his brutal usage adrift on the turbid river waves that they felt assured would float him down to a sure and swift death, the gang of ruffians returned to the cottage to complete their night's work.

Col. Seybert had dealt out plenty of bad whiskey to them to keep up their courage; and Nick Burley, besides satisfying his own vengeance upon Felix, had been offered a very handsome reward by his master for gettin' him out of the way and takin' Hester to a lonely old cabin of his in the depths of the big forest.

But they found the pretty cottage empty, and they could only show their disapprobation of the fact by despoilin' and ruinin' the cozy nest from which the bird had flown.

Hester had recovered from her faintin' fit jest as they wuz takin' Felix to the river; she discovered by their shouts which way they had gone, followed them at a safe distance, and when they had disappeared she by almost a miracle swam out to the boat which had drifted into a bayou, brought it to shore, and nursed him back to life agin.

And for weeks they remained in hidin', not darin' to return to their dear old home that they had earned so hardly, and Felix not dreamin' of claimin' his honest rights as a duly elected Justice of the Peace.

No, he felt that he had had enough of political honors and preferments—if he could only escape with his life and keep his wife and boy wuz all he asked.

At last he got a note to Victor, who aided him in

his flight to another State, where he patiently commenced life agin with what courage and ambition he might bring to bear on it, with his mind forever dwellin' on his bitter wrongs and humiliation, and on memories of the old home left forever behind him—that pretty home with the few acres of orchard and garden about it. And remembered how he and Hester delighted in every dollar they paid towards it, and how they had a little feast, and invited in their friends that sunny June day when the last dollar wuz paid, and it wuz their own.

And remembered how proudly they had labored to finish and furnish the little home. How Hester had worked at washin' and ironin' and bought the paper and paint, and pretty curtains and carpet, and how infinitely happy they had been in it.

How after his hard day's work he would work in the little sunshiny garden and orchard settin' out fruit trees, plantin' berry bushes and grape-vines, and how they had together gloried over all their small successes, and thought that they had the very coziest and happiest home in the world.

Wall, they had lost it all. The honor of bein' an American citizen bore down pretty heavy on him, and he had to give it up.

Wall, twice did Felix try to get a home for himself and his wife in the Southern States.

But both times, on one pretext or another, did the dominant power deprive him of his earnings, and take his home from him.

Felix had a good heart; and once, the last time he tried to make a home under Southern skies, this good heart wuz the cause of his overthrow.

He barely escaped with his life for darin' to harbor a white teacher who had left his home and gone down South, followin' the Bible precepts " to seek and save them that was lost, and preach the Gospel to every creature."

He taught a small colored school week days and preached in an old empty barn on Sundays.

Little Ned went to his school and wuz greatly attached to him.

But when he wuz ordered to leave the State within twenty-four hours, because " he wuz tryin' to teach them brute cattle jest as if they wuz humans"—

Bein' frightened and made sick by the violence of his discharge and the stingin' arguments with which they enforced their orders, Felix opened his poor cabin-door and sheltered him; then agin his home wuz surrounded with a band of armed, masked men, and they only managed to escape with their lives, and Felix agin left all his poor little improvements on his home behind him.

He and his family and the white teacher, bruised but undaunted, got to the railroad by walkin' almost all night, and so escaped out of their hands.

The young teacher married soon after a rich Northern woman with kindred tastes to his own, and they both betook themselves imegiatly after their marriage to a part of the South a little less ardent in hatred to the Freedmen's Bureau, where they are doin' a good work still in teachin' a colored school.

But the next time Felix made a start in life he commenced it in a Northern city.

There the best thing he could get in the way of a home for his wife and child wuz a room way up on the top of a crazy old tenement-house tenanted by noisy, drunken, profane men and women.

For drunkenness, and brawls, and sickenin' hor-

FELIX AND THE TEACHER.

rors are not confined to Southern soil; they are also indigenous to the North.

And the gaunt wolves of Sin and Want howl to the moon under the Northern skies as well as Southern.

And stayin' there—not livin'—workin' hard as he did through the day, and uninvitin' as his home wuz after his labor wuz over, he could set down for a few minutes with Hester, only to have their quiet broken by drunken brawls, and oaths, and fights, and all sounds and sights of woe and squalor.

In such circumstances as these the teachings and importunate words of Victor about colonization fell upon a willin' ear.

For the seeds that had laid in Victor's heart, waitin' only the warm sun to bring them to life, had sprung up into full vigor and bloom under the influence of Genieve's prophetic words, and afterwards by his own observation and study.

Victor come to believe with his whole soul and heart that the future of his race depended upon their leavin' this land and goin' fur away from all the cursed influences that had fettered them so long here and found a new home and country for themselves —a New Republic.

And as Felix, with whom Victor had been in constant correspondence, read these glowin' words and arguments, they fell upon good ground.

Truly the soil in Felix' breast had been turned, and ploughed, and made ready for the seed of liberty to be planted and spring up.

All of the time while he wuz gettin' his education so hardly, spendin' every hour he could possibly spare from his work in endeavorin' to fit himself for a future of freedom and usefulness—all this while he had been told, been taught in sermons and religious and secular literature, and read it in law books and statutes, that merit wuz the only patent of nobility in this country, that merit would win the prizes of life.

To this end he had worked, had shaped his own life to habits of honesty and industry; he had surrounded himself with all the safeguards possible to keep him in the right path, chose for his intimate friends young men who cherished the same lofty ideals that he did.

He attended church constantly, became an earnest Christian, had obtained an excellent education, and then it wuz not strange that he should look about him to try to behold the rewards that merit wins. One illustration of this reward of merit we have jest given—when he wuz elected Justice of the Peace.

That wuz a fair sample of the rewards of merit offered to his race.

He wuz not alone in it; no, he looked about him, and he saw thousands and thousands of young colored men who had studied jest as hard as he had—they too had dreams of this great truth that had been dinned in their ears so long—that Christianity, education, and merit will win all the prizes of life.

They studied, they worked hard, they pursued lofty ideals, and when they left their schools they wuz Christians, they wuz educated, they wuz meritorious. Their minds wuz bright and well equipped, their tastes wuz refined, they wuz good.

Of what avail wuz it all, so Felix asked himself, when they wuz pushed back to the wall by brazen audacity and ignorance—and intolerance and ignorance and immorality, if encased in a white skin, might snatch all the prizes out of their hands and take their places in the front ranks of life.

In many States in the South they could not get the place of a policeman if it depended upon the integrity of the ballot.

What sort of an education, a finishing school, wuz this for the young colored man of the South? Wuz such unblushin' fraud, and lies, and cheatin', and heart-burnings, and sickenin' disappointments, and deeds of violence, a wholesome atmosphere for young people to learn morals in?

Felix, as he looked about him and saw the thousands and thousands and thousands of young men, graduates of schools and members of churches, in jest the same condition as he himself wuz—he might be pardoned if he asked himself if the long horror of the War had been in vain.

If Lincoln and Grant and all the other pure souls had toiled and died in vain.

If the millions of dollars given by Northern philanthropy, and the noble lives of sacrifice in teachin' and preachin', had been given in vain.

He might be pardoned if he said:

"Give these young colored people new doctrines or new laws; teach them less Christianity by book and a little more practical religion and justice by object lesson; give these law-abiding, native-born citizens of this Republic a tithe of the rights and privileges enjoyed by the lowest criminal foreigner newly landed on our shores, or else let this addition be made to their creeds:

"'Merit has nothing to do in determining a man's future life.'

"'Injustice shall conquer in the end.'

"'Fraud shall be victor over honest and Christian endeavor.'

"'The colored man, by reason of his dark complexion, shall be forever deprived of all the blessings and privileges of the Government he risked his life to save.'"

Put this into the creeds you teach the young colored men and women, and they will at least respect you for bein' sincere and truthful.

Felix felt all this, and more too—more than I could set down if my pen wuz as long as from here to the moon, and longer.

And feelin' as he did, is it any wonder that all his mind and heart wuz sot on this skeme of Victor's, and all his hopes and aims pinted towards a new home, where he could take his wife and child and be free? where he felt that he could own them and own a right to make a home for 'em—a home where the American eagle, proud bird of Liberty, could nevermore tear him with her talons, or claw his trustin' eyes out with her sharp bill?

He felt this, but the eagle wuzn't to blame—it wuz her keepers, if he had only known it. The eagle wuz in a hard place. I felt real sorry for the fowl, and have for a number of times. She has been in many a tight place before now—places where it wuz all she could do to squeeze out her wings and shake 'em a mite.

Wall, Felix worked hard, and so did Hester, with this end in view—to go fur away and be at rest.

Felix, after many efforts, got a place as workman on a big buildin' that wuz bein' put up; and Hester got a place as fine washerwoman and laundress with good wages.

They lived cheap as they could, and at the time when I first hearn about 'em (from Genieve) they had got about the amount saved that Victor thought they would require.

Felix wanted at least four or five hundred dollars to start with. You see, he and Victor could look ahead, which is more than some of their mother's race can do.

Felix knew he had got to have something to live on for the first year after he got to the Promised Land. He didn't mean to pin his faith onto anybody or anything. He felt that his family's safety and well-bein' depended on him, and he wuz bound to labor with that end in view.

And Victor wuz workin' as hard as Felix; workin' quietly and secretly as possible, deemin' that the best way to avert danger from them and make success possible.

He wuz workin' as a standard-bearer, a tryin' to make his people hear his cry to move forward into the Promised Land, into their own land, from whence they had been torn with violence, but to which they should return with knowledge and wisdom learned in the hard school of martyrdom and slavery.

He knew that to preach this doctrine to all his people would be like tryin' to stop the course of the wind by a shout.

The old, the feeble, and those who wuz attached by strong ties of love or gratitude to this Western land —and Heaven knows there wuz many such who had received such kind treatment from the dominant race (if kindness is possible in slavery) that their hearts wuz knit to the spot where their old masters and mistresses wuz—

These people he did not seek to disturb with

"THE OLD, THE FEEBLE."

dreams of new homes in a freer land—love makes labor light—they wuzn't unhappy.

And then there wuz many who had got peaceful homes in settlements and cities who wuz contented and doin' well—or, that is, what they thought well—these Victor did not seek to change.

But for the young, the educated, the resolute, the

ambitious he tried to influence their eager, active minds with his own ideal of a New Republic.

Where his people, so long down-trodden, might have a chance to become a great nation, with a future glorious with a grandeur the colder white race never dreamed of.

When Victor heard scoffin' prophecies of the negro's incapacity to govern himself or others, he thought of the example of that hero saint, Toussaint L'Ouverture. How he, a pure negro, with no white blood in his veins, carved out the freedom of his race.

How, brave as a lion, this untaught man fought aginst overwhelmin' odds, and won battles that the best-trained soldier would almost have despaired of; surmounted difficulties and won victories that would have proved well-nigh impossible to a Washington or a Napoleon. How, untaught in diplomacy, he reconciled conflictin' interests that would have baffled our wisest statesmen.

Clement and merciful, for he always shrank from causin' bloodshed till war or ruin wuz inevitable.

Generous, for when the storm burst his first thought wuz to save his master's family.

Wise and prudent, he founded and ruled over a peaceful and prosperous republic till he wuz betrayed to his ruin—not by the black race, but by the cupidity, and treachery, and envy of the white race.

Perished by starvation in a dungeon for the sole fault of bein' superior and nobler than the white people who envied his success and sought his overthrow.

Victor thought if one of his own race could do this

marvellous thing, amidst such warrin' and diverse elements and opposin' races, what would it not be possible for his people to do in a new and free country, in a state of peace and quiet, with only the interests and advancement of this one race to look after.

He dreamed in his hopeful visions of a fresh new civilization springin' up anew in the soil that had nurtured the first civilization.

For in the East, where the star had first shone and travelled on to the West, then back agin to the mystical wonder-laden East—thither did Victor's rapt eyes follow it. And Genieve, too, how she dreamed and longed for that new kingdom!

All through their dreary servitude, tortured and wretched, it seemed as if God gave to the believers amongst this people songs in the night, as if His spirit breathed through the simple hymns they sung to lighten the hours of bondage.

Some spirit, some inspiration seemed to breathe through their songs that brought tears to eyes unused to weepin'.

The most cultured, the most refined found, in spite of themselves, that they had wet cheeks and beatin' hearts after listenin' to these simple strains.

It could not have been for their musical worth—for they had little; it could not have been for their literary value—for they had none.

What could it have been in them that charmed alike prince and peasant but the spirit of the Most High, who come down to speak hope and cheer to His too burdened and hopeless ones and lighten their captivity?

Genieve thought that when this people, whom God chose to honor in this way, and whom He had led in such strange ways out of the jungles of ignorance in Africa, through the hard school of American slavery, out into liberty—she dreamed it was for the express purpose of educating her race so they might go back and redeem this dark land ; and then she fancied that the Presence that had stayed with them through the dark night of sorrow would in the full day of their civilization shine out with a marvellous light, and they would be peculiarly under His care.

She dreamed that this child-like, warm-hearted race would indeed " see God" as the colder and more philosophical races could not.

So, as I begun to say—but what a hand to eppisode I am, and what a digressor I be—and I believe my soul it grows on me—

Wall, as I begun to say more'n half an hour ago, if it wuz a minute,

Col. Seybert thought he had another cause of enmity aginst Victor, for he had strong proofs that it wuz he who had helped release Hester from his clutches.

And although it wuz kept secret as possible, yet rumors had reached Col. Seybert of Victor's dreams of the colonization of his race.

And to this Col. Seybert wuz opposed with all the selfishness and haughty arrogance of his nature. Why, who would work his big plantations if it wuz not for the blacks ? And if this movement should succeed he knew it would draw off the best, and most intelligent, and industrious element, and the ones left in the South would charge double wages, so he reasoned.

And as to Victor, he vowed to himself with a big

"HIS OVERSEER."

round oath that he should *not* go. He *should not* leave him.

Why, who would look after his interests as he always had—who would keep his affairs from goin' to ruin durin' his long sprees? Where could be found another servant with his absolute honesty, and intelligence, and care for his interests?

Why, as he thought of it, all the old slaveholdin' instinct of compellin' his inferiors, the hereditary impulse to rule or ruin rose in him, and his face grew red with wrath, and he vowed agin, with a still more sonorous oath, "That Victor should not go," and he added, with a true slave-driver's emphasis, "*not alive.*"

His overseer and kindred spirit, Nick Burley, hated Victor; for, added to the hated knowledge that Victor wuz his superior in every way, wuz the belief that he had befriended Felix. At all events, Victor and Felix wuz close friends always, and Burley hated Felix worse if possible than he did Victor.

But to Victor and Genieve all these shadows lay fur away on the horizon almost unseen, and anyway almost forgotten in the clear sunshine of their happiness.

For true love will make sunshine everywhere.

"A LITTLE TUMBLE-DOWN COTTAGE."

## CHAPTER VI.

ABOUT half a mile from Belle Fanchon, on the road that led to Eden Centre, stood a little tumble-down cottage where an old colored woman lived with her granddaughter and grandson.

Cleopatra, shortened into Aunt Clo', wuz picturesque-lookin' even in her rags. She wuz taller by far than common wimmen, with a portly figure, that did not show any marks of privation, although it wuz difficult to tell what the family lived on, for it wuz the exception instead of the rule to see any one of 'em employed in any useful labor.

Once in a great while Aunt Clo' would go out for a day's work washin' or cleanin' house, or any other work she could perform.

At such times, although she professed to have great "misery" in her back, her arms, her legs, and, in fact, "all her bones," yet she did a good day's work, but with groanings scarcely to be uttered.

She always seemed serenely gracious in receivin' anything that Maggie gave her, evidently considerin' it wuz only her due.

But although her day's works wuz exceedingly unfrequent, and her granddaughter Rosy and the boy Abe wuz hardly ever seen to perform any labor, yet they showed no signs of starvation, certainly.

As a reason for this state of things the neighbors' hen-roosts and corn-fields might have given evidence.

Rosy, the young granddaughter, wuz utterly without morals of any savin' kind. She wuz rather

CLEOPATRA.

pretty for a full-blooded African. A empty-headed, gigglin', utterly depraved study in black.

Not one of the family could read or write, or hardly tell the time of day. Two large dogs formed part of their household, and they seemingly possessed more intelligence than either of the human residents.

Rosy used often to come to Maggie's kitchen to ask for things they wanted. For one peculiarity of this family wuz that they seemed only serenely performin' their duty when they begged for anything they wanted.

One day, as she sot before me arrayed in cheap, dirty finery, I said to her:

"Rosy, can you read or write?"

"No, missy."

"Wouldn't you like to learn to?"

"I d'no, missy."

"There is a colored school only a little ways from here, where a good many of your people are learnin' to be good scholars. Why don't you go to it?"

"I d'no, missy."

"If you will go I will give you the books you will want. Will you go if I will get them for you?"

"Yes, missy."

A most unblushin' falsehood, as I learned afterwards. For she sold the books as soon as I gave them to her at the little store at the Corners, sold them for a string of yellow glass beads and a cheap cotton lace collar.

And when I taxed her with this, she denied it at once.

And when I told her that I saw the books at the store myself, she said she had lost the books on her way to school, and the beads and collar had been given her.

"'Fore de Lawd dey had."

What could any one do with such ignorance, and falsehood, and utter lack of principle?

And as Maggie said, "The South is overrun with just such characters as these."

Not all of them about there wuz so, she said, not

by any means; some of them wuz earnest Christians, good scholars, good inhabitants.

But thousands and thousands of those who wuz slaves, bred to concealment and lies in self-defence, taught all kinds of vice by the system under which they wuz born and nurtured, seem to have no sense of what is right and what is wrong; they will steal with no compunction of conscience; lie when the truth would serve them better; will only work when compelled to, and are low and depraved every way.

"What is to be done with them?" sez I. And Maggie said and I thought there wuz but one answer to this, wherever they be, for movin' their bodies round won't purify their souls to once nor quicken their intellects imegiatly.

Give them the Bible, teach them, arouse them from the dark sleep of sin and ignorance, learn them to stand upright and then to walk.

Givin' such men the right to vote and control by their greater numbers the educated race is as simple as it would be to set a baby that had never took a step to runnin' a race for a prize with an athlete.

The baby has got to stand on its feet first, get a little strength in its soft, unused muscles, then it has got to learn to walk, then to run, and so on; after long patience and teachin', it can mebby win its race by runnin' and leapin'; but not at first, not before it can creep.

Why, for a time after I first went South things looked so new and strange to me, and my daughter Maggie wuz so firm in her belief, that I seemed to think jest as she did, and we would talk for hours and hours, and agree jest as well as two human creeters could agree. And I guess I even outdone her in drawin' metafors, and drawin' 'em to great distances, as my way is.

For I am always one to speak out and tell how things look to me to-day; if they look different to-morrow under the light of some different knowl-edge, why, then I'll speak out agin and tell that when the time comes.

And some of these beliefs Maggie and I pro-mulgated to each other, I believe now jest as strong as I did then, and some of my idees got sort o' modi-fied down in the course of time. Of this more and anon.

But then Maggie would talk to me, and I'd say to Maggie:

Why, lettin' such ignorant and onexperienced men rule the country, rule free, educated, cultured men and wimmen, is as foolish as it would be to put a blind man onto a wild, onbroke horse, and tell him to guide it safe when it wuz led right along by pits, and canyons, and kasems, and helpless ones and infants are layin' right in its path, and lots of mean, ugly creeters ready to ketch holt of the bits and back him off out of their way.

Why, that blind man couldn't do it. Why? be-cause he hain't got any eyes, that is why.

He don't know which line to pull on, for he hain't got no eyes to see which way the danger lays, nor which side on him folks are a layin' in his track.

He hain't to blame, that blind man hain't, nor the horse hain't to blame, nor the helpless ones he is a tromplin' over and a stompin' and a kickin'.

"Who is to blame?" Why, the ones that lifted him onto the horse.

Wall, say some, the blind man wuz lifted onto the horse in the first place to get him out of danger; he wuz jest on the pint of sinkin' down into the deep mud and quicksand; he wuz lifted onto the horse as a war measure, a way of safety to him out of his danger.

Wall, I sez, that wuz all right; I presume they thought the horse could bear him out safely amongst the pitfalls a layin' on every side of him, and I dare presume to say they didn't realize that the man wuz so blind, or that so many wuz goin' to be trompled on by the heels of the horse.

But now, I say, they have gin it a fair trial, they see it didn't work; they see that a blind man can't ride a wild horse over a dangerous road with safety to himself, or the horse, or the helpless ones in his way.

"Wall, what will you do?" you say.

Wall, Maggie spozed the case, and I did; we said, spozin' the ones that lifted that blind man up onto the horse should take him off on it a spell as easy as they could, so's not to hurt his feelin's, and then go to doctorin' the man's eyes, to try to get him so he can see; hold the horse for him till he can see; curb the horse down so it will go smoother some; encourage the man by tellin' him the truth that you are a keepin' the horse for him, and he is a goin' to get up onto him agin and ride him as soon as he can see, and the sooner he gets his eyesight the sooner he can ride.

Give him the sure cure for his blindness, and then

ROSY.

if he won't lay holt and cure himself, let him go afoot as long as the world stands.

Give the black man and the poor whites plenty of means for study and self-improvement. Give them the Bible and good schools, plenty of religious and seckular teachers, and I believe they will improve, will become safe guides to foller and to guide themselves, whether in this land or in another, wherever their future may lay.

Sez Thomas Jefferson: "The same rule would work well to the North as well as the South."

"Heaven knows it would," sez I. It hain't becomin' in us to cast motes and forget beams. Heaven knows that our criminals, and paupers, and drunkards, and the foreign convicts and jail-birds landed on our shores are not safe gardeens to trust our life and liberties to.

This mass of ignorance and vice, native and foreign, that swarms to the polls, bought for a measure of whiskey, ought to be dealt with in the same way.

Men who can't read the names on the ballots can't see deep enough into the urena of political life to be safe guides to foller, to be safe gardeens to the helpless wimmen and children committed to their care.

Liberty is too priceless a jewel to be committed into such vile hands, such weak hands, hands that would and do barter it away to the highest bidder.

Liberty and Freedom sold for a glass of beer. The right of suffrage, the patent of our American nobility, to be squandered and degraded for a pipeful of tobacco. The idee!

And kneelin' in churches, sez I, and settin' apart in their own homes are royal souls, grand, educated lovers of their country and their kind, who would for duty's sake reach out one hand to take the ballot, and cling with the other to the cross of the Crucified.

Them who have agonized over the woes and wrongs of the world, and tried with anointed vision to find out the true wisdom of life and right livin'— have spent their whole noble lives for the good of poor humanity—

They must kneel on in silence, and stay in seclusion, and see the freedom of their children and the children of humanity bought and sold, and sunk in the dirt, and trailed in the mire by them who have never given a thought to righteousness and right livin'.

The black man would never have been freed from his chains of bondage had not a necessity arisen. God's great opportunity comes on down the ages; let us be ready for it. He sees wrongs, and woes, and incomparable sufferings plead to Him for redress.

The heavens are very still. The prayin' ones hear no reply to their tears, their lamentations, their despairin' cries.

The heavens are very calm, and blue, and fur away.

But at last man's necessity, God's great opportunity comes; the oppressors are driven into some corner by their own deeds, till the only way for them to get out in safety is to answer the prayers of centuries and let the oppressed go free.

Man's necessity has come; they endure plague after plague, and depend on their own strength and keep up their own proud wills, and harden their hearts, and refuse to answer the pleadings of justice.

But bimeby the plagues increase, their troubles grow greater and greater, they encompass them about, there is no way out only to liberate the great throng that stands between them and safety. And bimeby, when there is a dead one in every house, and weepin' is on every side, and the mourners go about the street, and the mountains are behind, and the sea in front, and there is no way out only to liberate the oppressed, why, then there is a "military necessity."

God's opportunity has come. Rather than perish themselves they will let justice be done, let the oppressed go free.

Now, here is another Egypt. A long-oppressed, ignorant race is set up too sudden as a ruler over an educated, intelligent, intolerant one, for in many places the white race is in the minority.

But it will not yield to the misrule of ignorance.

The white people are bitter, arrogant, and oppressive under their new conditions.

The blacks, nursin' their old and new wrongs, are burnin' for vengeance on their oppressors. They will not suffer much longer and be still

A great struggle is impendin'. I spoze the Nation thinks—and it is naterel for anybody to think—that the black vote cannot be put down legally sence the right of suffrage wuz gin 'em. They think it couldn't be taken from them for a long time without a war followin'; they think they would fight their way to the poles, and it would seem naterel that they should, sez I, and so sez Maggie.

"Then what can be done?" sez Maggie; and then wuz the time that I sez, and I felt real riz up when I sez it:

There is one thing that might be *tried*—give the ballot to the white women of the South, and to the black women too, if they can come up to the standpoint of intelligence. Let a certain amount of education and intelligence be the qualification to the ballot.

This is your peaceful passin' through the Red Sea of the present. The waves may stand up pretty high on each side; 'loud talk, and fears for womanly modesty, fears for man's supremacy, fears for the dignity of the ballot will blow up pretty high waves on both sides.

But, sez I solemnly, if the Lord is the Leader, if He stands in front of the army, and it is His hand that beckons us forward, and He who passes over in front of the army, we shall pass through in safety, and the nation will be saved.

The supremacy will remain in the hands of the educated men and women of the South till the illiterates become safe leaders to themselves and others by education and the civilizing influences of the Bible and good teachers.

The supremacy would be taken out of the whiskey bathed hands of the loafer rabble in Northern cities, and remain in the safer hands of educated men and women, till the lower classes rise up by the same safe means of education and enlightenment, when they too will become safe leaders and teachers of the best. And I sez, How will this Nation find any safer means, any fairer way?

It offers safety to the imperilled present, it offers a hope, an incentive for the strugglin' future.

The poorest boy and the poorest girl would have this hope, this incentive to learn—for the royal road is free for all, beggar or child of wealth. The path opens right up from the alley to the President's chair, from the tenement to the Capitol, jest as sure as from the mansion house or the university.

It is safe another way, so it seems to me, because it is right and just.

Justice may seem to lead through strange ways sometimes—thorny roads, steep and rugged mounts, and deep, dark wildernesses, while the path of expedience and pleasant selfishness may seem to open up a flowery way.

But every time, every single time, Justice is the safe one to foller. And it is she who will lead you out into a safe place, while the rosy clouds that hang over the path of selfish expedience will anon, or even sooner, turn black, and lower down, and close up the way in darkness and despair.

This seems to me a safe way for the imperilled South while it is passin' through this crisis, and the light shines jest as fair and fresh in the newer day that gleams in the distance. It is shinin' in the eyes of them that see fur off, fair and beautiful, the New Republic, where there are equal rights, educated suffrage, co-operative labor. Oh! blessed land beyend the swellin' waves of the unquiet Present!

Genieve sees it plain, and so duz Victor. And thousands and thousands of the educated and morally riz up of the colored race see it to-day, and are a strivin' towards it.

"HE WUZ GLAD TO SET DOWN."

## CHAPTER VII.

ONE mornin' I sot off for a walk, bein' set so much of the time, and used as I wuz to bein' on my feet.

I told Josiah I believed I'd lose the use of my lims if I didn't walk round some.

"Wall," he said, "for his part, he wuz glad to set down, and set there."

That man has always sot more or less. He hain't never worked the hours that I have, but I wouldn't want him told that I said it. Good land! it would only agrevate him; he wouldn't give in that it wuz so.

But anyway, as I say, I sot out most imegiatly after breakfast. I left Maggie pretty as a pink, a takin' care of the children with Genieve's help. And my Josiah a settin', jest a settin' down, and nothin' else.

But I didn't care if he growed to the chair, I felt

that I must use my lims, must walk off somewhere and move round, and I had it in my mind where I wuz a goin'.

I knew there wuz a little settlement of colored folks not fur from Belle Fanchon by the name of Eden Centre. Good land, what a name!

But I spoze that they wuz so tickled after the War, when they spozed they wuz free, and had got huddled down in a little settlement of their own, that they thought it would be a good deal like Paradise to 'em. So they named it Eden Centre.

As if to say, this hain't the outskirts and suburbs of Paradise—not at all. It is the very centre of felicity, the very heart of the garden of happiness, Eden Centre.

Wall, I thought I'd set out and walk that way.

So I wended my way onwards at a pretty good jog with my faithful umberell spread abroad over my head to keep the too ardent rays of the sun away from my foretop and my new bunnet.

Part of the way the road led through a thicket of fragrant pines, and anon, or oftener, would come out into a clearin' where there would be a house a standin' back in the midst of some cultivated fields, and anon I would see a orange grove, more or less prosperous-lookin'.

Jest a little way out of Eden Centre I come to the remains of a large buildin' burned down, so nothin' but some shapeless ruins and one tall black chimbly remained, dumbly pintin' upwards towards the sky; and owin' to a bend in it, it wuz shaped some like a big black interrogation mark, a risin' upwards aginst the background of the clear blue sky.

It looked curius.

And jest as I wuz a standin' still in my tracks, a ponderin' over the meanin' of it, and a leanin' on the rough fence that run along by the roadside, a old darkey come along with a mule hitched onto a rickety buggy with a rope.  And I akosted him, and asked him what wuz the meanin' of that big black chimbly a standin' up in that curius way.

He seemed awful ready to stop and talk.  It wuz the hot weather, I spoze.  And the mule had called for sights of labor to get him along, I could see that —and he sez :

" De Cadimy used to stand dar."

Sez I, " The school-house for the colored people ?"

" Yes," sez he.

" How did it come to be burned down ?" sez I.

" De white folks buhnt it down," sez he calmly.

" What for ?" sez I.

" 'Cause dey didn't want it dere," sez he.  " Dat's what I spoze wuz de influential reason."

And then he went on and told me the hull story, and mebby I'd better tell it a little faster than he did.  It took place some years before, but he had lived right there in Eden Centre, and wuz knowin' to the hull thing.

A white minister had come down from the North, a man who had some property, and wuz a good man, and seein' the grievous need of schools for the black man, had used his own money to build the academy.

He tried to get land for the school nearer the city, where more could be helped by it, but nobody would sell land for such a purpose.

Finally, he come here, and on this poor tract of land that the negroes owned he put up his buildings.

It took about all the money he had to build the house and get the school started.

He had jest got it started, and had fifty pupils— grown people and children of the freedmen—when some ruffians come one stormy night and set it on fire.

The white prejudice wuz so strong aginst havin' the colored race taught, that they burned down the buildings, destroyed all the property that that good man had spent there.

It wuz on a cold, stormy night. His wife wuz ill in bed when the fire broke out; the fright and exposure of that night killed her.

Not a white man dast open his door to take the family in, though the white Baptist preacher at Wyandotte, when he hearn on it, he jest riz right up in his pulpit the next Sunday night, mad with a holy wrath at what had been done in their midst.

He riz right up and told his flock right to their faces what he thought of such doin's.

They said he stood there with his handsome head throwed back, and sez he, brave as a lion (and fur better-lookin'), sez he:

"Such outrages are a shame to humanity. Men war against principles and issues, not against helpless women and children;" and sez he, "If they had fled to me for safety, I would have opened my doors and taken them in."

Oh, how they glared at him, and how the threatenin', scowlin' faces seemed to close round him, and his wife's heart almost stopped beatin'; she could fairly hear the report of the pistol-shot and feel the sharp knife of the assassin.

When all to once his little girl, only three years old, who had come to church that night, she see the black looks and heard the muttered threats aginst her papa. And she slipped down unnoticed and come up to him, and pressed up close aginst him, and tried to creep up into his arms as if she wanted to protect him, the pretty creeter.

He sez, " Hush, darling, you mustn't come to papa."

But she wouldn't go ; she made him take her up in his arms, and from that safe refuge she shook her tiny fist at the crowd, and cries out :

" You just let my papa be ; you shan't hurt my good papa."

Wall, the tears jest run down that preacher's face, he wuz that wrought up with divine fervor and principles before, and this capped the sheef.

Wall, they jest about worshipped that child, the hull flock did, and they loved their minister and his wife ; and men love bravery and admire courage, and they felt the power and pathos of the scene, and the tears stood in many a eye that had flashed with threatenin' anger only a minute before.

And so that storm lulled away and died down.

(I have been leadin' this horse behind the wagon, as it were.) Maggie told me this little incident afterwards (and now to hitch my horses agin where they belong, side by side, and in front of the mule) (metafor).

After the buildings wuz destroyed and the threats aginst them so awful and skairful, this poor man and his sick wife and child jest run for their lives; nobody dast to take 'em in; they went from place to place, only to be driven away, in the peltin' storm

THE OLD NEGRO.

too, till at last they found a poor refuge in a black man's cabin, where the baby died the next day. But so bitter wuz the feelin' aginst these teachers that this black man who took them in wuz found lyin' dead a few days after with a bullet through his heart.

Finally, they succeeded in gettin' to the cars and gettin' back North, where the wife died within a week's time.

And the sorrow over this loss, the exposure and agitation of that time, and the failure of his life plans jest killed that good man too. He died broken-hearted within a year.

All they had meant, all they had wanted wuz to carry out the Saviour's principle, "Carry the Gospel to every creature."

Then why didn't they have a chance to do it? I couldn't tell, nor Josiah couldn't, nor nobody. No wonder the tall black chimbly stood there a pintin' up into the heavens like a great interrogation mark, a askin' this solemn and unanswered conundrum:

"Why evil is allowed to flourish and the good to be overthrown?"

Yes, it wuz a conundrum that I couldn't get the right answer to; but I thought more'n probable the Lord could answer it, and would in His own good time.

And as I looked at it I thought mebby that onbeknown to me, or Josiah, or anybody, that tall black ruin was doin' a silent work in the hearts of Victor and Felix and many other of the young, intelligent, and resolute amongst this dark race.

Felix livin', as he had, under the very shadder of it, so to speak, who could tell what influence it had in carvin' this wrong down on the livin' tablet of his heart, so it might be answered in all the work he might do in the future amongst his people?

And Victor, how often had his sad eyes rested on it, who knew how such an object lesson wuz strikin' deep truths in his great heart. Bible truths such as—

"A house divided against itself cannot stand."

And how it stood up black before him a askin' him this everlastin' and momentous question:

"How long his people could endure such cruel wrong and outrage?"

And mebby sometimes, as the moon shone bright on it, it loomed up in front of him some like a pillar, and he heard a voice fallin' out of the clear illumined sky:

"I have seen, I have seen the afflictions of my people which are in Egypt; and lo, I am come to deliver them." "Get thee out of this land!" "Lo, I will send thee."

But I am a eppisodin', and to resoom.

I have only put down the heads of the old darkey's remarks, jest the bald heads—he flowered off the subject with various metafors and many big words, not always in the right place, nor pronounced as the world's people pronounce them, but with deep earnestness.

And then I asked him about Eden Centre and how affairs had gone there.

And he told me with more flourishes and elocution all the hard trials they had gone through, with perils from foes and perils from false friends, from ignorance, from avarice, and etc., etc., etc.

It wuz deeply interestin' to me and to him too, but finally he glanced up at the sun, and straightened up in the buggy-seat, and told the old mule and me at the same time

"That they must hurry or they would be too late for the funeral."

And I asked him where the funeral wuz to be, and he stood up in the rickety buggy and pinted with his whip to a little cluster of houses only a short distance away.

And I made up my mind then and there that I would jest go acrost lots and attend to that funeral myself.

So I made my way through a broken place in the fence and sot out for the funeral.

I got there after a short walk through the ruther sandy path, though some flower-besprinkled. I knew which wuz the mournin' cabin by the mules and old horses hitched along the fence in front of it.

I went in and obtained a seat near the door. It seemed that it wuz the funeral of a young man taken sick at the place where he worked and come home to die. He had been waiter in a hotel at Wyandotte. The mournin' was evidently sincere; certainly it wuz loud and powerful.

The minister seemed to want to administer consolation to the mournin' group; his text wuz choze with distinct reference to it, and his words wuz meant to cheer. But he got his metafors mixed up and his consolation twisted.

But mebby they took it all straight and right, and if they did it wuz all the same to them.

His text wuz choze from the story of the child's death in the Old Testament, and the words wuz these:

"We shall go to him, but he shall not return to us."

The minister wuz a short, thickset negro, with a high standing collar, seemin' to prop up his head, and a benevolent look in his eyes and his good-natured mouth.

"GAWGE PERKINS AM DAID."

He fixed his eyes upon the congregation after he had repeated the text, and sez:

"Gawge Perkins am daid; he wuz a waitah at Wyandotte, an' of cose he died."

It seemed that to him this wuz a clear case of cause and effect, which he did not explain to his audience.

"Of cose he died. Now, dar am in dis audnance many no doubt dat tink dey have got riches, an' honoh, an' fame; but Gawge Perkins am daid, an' you have to go and see Gawge Perkins.

"An' you may tink you are gay, an' happy, an' in high sperits; but dis fac' remains, an' you can't get round dis fac', Gawge Perkins am daid, an' you have got to go and see Gawge Perkins.

"But dar am one consolation, Gawge Perkins can't come back to us."

Durin' the sermon he spoke of the last day and the sureness of its comin', and the impossibility of tellin' when it would come.

"Why," sez he, "it hain't known on earth, nor in heaven; de angels am not awaih of de time; why, Michael Angelo himself don't know it."

But through the whole sermon he dwelt on this great truth—that they must all go to see George Perkins, and, crowning consolation, George Perkins could not come back to them!

The mourners seemed edified and instructed by his talk, so I spoze there wuz some subtle good and power in it that mebby I wuzn't good enough to see.

And I have felt jest so many a time when I have heard a white preacher hold forth for two hours at a Jonesville funeral till my limbs wuz paralyzed and my brain reeled; and the mourners had added to their other affliction, almost the num palsy. Their legs would go to sleep anyway, and so forget their troubles (the legs).

As the colored graveyard wuz only a little ways from the cabin, I followed the mourners at a short distance, and saw George Perkins laid in the ground to take his long sleep, with tears and honest grief to hallow the spot.

What more, sez I to myself, could an emperor

want, or a zar? A quiet spot to rest in, and a place in the hearts left behind.

After the funeral crowd had dispersed I sot down under a pine-tree with spreading branches, and thought I would rest awhile.

And even as I sot there another funeral wended its way into the old yard, which did not surprise me so much, nor would it any deep philosopher of human nater. For we well know when things get to happenin' they will keep right on.

Human events go by waves, as it wuz—suicides, joys, broken dishes, griefs, visitors, etc., etc. So I sot there a moralizin' some on the queerness of this world, as I see the rough coffin a bein' lowered into the ground.

But one thing struck me as being singular—there wuz no mourners to be seen.

After a while I got up and asked a cheerful-lookin' negro " where the mourners wuz?"

" Wall, misses," sez he, " I spoze I am about as much of a mourner as there is."

He looked anything but mournful, but he went on :

" I married dis ole man's stepdaughter, an' consequentially she died. An' den dis ole man got a kick from a mule, an' laid he flat on his back ; den he got his head stove in with a chimbly fallin' on it ; den de airysipples sot in, an' de rheumaticks, an' nurality, an' foh years desese has jes' fed on him, an' de ultamatim of it wuz he died. An' I spoze I am jes' about as much of a mourner heah as you'll find."

And sayin' this, the radiant-faced mourner turned away and joined some friends.

As I turned back I met the colored preacher and his wife, who wuz evidently takin' a short road home acrost the graveyard.

She wuz a good-lookin' mulatto woman, and I

ONE OF THE MOURNERS.

passed the time of day with her by sayin', "How do you do?" and etc.

And bein' one that is always on the search for information, I fell into talk with her and her husband, and likin' their looks, I finally asked him what his name wuz.

And he said, " My name is Mary Johnson."

Sez I, " You mean your wife's name is Mary."

" No," sez he, " my name is Mary."

And then he went on and told me that he wuz the youngest of twelve boys, and his father wuz so mad at his havin' been a boy that he named him, jest in spite, Mary.

Wall, we had quite a good visit there, but short.

He told me he had been a slave in his young days.

And I asked him if his master had abused him, and he told me, and evidently believed every word he said, that his master wuz the best man this side of heaven.

And sez he, " Freedom or not, I never would have left him, never. If he had lived," sez he, " I would have worked for him till I dropped down." And then he went on and related instances of his master's kindness and good-hearted generosity, that made me stronger than ever in the belief I had always had, that there are good men and bad men everywhere and under all skies.

And he told me about how, after his master died, and the grand old plantation broken up, the splendid mansion spoiled by the contendin' hosts, and everything dear and sacred scattered to the winds— how his young master, the only one left of the happy family, had gone up North and wuz a doctor there.

Buryin' in his heart the scenes of his old happy life, and the overthrow of all his ambitious dreams, he wuz patiently workin' on to make a home and a livelihood fur from all he had loved and lost.

I declare for 't, I most cried to hear him go on, and his wife joinin' in now and then; they told the truth, and are Christians, both on 'em, I hain't a doubt.

Finally, we launched off on other subjects—on religion, etc.—and at the last he made a remark that gin me sunthin' to think on all my way home to Belle Fanchon.

For I give up goin' to Eden Centre that day. Good land! I had talked too much—I am afraid it is a weakness with me—anyway, there wuzn't any time.

We wuz a talkin' on religion, and faith, and the power of prayer, etc., and he sez:

"I enjoy religion, but I have got too much confidence in God."

Sez I, "You mean you lack confidence in God."

"Yes, that is it, I lack confidence in God, for I find that when I pray to Him for anything, if I don't get an answer to it to once I make other arraingments."

And I thought as I wended my way home, "Oh, how much, how much is Samantha and the hull human race like Mary Johnson; we besiege the throne of grace for some boon heart longed for and dear, and if the Lord does not answer at once our impassioned pleadin's, we make other arraingments.

But I am a eppisodin'.

When I got back from my walk I went into the kitchen to get some cool water to put some posies in I had picked by the way, and there sot old Aunt Clo', and most imegiatly after my entrance she announced to me that Rosy, her granddaughter, had got a little boy, and that Dan, Maggie's colored coachman, wuz the father of it.

Aunt Clo' did not seem to be excited in any way about it; she simply told it as a bit of news, rather onpleasant than otherwise, as it necessitated more work on her part.

As for the immorality, the wrong-doing connected with it, she showed no signs of feelin'.

But Maggie wuz aroused; there wuz a pink spot on both cheeks when I told her about it.

She wuz settin' in her pretty room, and near her lay Boy asleep on some cushions on the sofa. She wuz readin' a love letter from Thomas Jefferson, for he wuz away for a few days, and his letters to her wuz always love letters.

There she sot in her safe and happy love-guarded home, by the side of Boy, whom she held clost in her heart because he wuz the image of her lover husband, Thomas J. Allen.

There she sot in her pretty white dress, with her pure, happy face—the flower, so I told myself as I looked at her, of long years of culture and refinement, and I couldn't help comparin' her in my mind with the ignorant and onthinkin' soul that another boy had been give to.

But I told Maggie, for I thought I had ought to, and her eyes grew darker, and a red spot shone on both cheeks; and sez she the first thing:

"Dan must marry her at once."

Sez I, "Mebby he won't."

"Why, he must," sez Maggie; "it is right that he should; I shall make him."

"Wall," sez I, "you must do what you think is

right. I am fairly dumbfounded, and don't know what to do," sez I.

Maggie got up sort o' quick and rung the bell, and asked to have Dan sent up to her room.

And pretty soon he come in, a tall, hulkin' chap, good-natered but utterly irresponsible, so he seemed to me, black as a coal.

And Maggie laid his sins down before him as soft as she could and still be just, and ended by tellin' him that he must marry Rosy.

This seemed to astound him that she should ask it; he looked injured and aggrieved.

But Maggie pressed the point. He stood twirlin' his old cap in his hand in silence.

He did not deny his guilt at all, but he wuz surprised at the punishment she meted out to him.

Finally he spoke. "I tell you what, Miss Margaret, it is mighty hard on a fellah if you make a fellah marry everybody he pays attentions to."

He looked the picture of aggrieved innocence in black.

But Maggie persisted. She told him he could move into a little buildin' standin' on the grounds; and as he was fairly faithful and hard-workin', Maggie thought he would get a good livin' for his wife and son.

"And you will love your child," sez Maggie, lookin' down into Boy's sleepin' face.

Finally, after long arguments and persuasions on Maggie's part, Dan promised to marry Rosy.

And to do him justice he did marry her in a week's time, and they moved into a little thatched cabin at the bottom of the grounds.

Dan wuz good-natered, as I said, and a good coachman and gardener when he chose to work; and Maggie and I took solid happiness in fittin' up the little rooms so they looked quite pleasant and homelike.

Rosy, as her little baby grew and thrived, manifested a degree of love for it that wuz surprisin' when one took into consideration the utter barrenness and poverty of the soil in which the sweet plant of affection grew.

And it actually seemed as if the love she had for the child awakened a soul in her. Frivolous and empty-headed enough she wuz to be sure, but still there wuz an improvement in her datin' from the hour when her baby first became a delight to her.

Dan too grew more settled in his behavior. His drinkin' spells, which he had always had periodically, grew further and further apart, and with the dignity of a father and householder added to him, it seemed to add cubits to his moral stature.

Ignorant enough, and careless and onthinkin' enough, Heaven knows, but still there wuz a change for the better.

Little Snow, sweet angel that she wuz, never tired of flittin' down the pleasant path bordered with glossy-leaved oleanders and magnolias, to the little whitewashed cottage, to carry dainties to Rosy sent by Maggie, and to baby Dan when he got large enough to comprehend her kindness.

And it wuz a pretty sight to see Snow's rose-sweet face and golden curls nestlin' down by baby Dan's little ebony countenance.

"YOU CAN REPAIR YOUR DWELLIN' HOUSE."

## CHAPTER VIII.

HOW true it is that though you may move the body round from place to place, you can't move round or move away from the emotions of the soul that are firm and stabled.

You can change your climate, you can repair your dwellin' house, you can fill your teeth and color your hair, but you can't make a ardent, enthusiastic man into a sedate and stiddy one, or chain down a ambitious one and make him forget his goles.

Now, Josiah Allen had been happy as a king ever sence he had come South to our son's beautiful home.

He had seemed to enjoy the change of scene, the balmy climate, and the freedom from care and labor.

But that very freedom from toil, that very onbroken repose wuz what give him and me a sore trial, as you can see by the incident I will tell and recapitulate to you.

You see, Josiah Allen, not havin' any of his usual work to do, and not bein' any hand to sew on fine sewin', or knit tattin', or embroider tidies and splashers, etc., he read a sight—read from mornin' till night almost.

And with his ardent, enthusiastic nater he got led off "by many windy doctrines," as the text reads.

He would be rampant as rampant could be on first one thing and then another—on the tariff, the silver bill, and silo's, and air ships, etc., etc.

And he would air all his new doctrines onto me, jest as a doctor would try all his new medicines on his wife to see if they wuz dangerous or not. Wall, I spoze it wuz right, bein' the pardner who took him for worse as well as better.

And for family reasons I ever preferred that he should ventilate his views in my indulgent ear before he let 'em loose onto society.

And one mornin', havin' read late the night before and bein' asleep when I come to bed, he begun promulgatin' a new idee to me as he stood by the washstand a washin' him in the early mornin' sunshine.

He wuz full of enthusiasm and eagerness, and did not brook anything of the beautiful mornin' scene that wuz spread out in the open winder before him.

The cool, sweet mornin' air a comin' in through the clusters of climbin' roses, and through the tall boughs of a big old orange-tree that stood between him and the sunshine.

Its glossy green leaves wuz new washed by a shower that had fell over night, and it looked like a bride decked for her husband, with garlands of white and pink posies, and anon the round, shinin' globes of the ripe fruit hangin' like apples of gold right in amongst the sweet blows and green leaves.

And way beyend the fields and orchards of Belle Fanchon stood the tree-crowned mountain, and the sun wuz jest over the top, so the pine-trees stood out dressed in livin' green aginst the glowin' sky.

It wuz a fair seen, a fair seen.

But my companion heeded it not. He had read some eloquent and powerful speech the evenin' before, and his mind had started off on a new tact.

His ambition was rousted up agin to do and to dare, as it had been so many times before (see accounts of summer boarders, tenants, political honors, etc., etc., etc., etc., and so forth).

And sez he, a holdin' the towel dreamily in his hands, "Samantha, my mind is made up."

I had not roze up yet, and I sez calmly from my piller, where I lay a drinkin' in the fair mornin' scene:

"It wuzn't a very hefty job, wuz it?"

Sez he, with about as much agin dignity as he had used before:

"You can comment on the size of my mind all you want to, but you will probable think different about the heft of it before I get through with the skeme I am jest about to embark on."

And he waved the towel some like a banner and wiped his whiskers out in a aggressive way, and stood up his few hairs over his foretop in a sort of a helmet way, and I see by his axent and demeanors that he really wuz in earnest about sunthin' or other, and I beset him to tell me what it wuz. For I am deathly afraid of his plans, and have been for some time.

But he wouldn't tell me for quite a spell. But at last as he opened the chamber-door for a minute, and the grateful odor of the rich coffee and the tender, brown steak come up from below, and wuz wafted into his brain and gently stimulated it, he sort o' melted down and told me all about it.

He wanted to jine the Pan American Congress as a delegate and a worker.

Sez he, "Samantha, I want to go and be a Pan American. I want to like a dog."

"What for?" sez I. "What do you want to embark into this enterprise for, Josiah Allen?"

"Wall," sez he, "I will tell you what for. I want to enter into this project because I am fitted for it," sez he, "I have got the intellect for it, and I have got the pans."

Wall, I see there wuz some truth in this latter statement. For the spring before, nuthin' to do but Josiah had to go and get pans instead of pails to use in a new strip of sugar bush we had bought on.

I wanted him not to, but he wouldn't give in. And of course they wuz so onhandy he couldn't use 'em much of any, and there we wuz left with our pans on our hands—immense ones, fourteen-quart pans. The idee!

Wall, the pans wuzn't of any earthly use to us, only I could make a few on 'em come handy about the house, and I had give a few on 'em to the girls, Tirzah Ann and Maggie.

And then they wuz packed away up on the store-room shelves—most seven dozen of 'em ; and truly, take them with our dairy pans, why I do spoze we had more pans than anybody for miles round either way.

"AND I HAVE GOT THE PANS."

Wall, he wuz jest bound to go ; he said he felt a call. Sez he, "There is things a goin' on there amongst them Pan Americans that ought to be broke up ; and," sez he, "they need a firm, noble, manly mind to grapple with 'em. Most the hull talk of all of 'em that come from different countries is about our pleasant relations with one another; and they own up that their chief aim is to draw our relations closter together. Samantha, that has got to be stopped."

And he went on with a look of stern determination onto his eyebrow that it seldom wore.

"No man begun life with a firmer determination than I did to do well by the relations on your side, and as for the relations on my own side, I laid out to jest pamper 'em if I had the chance; but," sez he, as a gloomy shadder settled down onto his countenance, "enuff is enuff. I have had Lodema Trumble fourteen weeks at one hitch; I have had Cousin Peter on my side, and Cousin Melinda Ann on yours, and aunts of all sorts and sizes, and have been grandsoned till I am sick on't, and uncled till I despise the name; and as for cousinin', why I've had 'em, first, and second, and third, and fourth, up to sixth and seventh; I have been scolded at, complained on, groaned over, and prayed at, and sung to, and tromboned, and pickelowed, and nagged, and fluted, and preached at—"

Sez I sternly, "Don't you go to sayin' a word aginst John Richard Allen, that angel man."

"I hain't said nothin' aginst that angel man, have I? Dumb him, he'd talk anybody to death."

"What are you doin' now, this minute, Josiah Allen?"

"I am a talkin' sense, hard horse sense, and you know that I have been fifed, and base-drummed, and harrowed, and worried, and eat up, and picked to pieces down to my very bones by relations on both of our two sides, and I have stood it like a man. I hain't never complained one word."

I groaned aloud here at this awful story.

"Wall, I hain't never complained much of any. But when the Nation takes it in hand and wants to draw our relations closter and closter, then I will interfere. For that is their main talk and effect, from what I can make out from this speech," sez he, a pintin' to a newspaper.

"I will interfere, Samantha Allen, and you can't keep me from it. I will stop it if a mortal man can. Anyway, I will boldly wade in and tell 'em my harrowin' experience, and do all I can to break it up. For as I told you, Samantha Allen, I have had more experience with relations than any other human bein' on the face of the globe; I have got the intellect and I have got the pans."

Oh, how I did have to talk to Josiah Allen to try to diswaide him from this rash enterprise!

"Why," sez I, "this meetin' hain't a goin' on now; you are mistook."

But he knew he wuz in the right on't. And anyway, he said he could tell his trials to some of the high officers of that enterprise and influence 'em.

"I want to influence somebody, Samantha," sez he, "before it is too late."

And so he kep' on; he didn't say nuthin' before our son and daughter, but every time he would get me alone, whether it wuz in the seclusion of our bed-chamber, or in a buggy, or on the beautiful grounds of Belle Fanchon, then he would begin and talk, and talk, and talk.

The family never mistrusted what wuz a goin' on. Lots of times to the table, or anywhere, when the subject came round anywhere nigh to that that wuz uppermost in his brain, he would give me a wink, or step on my foot under the table.

"I AM NEEDED THERE."

They never noticed the wink, and their feet didn't feel the crunch of his boot toe—no, I bore it in silence and alone.

For how could they see the tall mountain peaks of ambition that loomed up in front of that peaceful, bald-headed man—precipitous mounts that he wuz in fancy scalin', with the eyes of a admirin' world lookin' up to him?

No; how little can them a settin' with us round the same table see the scenes that is passin' before the mental vision of each. No, they can't do it; the human breast hain't made with a winder in it, or even a swing door.

No; I alone knew what wuz a passin' and a goin' on in that beloved breast.

To me, as he always had, he revealed the high bubbles he wuz a throwin' up over his head, and had always throwed ever and anon, and even oftener, bubbles wrought out of the foamin' suds of hope and ambition, and propelled upwards out of the long-stailed pipe of his fancy, floated by the gusty wind of his vain efforts.

And it wuz to me he turned for comfort and solace when them bubbles bust over his head in a damp drizzle (metafor).

But to resoom and continue on.

He talked, and he talked, and he talked; he said he wuz bound to start for Washington, D. C.

Sez I, "Are you crazy?"

Sez he, "It hain't no further from here than it is from Jonesville, and I am needed there."

Sez he, "I am goin' there to offer my services as a International Delegate, as a Delegate Extraordinary," sez he.

And I sez, "I should think as much; I should think you would be a extraordinary one."

"Wall," sez he, "in national crysisses they have delegates by that name—I have read of 'em."

"THE BUTTER-MAKER UP IN ZOAR."

"Wall," sez I, "they couldn't find a more extraordinary one than you are if they combed the hull country over with a rubber comb."

Wall, the upshot of the matter wuz that I had to call in the help of Thomas Jefferson. I knew he wuz all in the family and would hush it up, jest as much as I would.

He interfered jest as his father wuz a packin' his portmanty to start for Washington, D. C., to offer his services as a extraordinary delegate, and set up as a Pan American.

Thomas J. argued with his Pa for more than a hour. He brung up papers to convince him he wuz in the wrong on't. He argued deep, and bein' a lawyer by perfession, he knew how to talk rapid and fluent. And finally, after a long time, by our two united efforts, we quelled him down, and he onpacked his shirt and nightcap from his portmanty and settled down agin into a private citizen.

And owin' to Thomas J.'s efforts and mine, undertook at once by letter (for we feared the effects of delay), we sold the most of them pans at a good price to the butter-maker up in Zoar, and a letter wuz writ to Ury and Philury to deliver 'em.

So, some good come out of the evil of my skair and my pardner's skeme.

"JOSIAH GIVE UP."

## CHAPTER IX.

WALL, Josiah give up and crumpled down along the middle of the forenoon, and he looked happy as a king after he give up his project (it wuz only ambition that wuz a goarin' him and a leadin' him around).

And he and Snow (the darlin'!) had gone out a walkin' in the grounds—

And I wuz a settin' alone on the veranda by the side of Boy's cradle, Genieve havin' gone to the village to get some thread—

When Victor come over on a errant. He come to bring a note over from Mrs. Seybert to my daughter Maggie, and I told him I would give it to her jest as soon as she returned and come back. She had gone out ridin' with Thomas Jefferson.

And I, feelin' kinder opset and mauger through what I had went through with my pardner, thought it would sort o' take up my mind and recooperate me to talk a little with Victor (I had always liked him from the first minute I see him).

And so at my request he sot down on the veranda, and we had a little talk. I guess, too, he was dretful willin' to talk with me, so's to sort to waste the time and linger till Genieve got back.

And before some time had passed away I turned the conversation onto that skeme of hisen. I had hearn a sight about it first and last, and kinder hankered to-day (for reasons given prior and beforehand) to hear more.

And he went on perfectly eloquent about it—he couldn't help gettin' all worked up about it every time he got to talkin' about it; and yet he talked with good sound sense, and he see all the dangers and difficulties in the way, and his mind wuz sot on the best way of surmountin' and gettin' over 'em.

Genieve's mind wuz such she naterelly looked so sort o' high that she couldn't see much besides the sun-lit glorified mountains of the high lands and the beauty of the Gole.

But Victor see the rough road that led down through rocky defiles and through the deep wilderness; he see and counted all the lions that wuz in the path between this and the Promised Land, and his hull mind wuz sot on gettin' by 'em and slayin' 'em; but he heard their roars plain, every one of 'em. The name of the two biggest lions that lay in the road ahead of him a roarin' at him wuz Ignorance and Greed.

One of 'em had black skin, black as a coal, and the other wuz light-complected.

How to get by them lions wuz his first thought, for they lay watchin' every move he made at the very beginnin' of the road that led out to Canaan.

The animal Ignorance wuz too gross and heavy and sensual to even try to get out of the path where it must have known it wuz in danger of bein' crushed to death and trampled down; it wuz too thick-headed to even lift its eyes and look off into a more sunlighted place; it lay there, down in the dark mud, as heavy, as lifeless, as filthy as the dark soil in which it crouched.

Its huge black form filled up the way; how could Victor and them like him lift it up, put life and ambition in its big, heavy carcass, and make it move off and let the hosts go forward?

The beast Greed lifted its long neck and fastened its fiery eyes on Victor and his peers, and its mighty arms, tipped with a thousand sharp claws and talons, wuz lifted up to keep them back—force them back into the prison pens of servitude.

Victor see all this that Genieve couldn't see, not bein' made in that way; he see it, but, like Christian in his march to the Beautiful City, he wuz determined to press forward.

And as I sot there and looked at him and hearn him talk, I declare for't I got all rousted up myself with his project, and I felt ready, and told him so, to help him all I could consistently with my duties as a pardner and a member of the Methodist meetin' house.

And as I hearn him talk, I seemed to be riz up more and more, and able to see further than I had seen, and I felt a feelin' that Victor wuz in the right on't. I thought back on how eloquent Maggie and I had growed on the race question, and I felt that I wouldn't take it back. No; I had spoke my mind as things seemed to me then, and if the two races wuz goin' to be sot down together side by side, I felt that the idees we had promulgated to each other wuz right idees; but the more Victor talked the more I felt that his idees wuz right to separate the two races, if it wuz possible to do it.

His talk made a deep impression onto me, and I went on in my mind and drew some metafors further, it seemed to me, than I had ever drawed any, and eppisoded to myself more eloquent than I had ever eppisoded.

I hain't one to go half way into any undertakin', and I made up my mind then and there that if Victor and Genieve married and sot off for this colony in Africa, that I would set 'em out with a bushel of my best dried apples, and mebby more. And some dried peaches, and a dozen of them pans—I thought they would come handy in Africa to ketch cocoanut milk, or sunthin'.

And I said I would give 'em a couple of hens in welcome, and a male hen and a pair of ducks, if he spozed he would get water enough to keep 'em contented. Somehow I kep' thinkin' of the Desert of Sarah—I couldn't seem to keep Sarah out of my mind.

But he said there wuz plenty of water where they wuz goin'. And he sot and promulgated his idees to me for some time. And I looked on him with admiration and a considerable amount of deep respect.

He wuz a tall, broad-shouldered, handsome fel low, with very courteous, winnin' manners.

He had a clear-cut, resolute face, and silky brown hair that fell down over a broad white forwerd, and a mustache of the same color.

His eyes would fairly melt sometimes, and be soft as a woman's, and then agin they would look you through and through and seem to be piercin' through the hull dark path ahead out into the light of safety.

And his lips, that wuz resolute and firm enough sometimes, could anon, or oftener, grow tremulous with feelin' and eloquence.

He wuz a earnest Christian, a professor of religion, and, what is fur better, a practicer of the same.

He give his ideas to me in full that day in confidence (and a desire to linger till Genieve got back).

Some of these idees he got from Genieve, some on 'em he learned from books, and kindred minds, and close observation, and remembrance of talks he had hearn when such things sunk deep in his heart, and some on 'em sprung up from seeds God had planted in his soul, onbeknown to him; in a woman we call it intuition.

But anyway, no matter by what name we call these seeds, they lay in the soul till the Sun of Occasion warms 'em into life, and then they open their star flowers and find the way to the Right and the True.

To Victor the welfare of his mother's people lay nearer to his heart than even Genieve, much as he loved her—than his own life, sacred as he held it, holding, as he believed it did, a mission for humanity.

It wuz his idee to transplant the Africans to some

place where they could live out their full lives without interference or meddlin' with from another people, that must, in the nature of things, be always an alien race and one opposed to the black race instinctively and beyond remedy.

I see jest how it wuz; I see that nobody, no matter how strong you should fix the medicine and how powerful the doses you might give, could cure this distemper, this instinctive, deep-rooted feelin' of antipathy and repulsion towards the negro.

I see that no amount of pills and plasters wuz a goin' to make the negro feel free and easy with the white race.

There is a deep-rooted difference of opinion, and difference of feelin', difference of aims, and desires, and everything between the two races.

It is as deep down as creation, and as endless as eternity, and can't be doctored, or tackled up in any way and made to jine and become one.

It can't be did, so there is no use in tryin'.

And any amount of flowery speeches or proclamations, or enactments, or anything, hain't a goin' to amalgamate the two races and make 'em blend into another and be a hull one.

No; a law may contain every big law word, and "to wit" and "be it enacted" and every clause that ever wuz claused, and every amendment that wuz ever amended, but it hain't a goin' to make any difference with this law that wuz made in a higher court than any they have in Washington, D. C.

And a speech may contain the hull floral tribe, all the flowers that wuz ever heard on; it may soar up in eloquence as fur up as anybody can go, and dwindle down into pathos as deep as ever wuz went.

But it is a goin' to blow over the subject jest like any whiff of wind; it hain't a goin' to do the job of makin' the two races come any nigher to each other.

Why, you see when anybody is a tryin' to do this, he hain't a fightin' aginst flesh and blood only, the real black and white flesh of the present, but he is a fightin' aginst principalities and powers, the powers of the long kingdom of the past, the viewless but unfightable principalities of long centuries of concentrated opinions and hereditary influences, the ingrained contempt and scorn of the superior race towards the inferior in any other condition only servitude—the inbred feelin's of slavery, of lookin' up with a blended humility and hatred, admiration and envy, into the face of the dominant race.

The race difference lays like a gulf between the two people. You can't step over it, your legs hain't long enough; you can't bridge it over, there hain't no boards to be found strong enough; there it yawns, a deep gulf, and always will between the two races.

And when the Nation expected to jine these two forces and hitch 'em side by side to the car of freedom by a piece of paper with writin' on it, expectin' they would draw it along easy and stiddy, that wuz the time the Nation wuz a fool.

It would be jest as reasonable to hitch a wild lion from the jungles by the side of a sheep, and set 'em to drawin' the milk to the factory.

They might expect that if the team got to the factory at all, the sheep would be inside of the lion, and the milk too.

It won't do no good to go too hard aginst Nater. She is one, Nater is, that can't be went aginst not with any safety.

Mebby after centuries of trainin' and education, the lion might be learnt to trot along by the side of the sheep and dump the milk out all right at the factory door. But centuries after this had been done, the same instinctive race war would be a goin' on between the black people and the white.

You cannot make a soap-stun into a runnin' vine, or a flat-iron blossom out with dewy roses, or a thistle bear pound sweet apples—it can't be done, no matter how hard you work, or how pure your motives are.

So these things bein' settled and positive, Victor thought—and I'll be hanged if I could blame him for thinkin'—that the sooner his people got into a place of their own, away from the white race that had fettered them, and they had fettered so long, the better it would be for them.

He reasoned it out like this: " The Anglo-Saxons wuz here before we wuz, and they are a powerful nation of their own. They won't go; so what remains but to take ourselves away, and the sooner the better," he thought.

He had read, as I said, many books on the subject; but of all the books he had read, Stanley's description of some parts of Africa pleased him best.

He shrank from takin' his people into a colder climate; he had read long and elaborate arguments as to what cold wuz to do in changin' and improvin' the African.

But his common sense taught him that the Lord

knew better than the authors of these tracts as to what climate wuz best for His people.

He felt that it wuz useless to graft a pomegranate or a banana bush onto the North Pole. He felt that it wouldn't do the pole any good, and the grafts would freeze up and drop off—why, they would have to, they couldn't help it, and the pole couldn't help it either—the pole had to be froze, it wuz made so.

So he never had favored the colonization of his race in the colder Western States.

Nor had he quite liked the idee of their findin' a new home in the far South or in South America.

They would be still in an alien land, alien races would press clost aginst 'em.

No, a home in Africa pleased him best—in that land the Lord had placed the black people—it wuz their home accordin' to all the laws of God and man.

And if it hadn't been the best place for 'em, if they hadn't been fitted by nater for that climate, why he reasoned it out that they wouldn't have been born there in the first place.

He didn't believe God had made a mistake; he didn't believe He could.

Why, way down in the dark earth there never wuz known to be any mistake made, a wheat seed never sprung up into a cowcumber, a lily seed never blowed out into a daffodil.

No, there seemed to be a eternal law that prevented all mistakes and blunders.

And havin' sot down the black man in Africa, Victor felt that it wuz pretty sure to be the right and best place for him.

Stanley said that there wuz room enough in one section of the Upper Congo basin to locate double the number of negroes in the United States, without disturbin' a single tribe that now inhabits it; that every one of these seven million negroes might become owner of nearly a quarter square mile of land. Five acres of this planted with bananas and plantains would furnish every soul with sufficient food and drink.

The remainder of the twenty-seven acres of his estate would furnish him with timber, rubber, gums, dye stuffs, etc., for sale.

There is a clear stream every few hundred yards, the climate is healthy and agreeable.

Eight navigable rivers course through it. Hills and ridges diversify the scenery and give magnificent prospects.

To the negroes of the South it would be a reminder of their own plantations without the swamps and depressin' influence of cypress forests.

Anything and everything might be grown in it, from the oranges, guavas, sugar-cane and cotton of sub-tropical lands, to the wheat of California and the rice of South Carolina.

If the emigration wuz prudently conceived and carried out, the glowin' accounts sent home by the first settlers would soon dissipate all fear and reluctance on the part of the others.

But to make this available, it would have to be undertaken at once, says Stanley. For if it hain't taken advantage of by the American negro, the railways towards that favored land will be constructed, steamers will float on the Congo, and the beautiful forest land will be closed to such emigration by the rule, first come first served.

And then this beautiful, hopeful chance will be lost forever.

Victor read this, and more, from Stanley's pen, and felt deeply the beautiful reasonableness of the skeme.

With all the eloquence of which he wuz master he tried to bring these facts home to his people, and tried to arouse in them something of his own enthusiasm.

As for himself he wuz bound to go—as teacher, as missionary, as leader—as soon as he could; his mother's health wuz failing—his unhappy mistress needed him sorely—his preparations wuz not all completed yet.

There wuz several hundred young, intelligent negroes, most of them with families, who wuz workin' hard to get the money Victor thought would be necessary for a successful venture.

For besides the cost of transportation, Victor wanted them to be placed beyend the possibility of sufferin' and hardship while they wuz preparin' their land for cultivation.

But I sez, "Most probable this Nation will fit out some ships and carry you back to your old home." Sez I, "More than probable Uncle Sam will be glad of the chance to pay some of his debts, and clear the slate that hangs up behind the Capitol door, of one of the worst and meanest debts it ever had ciphered out on it, and held up aginst him."

But Victor smiled ruther sadly and looked dubersome.

He thought after the colony there wuz a assured success, thousands and thousands would go with their own money and help poorer ones to new homes there; but he didn't seem to put much dependence on Uncle Samuel's ever hitchin' up his steamships and carryin' 'em over.

But I sez real warmly, for I cannot bear any animyversions aginst that poor old man (only what I make myself in the cause of Duty)—sez I, "You wrong Uncle Samuel;" sez I, "You'll find out that he will brace up and do the right thing if the case is presented to him in the right light, and he brings his spectacles to bear on it.

"Why," sez I, "if I borry a cup of tea of Miss Gowdey, do I spoze that she will trapise over to my house after it?—and the same with flat-irons, press-boards, bluin' bags, etc.

"No, I carry 'em back agin, honorable.

"And if Josiah Allen borrys a plough or a fannin' mill, do you spoze he expects the neighborin' men he borrys 'em of to harness up and come after 'em? No, he carries 'em back.

"And how much more would he feel obligated if he had stole 'em, and me too; why we should expect to carry 'em back, or else get shot up, and good enough for us.

"Now," sez I, "you and your people wuz stole from Africa by Uncle Samuel, or, I don't spoze the old man did the stealin' with his own hands, but he stood by and see it done and winked at it, and allowed it; and so, he is responsible, bein' the head of the family.

"And if that old man ever calculates to make any

DEACON HUFFER.

appearance at all before the nations of the earth, if he ever calculates to neighbor with 'em to any advantage, he will jest carry them stolen creeters back and put 'em down onharmed on the sile he dragged 'em from.

"Good land! it won't be no job for him; it won't be no more for him than it would for my companion to take back a hen he had borryed from Deacon Huffer up to Zoar—or stole from him, I spoze I ort to say, in order to carry out the metafor as metafors ort to be carried."

I sez this in a real enthusiastic axent, and a very friendly one too towards Uncle Samuel; for I love that noble-minded but sometimes misguided old creeter—I love him dearly.

But Victor smiled agin that sort of a amused smile, and yet a sort of a sad one too. And sez he:

"I am afraid this Nation has not got your sense of honor."

He couldn't help, I see, a kinder wishin' that the Government would brace up and take over a few cargoes of 'em.

But he wuz dubersome.

But anyway he wuz bound they should get there some way. And I had a feelin', as I looked at him, that the dark waves in front of him would part some way, and he would pass over into the light, he and his race.

Wall, jest about as he finished up his idees to me, Genieve come in lookin' as pretty as a pink, and I got up and carried the thread into the house, willin' to leave 'em alone for a little while, and I spoze—I spoze they wuz willin' to have me go.

Yes, I hadn't forgot what courtship wuz, when Josiah Allen come over to see me, sheepish but affectionate.

And I remember well how he would brighten up when Mother Smith would be obleeged to go out to get supper, or to strain the milk, or sunthin' or other.

No, I hain't forgot it, and most probable never shall.

"UNDER THE WHITE CROSS."

## CHAPTER X.

LITTLE Snow wuz always askin' about the little girl who wuz a lyin' under the white cross and the rose-trees down in the corner of the garden at Belle Fanchon.

And she would ask me sights of questions about her. She would ask "if Belle Fanchon used to walk about and run as she did through the paths of the old garden, and pick the roses, and stand under the orange-trees, and hear the birds sing, and the laugh of the brook as it wound along amongst the flowers?"

And I would say, " Yes, I spoze so."

And then she would say, " What made her leave it all and go and lie down there under the grass?"

And I would say, " The Lord wanted her."

And she would say, " Will He want me?"

And I would 'hold her clost to my heart, and say, " Oh, no, darlin', Grandma hopes not, not for a long, long time, not till these old eyes are closed many and many a year," I would say.

"But if He *should* want me," she would go on to say earnestly, "I want to lie down by the little girl in the garden. She wouldn't be so lonesome then in dark nights, would she, if she had another little girl close by her?"

And then she would go on and describe it to me in her own pretty language: How when the moon shone silver bright and the shadows lay long and white over the little girl's grave like a big, lovin' hand, it would cover 'em both, and how on warm, sunshiny mornin's the birds would sing to both of 'em, and the roses and tall lilies bend down over both, and the rivulet would talk to 'em as it went dancin' by, and—

"Don't talk so, darlin'," I would say, "Grandma don't love to hear you."

And then mebby she would see the shadow on my face, and she would put up her little hand in that tender caress that wuz better than kisses, lay it on my cheek, and brush my hair back, and then touch my cheek agin.

And mebby the very next minute she would be a askin' me some deep question about Jack the Giant Killer or the Sleepin' Beauty.

She had a very active mind, very.

And she wuz a beautiful child. Josiah said, and said well, that she went fur beyond anything on the globe for beauty, and smartness, and goodness. And Josiah Allen is a excellent judge of children, excellent.

But, as I wuz a sayin', Snow loved to talk about

the little girl who had been mistress of this pretty place so long ago. She talked about her a sight. And if she had her way she would always go there to play, by the little grave—carry her dollies down there—Samantha Maggie Tirzah Ann, and the hull caboodle of 'em—she had as many as fourteen of 'em, anyway—and her dolls' cradles, and wagons, and everything. And she wuz never so happy as when she wuz settled down there in that corner.

Wall, it wuz pleasant as it could be. How clost the little rivulet did seem to hold the child's grave in its dimpled arm, and its song never said to me:

"My arm is warm and faithful, and is reaching out and reaching out to fold it round another of the nearest ones and dearest, and guard it, hold it safely from danger and from trouble."

No, I never heard this in its song, and I never heard any undertone of pity for hearts that would break with a new grief.

No, I only heard low murmurs of compassion in its liquid tones for the achin' hearts that had bent over this one little grave long ago.

But the trees always did seem to cast greener, softer shadows here, and the sunshine and moonlight to rest more lovingly on it than on any other spot in the hull grounds. And I didn't wonder at all at little Snow's fancy for it.

Oh, what a judgment that child showed in everything—it was a sight!

One mornin' I wuz a settin' out on the veranda, and I see her as usual a settin' out for that corner, Snow with her arms full of toys, and Genieve wheelin' Boy in his cart, and the front of that full of

Snow's babies settin' up stiff and straight, a starin' back with their round, blank eyes at Boy's pretty, laughin' face.

It wuz a lovely mornin'.

The dew sparkled on the grass, and the walks of white shinin' shells which had been washed clean by a brisk, short rain the night before, shone white and silvery through the fresh, green grass borderin' 'em on each side.

And the trees tosted out their shinin' green branches, and the glossy-leaved shrubs shook out their sweet-scented flowers on the balmy air.

The climbin' roses bloomed out sweet and pink, the orange-trees gleamed with the round globes of gold, and anon clusters of posys amongst the shinin' green leaves.

It wuz a fair seen, a fair seen.

And I sot enjoyin' it to the full, and as is the depraved and curius nater of men and wimmen, a enjoyin' it still more as I turned to it from the pages of a voluminous letter I had jest got and received from Philury.

Yes, as I read of the snow piles, and the dirty slosh of snow and mud that the Jonesvillians had to wade through under gray skies and cotton umberells, I sot with a deeper gratitude and a happier frame to my mind under the clear blue skies of the balmy South land, amongst the beauties and summer fragrance of Belle Fanchon.

There wuz another letter I hadn't read yet a layin' in my lap, and my joyful meditation and my comparisons that I had drawed, and drawed so fur, had took my mind from it.

But anon, as I turned back from the sight of Maggie and Thomas Jefferson a ridin' off through the sunshine towards the depot, I took up the other let-

THE JONESVILLIANS.

ter, and as I opened it I involuntarily uttered them words which have sounded out from my lips in so many crysisses of joy or pain. I sez:

"Good land! good land!"

The letter wuz from John Richard Allen, writ for him by a friend. It seems that he had seen in the village paper that we wuz in the South and where we wuz; and he lay sick and a dyin', as they said, in a little hamlet not a dozen miles away.

I read the letter, and then went imegiatly—for to think and to act is but a second or third nater to me—and waked up my pardner, who was stretched out on a bamboo couch on the other end of the piazza fast asleep, with the *World* a layin' outstretched and abject at his feet. And I then told him the startlin' truth that his own relation on his own side lay sick unto death less than a dozen miles from us.

Wall, that noble man riz right up as I would have had him rozen to meet the exigencies of the occasion.

He sez, "The minute our children get back we will take the pony and drive over and see him."

As I said, they had gone to the depot to meet visitors from Delaware—a very distinguished cousin of Maggie's on her own side, who had writ that he wuz a goin' to pass through here on his way further South, and he would stop off a day or two with 'em —he and his little boy, if it wuz agreeable to them.

I had hearn a sight about this rich Senator Coleman—Maggie's father, old Squire Snow, wuz dretful proud of him.

He had made himself mostly—or, that is, had finished himself off.

He went to Delaware as a teacher, and married a Miss Fairfax, a very rich young woman down there, settled down in her home, went into business, got independent rich, wuz sent to Congress and Senate, and had a hand in makin' all the laws of his State, so I hearn.

He wuz now takin' a tower through the Southern States with his motherless boy, little Raymond Fairfax Coleman, so he writ (he thought his eyes on him, and jest worshipped the memory of his wife).

Maggie and Thomas J. had met him in Washington the winter before, and they sort o' took to each other. And so he wuz a goin' to stop off a few days with 'em.

Wall, that program of Josiah Allen's wuz carried out to the very letter. When Thomas J. and Maggie come back (the Senator didn't come, he wuz delayed, and sent a telegram he should be there in a week or two), we sot off, a preparin' to come back the next day if John Richard wuz better, but a layin' out to stay several days if necessary.

We took clothes and things, and I a not forgettin', you may be sure, a bottle full of my far-famed spignut syrup.

Maggie see that we had a early dinner but a good one, and we sot sail about one o'clock—Snow a ridin' with us as fur as we dasted to take her, and a walkin' back agin, watched by her Ma from the gate.

Thomas J. and Maggie told us to bring John Richard right back with us if he wuz well enough to come, and they would help take care of him.

Wall, we got to the picturesque little place called Howletts Bridge about four o'clock, and imegiatly made inquiries for the relation on his side, and found out where he wuz stayin'.

He wuz boardin' with a likely Methodist Episcopal couple, elderly, and poor but well-principled.

And indeed we found him sick enough.

Miss Elderkin—that wuz the folkses name he wuz a boardin' with, good creeters as I ever see, if they wuz Southerners, and aristocratic too, brung down by loss of property and etc.—she told me that Cousin John Richard had been comin' down with this lung difficulty for years—overwork, and hard fare, and neglect of his own comfort makin' his sickness harder and more difficult to manage.

Sez she, "He is one of the saints on earth, if there ever was one."

And her husband said the same thing, which I felt that I could indeed depend upon, for as a general thing men don't get so diffuse a praisin' up each other, and callin' each other angels and saints, etc., and men hain't drawed away by their pities and their sympathies so easy as wimmen be, nor drawed so fur.

Wall, Mr. Elderkin put our pony in the barn, and she made us comfortable with a cup of tea and some toast with a poached egg on top of it. And then we went in to see the patient.

He wuz layin' in a front room, ruther bare-lookin', for the Elderkins wuz poor enough so fur as this world's goods go, but rich in the spirit.

And the bare floor, and whitewashed walls, and green paper curtains looked anything but luxurious, but everything wuz clean.

And on a clean, poor bed lay the relation on his side.

He looked wan—wanner fur than I expected to see him look, though I wuz prepared for wanness. His cheeks wuz fell in, and his eyes wuz holler, but bright still with that glowin' fire that always seemed to be built up in 'em. But the light of that fire seemed to be a burnin' down pretty low now. And he looked up and see us and smiled.

It wuz the smile of a homesick child fur away to school, when he sees his own folks a comin' towards him in the school-room.

Poor John Richard! His school wuz hard, his lessons had been severe, but he had tried to learn 'em all jest as perfect as he could, and the Master wuz pleased with his work.

But now he wuz sick. He wuz a sick man.

As I said, he smiled as he see Josiah and me advancin' onto him, and he held out his weak hands, and took holt of ourn, and kep' 'em in hisen for some time, and sez he:

" I am glad—*glad* to see you."

He wuz interrupted anon, and ever oftener, by his awful cough and short, painful breathin'. But he gin us to understand that he wuz dretful glad to see us once more before he passed away.

He wuzn't afraid to die—no, indeed! There wuz a deep, sweet smile in his eyes, and his lips seemed to hold some happy and divine secret as he sez:

" I am glad to go home; I am glad to rest."

But I sez in a cheerful axent, " Cousin John Richard, you hain't a goin' to die;" sez I, " By the help of God and my good spignut syrup I believe you will be brung up agin."

But he shet up his eyes. And I see plain, by the look of his face, that though he wuz willin' to live and work if it wuz God's will, he wuz still more ready to depart and be with Christ, which he felt would be fur better.

But it wuzn't my way to stand and argue with a sick man back and forth as to whether he wuz a goin' to die or not.

No, I laid to, helped by my trusty Josiah. And

"BOY LAUGHED."

in an hour's time we see a difference in his breathin', and anon he fell into a sweet sleep.

And when he waked up that man looked and acted better. And three days and nights did we stay by him, a doctorin' him up and a gettin' him nourishin' things to eat, and a talkin' encouragin' and pleasant things to him (good land! the soul and mind has got to be fed as well as the body if you don't want to starve to death inwardly). And lo and behold! when we left Howletts Bridge and returned to Belle Fanchon, who should accompany us thither but Cousin John Richard Allen!

He had consented, after a deep parley, to go there and rest off for a few weeks.

Maggie and Thomas J. took to him from the very first, and give him a hearty welcome and the best bedroom. They appreciated the noble, martyrous life he had led, and honored him for it.

And the children acted dretful tickled to see him. You needn't tell me but what Boy knew all about it when I introduced Cousin John Richard to him. To be sure, he wuzn't only six months old.

But if he didn't know him, and if he wuzn't glad to see the relation on his grandmother's side, what made him laugh all over his face, eyes and all?

I presume the Doctor would have called it "wind." But I called it perfect courtesy and good manners towards a honored and onexpected guest. That is what I called it. He acted like a perfect little gentleman, and I wuz proud of him.

Snow, the sweet darlin', went right up to him, with her little snowflake of a hand held out in a warm welcome, and kissed him jest as she did her Grandpa. Oh, what a child—what a child for behavior! I never see her equal, and don't expect to—nor Josiah don't either.

Wall, Cousin John Richard jest settled down in that sweet, lovin' home into a perfect, happy rest— to all appearances—and gained every day.

Victor and Genieve thought everything of him from the first time they laid eyes on him. And they couldn't do enough for him seemingly. They had heard about his life and labor amongst their own people, and they tried in every way to show their gratitude and affection.

Victor and he talked together for hours, and so did he and Genieve about the plans for the colony. And first I knew, Cousin John Richard told Josiah and me that he had made up his mind to go with them to Africa.

The Doctor had told him that a long sea voyage would be the best of anything for his lungs. And so, as he wuz bound to spend his life for this people, I couldn't see, and Josiah couldn't, why it shouldn't be in Africa as well as America, specially as he had a better chance to live by goin' there.

And so we gin our consents in our own minds, and showed our two willingnesses to him, and the matter wuz settled.

He had only two children left now, and they wuz married and settled down in homes of their own, and in a good business. So he had no hamperin' ties to bind him to this land. And he felt that the Lord wuz a pintin' out to him the path of Duty over the sea.

And I wuzn't the one to dispute him—no, indeed! And I felt that his calm good sense and undaunted Christian spirit and Gospel teachings would be a perfect boon to the colony.

So it wuz settled. And I imegiatly went to work, Maggie and I, to make him a full dozen of shirts, twelve day ones and six nights.

And we prepared him a better assortment of socks and handkerchiefs, and collars, and cuffs, and such than he had ever dremp of, I'll venture to say, sence he lost his companion, anyway.

Wall, it wuzn't more'n several days after this that the relation of Maggie's—Senator Coleman—bein' sot free from hampers, writ agin, and also tele-

RAYMOND FAIRFAX COLEMAN.

grafted, that he would be at the station that day at five o'clock.

So, Maggie and Thomas J. rid over agin, and bein' luckier this time, they come a ridin' back in due time with her relation a settin' up by her side, big as life, and the boy, Raymond Fairfax Coleman, a settin' on the front seat by Thomas Jefferson.

The boy's name seemed bigger than he wuz, bein' a little, pale runt of a child with long, silky hair and a black velvet suit—dretful small for his age, about seven years old. But I spoze his long curls of light hair and his lace collar made him seem younger, and his childish way of talkin'—he had been babied a good deal I could see. And when he would fix his big blue eyes on you with that sort of a confidin', perplexed, childish look in 'em, I declare for't he didn't look so old as Boy.

But he wuz seven years old, so his Pa told me.

His Pa wuz as big and important-lookin' as Raymond wuz insignificant. And I sez to Josiah the first chance I got, out to one side, sez I:

"I've hearn a sight from old Judge Snow about this relation of hisen bein' a self-made man;" and sez I, "If he did make himself, he did up the job in quite a good shape, didn't he?"

Josiah can't bear to have me praise up any man, married or single, bond or free, only jest himself, and he sez:

"If I had made him I would have put in some improvements on him. I wouldn't have had him so cussed big feelin' for one thing."

I wuz deeply mortified to hear him use that wicked word, and told him so.

But I couldn't help seein' that Josiah wuz right in thinkin' Senator Coleman wuz proud and high-headed, for truly he wuz. His head wuz right up in the air, and he sort o' leaned back when he walked, and over his portly stomach hung a glitterin' watch-chain that he sort o' fingered and played with as he walked about, and he had some diamonds a flashin' on his little finger, and his shirt-front, and cuffs.

His eyes wuz a bright blue and as bold and piercin' looking as Raymond's wuz gentle and helpless, and his mustache and short hair wuz a sort of a iron gray; and his face bein' florid and his features good, he made a handsome appearance; and Maggie, I

"WITH A JUMPIN' TOOTHACHE."

could see, wuz quite proud of the relation on her side.

Wall, we had a good warm supper all ready for

'em, Maggie's cook bein' sort o' helpless that day with a jumpin' toothache (it jumped worse after Maggie went away and she see in me a willingness to help her get supper).

I laid holt and got the most of the supper myself, and it wuz a good one, if I hadn't ort to say it.

Two plump spring fowls roasted to a delicate brown, some sliced potatoes warmed up in cream, some hot cream biscuit; and I had splendid luck with 'em—they wuz jest as light and flaky and tender as they could be. And some perfectly delicious coffee. I thought the fragrance of that coffee would steam up invitingly into Senator Coleman's nostrils, after a hard day's journey.

And if the relation had been on Thomas Jefferson's side I couldn't have set out to do better by him; I am good to my daughter-in-law—anybody will tell you so that has seen me behave to her.

Aunt Mela, the cook, by bendin' all her energies onto 'em, had made a tomato salad and some veal croquettes. I hain't partial to 'em, but want everybody to be suited in the line of vittles, and Maggie loves 'em.

And then on the sideboard wuz cake, and jellies, and fresh berries heaped up in crimson beauty on some china plates, and the table had posys on it and looked well.

The cook's teeth stopped achin' about the time the supper wuz all ready—it seemed to give its last hard jump about the time I made the biscuit. I had proposed to have her make 'em, but I see it wouldn't do.

Wall, Maggie wuz delighted with the supper, and her relation eat more than wuz good for him, I wuz afraid—five wuz the number of the biscuit he consumed (they wuzn't so very large), and three cups of coffee kep' 'em company.

Maggie told him who made 'em, and he complimented me so warmly (though still high-headed) that Josiah looked cross as a bear.

Wall, the Senator seemed to like it at Belle Fanchon first rate; and as for Raymond Fairfax Coleman, he jest revelled in the warm home atmosphere and the lovin' attentions that wuz showered down onto him.

Poor little motherless creeter! He played with Snow, lugged her dolls round for her, and dragged Boy in his little covered carriage, and seemed to be jest about as much of a baby as our Boy.

If you think our boy didn't have any other name than Boy, there is where you are mistaken. His name wuz Robert Josiah from his birth—after his two grandpas; but Thomas Jefferson wuz so pleased to think he wuz a boy that he got in the habit of callin' him Boy, and we all joined in and followed on after him, as is the habit of human bein's or sheep. You know how the him reads:

> "First a daughter and then a son,
> Then the world is well begun."

I spoze Thomas J. had this in mind when he wuz so tickled at the birth of Boy.

But howsomever and tenny rate, we all called him Boy. And he knew the name, and would laugh and dimple all over in his pretty glee when we would call him.

Wall, I would take little Raymond up on my lap,

and tell him stories, and pet him, and Maggie would mother him jest as she would Snow, and we wuz both on us sorry for him as sorry could be to think of his forlorn little state.

Riches, and fame, and even his big name couldn't make up for the loss of the tender counsels and broodin' love of a mother.

His father jest thought his eyes on him. But he couldn't seem to stop fumblin' that watch-chain of hisen, and stop a talkin' them big words, and descend from his ambitious plans of self-advancement to come down to his little boy's level and talk to him in a lovin' way.

Little Raymond looked up to his Pa with a sort of a admirin' awe, jest about as the Jonesville children would to the President.

I believe Senator Coleman had ambitions to be one. I believe my soul he did. Anyway, his ambitions wuz all personal. Havin' made himself so fur, he wuz bound to put all the adornin's and embellishin's onto his work that he could.

I see that he wanted to be made President to once, and the thought that the nation wouldn't do it rankled in him.

And the fear that somebody else wuz a goin' to get higher than he wuz in political life wore on him.

His sharp, piercin' eyes wuz a watchin' the evershiftin' horizon of our national affairs, the everchangin' winds of public favor, hopin' they would blow him up into greater prominence, fearin' they would dash him down into a lower place.

The feverishness of perpetual onrest seemed to be a burnin' him all the time, and the fear that he should do or say sunthin' to incur the displeasure of the multitude.

What a time, what a time he wuz a havin'!

You could see it all in his linement; yes, ambition and selfishness had ploughed lots of lines in his handsome face, and ploughed 'em deep.

I used to look at him and then at Cousin John Richard Allen, and contrast the two men in my own mind, and the contrast wuz a big and hefty one.

Now, Cousin John Richard's face wuz peaceful and serene, though considerable worn-lookin'. He had gin his hull life for the True and Right, had gone right on, no matter how much he wuz misunderstood and despised of men, and labored in season and out of season for the poor and downtrodden of earth, without any hope of earthly reward—nay, with the certainty of the world's contempt and criticism.

But the blame or praise of the multitude seemed so fur off to him that he could scarcely hear it; the confusin' babble seemed to him only like a distant murmurous background for the close voice of the Master, who walked with him, and told him what to do from day to day and from hour to hour.

"Blessed are ye if ye hear my voice."

"Ye that are strong, bear the burdens of the weak."

"If ye love me feed my lambs."

"And lo, I am with you to the end of the world."

These wuz some of the words Cousin John Richard heard, and his face shone as he listened to 'em.

He had not sent out his ships on earthly waters;

"THE RELATION ON MAGGIE'S SIDE."

and so, let the winds blow high or the winds blow low, he did not fear any tempestuous waves and storms reachin' their sails.

No, he had sent his ships into a safer harbor ; they wuz anchored in that divine sea where no storms can ever come.

And his face wuz calm with the heavenly calmness and peace of that sure harbor, that waveless sea.

Wall, the relation on Maggie's side seemed to take a good deal of comfort a walkin' round with his head up and his hand a playin' with that heavy gold chain.

Good land! I should have thought he would have wore it out—he would if it hadn't been made of good stuff.

And he would converse with Thomas Jefferson about political matters, and talk some with my Josiah and Cousin John—not much with the latter, because they wuzn't congenial, as I have hinted at ; and Cousin John Richard seemed to take as much agin comfort a bein' off with the children, or a layin' in the green grass a watchin' the butterflies, or a talkin' with Genieve and Victor.

And the Senator would compliment Maggie up to the skies. He wuz more'n polite to females, as is the way with such men ; and he would write letters by the bushel, and get as many of 'em or more, and telegrams, and such. And little Raymond, poor little creeter, I believe took more comfort than he had before for some time.

He wuzn't very deep, as I could see, he didn't act over and above smart ; but then, I sez to myself real ironikle, mebby this dulness is caused by lookin' at the sun so much (his Pa used as a metafor).

And then what could you expect of a child of seven? he wuzn't much more'n a baby. Good land! I used to hold Thomas Jefferson in my lap and baby him till he wuz nine or ten years old, and his legs dragged on the floor, he wuz so tall.

I thought like as not Raymond Fairfax Coleman would take a turn after a while and live up to the privileges of his name and be quite smart.

He took a great fancy to Rosy's baby, and it was as cunnin' a little black image as I ever see, jest a beginnin' to be playful and full of laugh.

Raymond would carry it down candy and oranges, and give him nickels and little silver pieces to put into his savings-bank.

I gin that bank myself to little Thomas Jefferson Washington, for that wuz the name his Pa and Ma had gin him—we called him Tommy. They gin him the name of Thomas Jefferson, I spoze, to honor the name of my son, and then put on the Washington to kinder prop up the memory of the Father of our Country, or so I spoze.

I gin him that bank to try to give his Pa and Ma some idee of savin' for a rainy day, and days when it didn't rain.

It wuz very nice, in the form of a meetin' house—you put the money down through the steeple.

I thought mebby, bein' it wuz in this shape, it would sort o' turn their minds onto meetin' houses and such moral idees.

Well, finally, one mornin' early we heard, clear

up in our room, Senator Coleman makin' a great hue and cry.

We hearn his voice lifted up high in agitation and exhortation, and I sez to my pardner:

"What under the sun is the matter with the relation on Maggie's side?"

And Josiah said, and it pains me to record it:

"He didn't know, and he didn't care a dumb."

He never liked Senator Coleman for a minute.

But as we descended down to breakfast we soon found out and discovered what wuz the matter. Little Raymond (poor little babyish creeter!), a not mistrustin' its real value, had took a valuable diamond locket and gin it to little Tommy.

It wuz a very valuable locket, with seven great diamonds in it. It wuz one that the Senator's dead wife had gin him when they wuz first married, and had their two names writ on it, and inside a lock of their two hairs.

It wuz one of the most precious things in the Senator's hull possessions; and thinkin' so much of it, he couldn't make up his mind to leave it to his banker's with the rest of his jewelry and plate, but he kept it with him, with a little ivory miniature of sweet Kate Fairfax when she first become his girlish bride.

The relation on Maggie's side did have one or two soft spots in his nater, and one of 'em wuz his adoration of his dead wife, and his clingin' love for anything that had belonged to her, and the other wuz his love for his child—more because it wuz her child, I do believe, than because it wuz his own.

Them two soft places wuz oasis'es, as you may

say, in his nater. All the desert round 'em wuz full of the rocky, sandy soil of ambition, feverish expectations, and aims and plans for political advancement.

Wall, Raymond had took this locket and gin it to Rosy's baby. His Pa had told him it would be hisen some time, and he thought it wuz hisen now.

Poor little creeter! he didn't have no more idee of the value on't than a Hottentot has of snow ploughs, or than we have as to what the folks up in Jupiter are a havin' for dinner.

And he sot by the winder a cryin' as if his poor little childish heart would break, and the Senator wuz hoppin' mad.

But neither the tears nor the anger could bring back the jewel—it wuz lost. Thomas J. of course had gone down to the coachman's cottage to make inquiries about it, accompanied by the distracted statesman. But of course Rosy had lied about it; she said little Tom, three days before, jest after Raymond had gin it to him, had dropped it into the river.

But nobody believed it. How could that infant have dropped it into the river more'n a mile off?

No; we all spozed that Rosy, a naterel thief and liar, had passed it on to some other thief, and it wuz all broke to pieces and the diamonds hid away and passed on out of reach.

The strictest search hadn't amounted to nuthin'. Wall, I didn't say much about it till after breakfast —my manners wuz too perfect for that, and then I wuz hungry myself. And I felt that I had some things I wanted to say, and I didn't want to say 'em on a empty stomach, and didn't want 'em hearn on one.

After breakfast the Senator begun agin on the subject, and kep' it up. And I did feel sorry for him from the bottom of my heart, for, if you'll believe it, as we sot there alone in the settin' room after breakfast, that man cried—or, that is, the tears come fast into his eyes when he talked about it.

And I gin the man credit where credit wuz due; it wuzn't the money worth of the gem that he cared for, though it wuz very valuable.

No; it wuz the memory of lovely Kate Fairfax, and the blendin' of their two names on it, and a part of their two selves, as you may say—the curl of her golden hair twisted in with his dark locks. And all the tender memories of the happy time when she gin him this jewel with her first true love, and he gin her his hull heart. Memories bitter-sweet now as he mourned his losses.

Wall, I see the Senator wuz all melted down and broke up; and as is my way, havin' the good of the human race on my mind and heart, and havin' to do for 'em all the while, I see that now wuz the very time for me to tackle the relation from Delaware about a matter that I had long wanted to tackle him on, concernin' a law of his own State—

A statute so full of burnin' injustice, and shame, and disgrace that it wuz a wonder to me, and had been for some time, that the very stuns along the banks of the Delaware didn't cry out to its Senators as they passed along to and from their law-makin' expeditions.

And when he wuz a goin' on the very worst about

Raymond's doin' such a dretful thing, and what a irreparable loss it wuz, I spoke up, and sez I, "Why, Raymond had a right to it, didn't he?"

"A right?" he thundered out in his agitation, "a right to throw away this priceless jewel? What do you mean, madam?"

"Why," sez I calmly (for I wuz a workin' for Duty and Right; and they always brace me up and keep me calm), "Raymond has passed the age of consent, hasn't he?" He wuz a few days over seven years old.

"What!!!" cries the Senator, "*what* do you mean?"

"Why, children in your State can consent to their own ruin if they are over seven."

"It is girls that can do this," hollered the Senator from Delaware, "it hain't boys."

But I went on calm as I could:

"What are a few diamonds, that can be bought and sold, to be compared to the downfall of all hope and happiness, the contempt and derision of the world, the ruin of a life, and the loss of a immortal soul? And your laws grant this privilege to children if they are a day or two over seven."

"That law was made for girls," cried the Senator agin in stentorian axents.

"Yes," sez I, "men made that law, and girls and wimmen have to stand it. But," sez I, lookin' and actin' considerable fierce, as the mighty shame and disgrace of that law come over me, "it is a law so infamus that I should think the old Atlantic herself (bein' a female, as is spozed) would jest rare herself up and wash over the hull land, to try to wipe out or bury the horrible disgrace that has been put upon her sect—would swash up and cover your little State completely up—it ort to, and hide it forever from the heavens and the eye of females."

That man begun to quail, I see he did. But the thought of Snow, the darlin', and our dear Babe at Jonesville nerved me up agin—the thought of them,

BABE.

our own treasures, and the hosts of pretty children all over our land, beloved by some hearts jest as dearly as our children wuz.

And I went on more fiery than I had went, as I thought, why Babe is old enough now, and Snow will be in a little while, to lay their sweet little lives down under this Jugernut built up by the vile passions of men, and goin' ahead of Isaac, lay themselves on the altar, take their own lives, and build up the fire to consume 'em.

"The idee of law-makers who call themselves wise makin' such laws as these!"

He stopped a handlin' that watch-chain of hisen, his head drooped, his hands dropped demutely into his lap. He murmured sunthin' almost mechanically about "the law being on the statute-book."

"I know it is," sez I. "I know the law is there. But let wimmen have a chance to vote; let a few mothers and grandmothers get holt of that statute-book, and see where that law would be."

Sez I eloquently, "No spring cleanin' and scourin' wuz ever done by females so thorough as they would cleanse out them old law books and let a little of God's purity and justice shine into their musty old pages."

Sez I, "You made a great ado about Raymond losin' that locket because it wuz precious with the memories of your lost wife—you treasured it as your most dear possession because it held a lock of her hair, because she gin it to you, and her love and tenderness seemed shinin' out of every jewel in it.

"But how would it be with a child that a mother left as a souvenir of her deathless love, a part of her own life left to a broken-hearted husband? Would a man who held such a child, such a little daughter to his achin' heart, do and make a law by which the child could be lost and ruined forever?

"No; the men that make these laws make 'em for other folks'es children, not their own. It is other fathers' girls that they doom to ruin. When they license shameful houses it hain't their own pretty daughters that they picture under the infamous ruffs, despised playthings for brutality and lust. No; it is some other parents' daughters."

My tone had been awful eloquent and riz up, for nobody but the Lord knew how deeply I felt all I

"MY TONE RIZ UP."

had said, and more than I ever could say on the subject.

And I spoze I looked lofty and noble in my mean —I spoze so.

Anyway, Senator Coleman quailed to a extent that I hardly ever see quailed in my hull life, and I have seen lots of quailin' in my day. And I pressed home the charge.

Sez I, "You say this law wuz made for girls; but what if this boy that your sweet Kate Fairfax left you had happened to be a girl, and had gin away all that makes life worth living, how would you have felt then, Senator Coleman?

"How would you feel a thinkin' that you had got to meet her lovin', questionin' eyes up in heaven, and when she asked you what you had done with her child you would have to say that you had spent all your life a tryin' to pass laws that wuz the ruination of her darlin'; that you had done your best to frame laws so that them that prey upon innocence and childish ignorance could go unpunished, and that the blood of these souls, the agony of breakin' hearts wuz a layin' at your door?

"How could you meet them sweet, lovin' eyes and have to tell her this?"

He jest crumpled right down, and almost buried his face in his white linen handkerchief, and give vent to some low groans that wuz damp with tears.

That man had never had the truth brung right home to him before, and he trembled and he shrunk before it.

And he promised me then and there that he would turn right round and do his very best to make laws to protect innocence and ignorance and to purify the hull statute-book all he could; and I felt that he had tackled a hard job, but I believed he would try his best. I guess he means to tell the truth.

And I wuz almost overpolite to him after this, not wantin' to do or say a thing to break up his good intentions; and when he went away he gin me a dretful meanin', earnest look, and sez he:

"You can depend upon me to keep my word."

And I believed he would.

Poor little Raymond cried when he went away, cried and wept.

But the Senator promised to let him come back before a great while for a good long visit—that comforted him a little. And we all kissed him and made much of him; and Snow, with the tears a standin' in her sweet eyes, offered to gin him the doll she loves best—Samantha Maggie Tirzah Ann—if it would be any help to him. But he said he had ruther have her keep it. And I believe he told the truth.

He is a good child.

"I HAD BEEN OUT A WALKIN'."

## CHAPTER XI.

I HAD been out a walkin' one day, and when I got back and went into the settin' room, I see there wuz a visitor there, and, lo and behold, when I wuz introduced to him it wuz Col. Seybert!

He wuz dretful polite—and I know well what belongs to good manners—and so I didn't turn my back to him and walk off with my capstrings a wavin' back in a indignant, scornful way.

No; he wuz a neighbor, and my son and daughter wuz a neighborin' with him, so I treated him polite but cool, and shook his hand back and forth mebby once or twice, and sez:

"I am well, and I hope I find you the same."

Oh, I know how to appear.

I then went and sot down some distance from him.

Genieve wuz a settin' in the next room holdin'

Boy in her arms—he wuzn't over and above well that day (cuttin' teeth). And I looked out and smiled at 'em both; I then went to knittin'.

If I should be obleeged to kiss the Bible and tell jest what I thought about Col. Seybert, I should say that I didn't like his looks a mite, not a mite.

He looked bold, and brassy, and self-assertive, and dissipated—he looked right down mean. And I should have said so if I hadn't never hearn a word about his treatment of Victor, or his deviltry about Hester, or anything.

You know in some foreign countries the officers have to give you a passport to pass through the country. And when you are a travellin' you have to show your papers, and show up who you be and what you be.

Wall, I spoze that custom is follered from one of Nater's. She always fills out her papers and signs 'em with her own hand, so that folks that watch can tell travellers a passin' through this world.

Nater had signed Col. Seybert's passport, had writ it down in the gross, sensual, yet sneerin' lips, in the cold, cruel look in his eyes, in his loud, boastin', aggressive manner.

Yet he wuz a neighbor, and I felt that we must neighbor with him.

After I come into the room, he begun, I spoze out of politeness, to sort o' address himself to me in his remarks. And he seemed to be a resoomin' the conversation my comin' in had interrupted.

And anon, he begun to went on about the colored people perfectly shameful.

And as my mind roamed back and recalled the

various things I had heard of his doin', I most imegiatly made up my mind that, neighbor or not, if this thing kep' on I should have to gin him a piece of my mind.

And there Genieve sot, the good, pretty, patient creeter, a hearin' her own people run down to the

POOR WHITE.

lowest notch. I felt as if I should sink, but felt that before I *did* sink I should speak.

He went on to tell what a dretful state the country wuz in, and all a owin' to the colored race; and sez he:

"The niggers don't take any interest in the welfare of the country. What do they care what becomes of the nation if they can get their pan of bacon and hominy?

"A mule stands up before their eyes higher than any idea of Justice or Liberty.

"They are liars, they are thieves, they are lazy, they are hangers-on to the skirts of civilization, they can never stand upright, they have got to be carried all their days. And it is this mass of ignorance, and superstition, and vice that you Northerners want to see ruling us white men of the South.

"They can't read nor write, nor understand an intelligible remark hardly; and yet these are the men that you want to have vote and get put in as rulers over us.

"Well, we will not submit to it, that is all there is about it; and if war comes, the sooner the better, for we will die fighting for our freedom. It is bad enough for us Southerners to be ruled by Northern men, but when it comes to being ruled by beasts, animals that are no higher than brutes, we will not submit."

Sez I, for I would speak up, and I did:

"Hain't there plenty of intelligent educated colored people now, graduates of schools and colleges—lawyers, teachers, ministers, etc., etc.?"

"Oh, yes, a few," he admitted reluctantly.

I knew there wuz a hundred thousand of 'em, if there wuz one.

And I sez, "Hain't the condition of your poor whites here in the South about as bad as the negroes, mentally and morally and physically?"

"Well, yes," he admitted that it wuz. "But,"

sez he, "that don't alter the dangerous state of affairs. The interests of a community cannot be placed in the hands of an ignorant, vicious rabble without terrible peril and danger. And when it is too late the country will awake to this truth."

His axent wuz very skairful, and reproachful, and rebukin', and despairin', and everything. And so, thinkses I, I will ventilate some of them views that had gone through my mind when I first begin to muse on the Race Problem, before I had heard so much of Victor and Genieve's talk and Cousin John Richards'es.

Thinkses I, "It won't do no hurt to promulgate 'em anyway," for I truly felt that if they wouldn't do no good, they wouldn't be apt to do no hurt.

And then, when there is a big conundrum gin out to a individual or a nation, it stands to reason that there must be more than one answer to it—or, that is, folks will try to answer it in more than fifty ways.

And anyway, this wuz part of one answer to the conundrum, though folks might be dubersome of its bein' the right one; anyway, I sez, sez I:

"Hain't your Southern wimmen of the higher classes high-minded and educated ladies?"

"Yes, God bless them," sez he, "they are as pure, and good, and high minded as angels; and to think of these lofty-souled, spiritual creatures being under the rule of these beasts of burden."

(Thinkses I, no thanks to him if they are good and pure, the mean, miserable snipe.)

But I sez, "If these wimmen are so good and noble, of course you wouldn't be afraid to trust 'em. Why not let 'em vote, why not have a educated, moral vote, that would take the power out of the hands of the low and vile, black and white, and place it in the hands of the educated and moral, and whether in this country or another" (sez I, as I thought to myself of Victor's plan), "whether in this Republic or a new colony, it would be a right way, a safe way."

"I don't believe in women voting," sez Col. Seybert, with a strong, witherin' emphasis. "I don't believe in it—and they don't; you couldn't get our women to vote."

"How do you know they wouldn't? You say they are high-minded and pure as angels. Now, an angel, if she see that the best good of the greatest number depended on her votin', she would jest lift her wings right up and sail off to the pole and vote. I believe it as much as I believe I am alive.

"If the wimmen of the South are as lofty principled as you say they are, and they wuz convinced that they could rescue their beloved land from danger by sacrificin' their own feelin's if necessary, to keep the balance of power in the educated classes, why, they would walk up and vote. I believe it jest as much as I believe I am standin' here.

"The same bravery that met the terrible reverses of the War with a smile hidin' a breakin' heart, that endured privation, and almost starvation, for their love to the cause, that same spirit hain't a goin' to falter now. Let them know that they can do great good to the imperilled South. Let them know that the country wants an intelligent, educated vote. Let the test of intelligence and a certain amount of education and morality be required. And then let every one of 'em vote, male or female, bond or free, black or white.

"I don't spoze you could bring up, if you should hunt for weeks, any good reason aginst this plan. I don't spoze you would find any skairful and dangerous objection to it. I don't spoze, really and honestly, that it *could* be apt to do any harm. And then, on the other hand, you could bring up lots of reasons as to why it might do good; lots of 'em hefty reasons too—and good sound moral ones, every one of 'em.

"The supremacy would for years and years, or as long as safety demanded, remain in the hands of the white race." (I didn't, in my mind, come out aginst Victor's plans, but I knew that this would be a good thing for them that wuz left behind in the exodus and them that went too, a helpful, encouragin' thing.)

"And jest as soon as the negro and the poor whites get fit for it, as soon as they had fitted themselves morally and intellectually for the right of suffrage, why it is only justice that they should have it.

"It would ensure safety to the South to-day, and it would open a bright and fair to-morrow, whether in this land or any other, where the colored men and wimmen can stand free and equal with the white race, where the low, ignorant ones of the white people can come up on another plane and a higher one, where they can read this text a shinin' with the gold letters of Justice and Common Sense, where they glitter now with the sham gildin' of absurdity—

"'All men are free and equal.'

"For a low, vicious, ignorant person, be he black or be he white, is *not* equal to a high-minded, intelligent one. And the law that sets them two up side by side is an unjust and foolish law.

"But the light of the fair to-morrow is a shinin' down; its light beckons, it inspires, it helps forward.

"It is a *sure* thing. Jest as soon as a man or woman is fit to vote they can vote. If they prepare themselves in ten years, there the golden prize is a waitin' for 'em. If they fit themselves in one year to reach it, so much the better.

"It is a premium set upon effort for men and wimmen, black and white, upon noble endeavor, upon all that lifts a man above the animals that perish.

"To make one of the rulers of a great republic, a great country, what can stimulate a young man or a young woman more than this? And every prize that is open to the cultured and educated now will in that time be open to them; they can aspire to the highest place jest as soon as they become worthy of it.

"All the teachers in colored schools testify that the ability of the colored boys and girls is fully equal to the white. In Jonesville," sez I, "my own native place, a little colored boy led the roll of honor, wuz more perfect in school than the children of ministers or judges, and they white as snow, and he as black as a little ace of spades."

Sez I, "The idees I have promulgated to you would be apt to light up one side of the Race Problem."

"You have got to put the niggers down," sez Col. Seybert, as onconvinced as ever, so I see. "That is the only way to get along with them."

Sez I, "That time has gone by, Col. Seybert.

"The time when it wuz possible to do this has passed; if you want to make a man, black or white, stay in a dark dungeon, you mustn't break his chains and show him the stairs that climb up to the sunshine and to liberty.

"If he has dropped his chains onto the damp, mouldy pavement, if he has stood on the very lowest of them steps and seen way up over his head the warm sun a shinin' and heard the song of birds and the distant rushin' of clear waters, you never can put him back down into that dark, damp dungeon agin, and slip his hands into the fetters and keep him there.

"No; he has had a glimpse of the wideness and glory of liberty, and you never can smother it agin.

"If this Nation had wanted to keep on a Nation of slaveholders and slaves, it ortn't to have let the light of Christianity and education shine down onto 'em at all; it ortn't to have broke their chains and called 'em free.

"They will never resign that glorious hope, Col. Seybert; they will press forward.

"They have crouched down and wore their fetters long enough; they are a goin' to stand up and be free men and free wimmen.

"And for you or for me to try to put our puny strengths in the way of God's everlastin' decree and providence would be like puttin' up our hands and tryin' to stop a whirlwind. It would whirl us out of the way, but its path would be onward.

"The negroes will be a free people, a powerful, God-fearin', patient, noble one."

Col. Seybert wuzn't convinced. Fur from it. He made a motion of extreme disgust. But I turned my head a little, and over Col. Seybert's shoulder, back behind him, I see a face.

It wuz a face illumined, riz up, inspired, if ever a face wuz upon earth. A noble purpose shone through it and made it a grand face.

It wuz Victor; he had heard every word I had said and believed every word, only he had fitted the words to suit his own meaning.

I felt this by the rapt expression of his countenance, and also by that free-masonry of the spirit that binds the souls of the true lovers of Humanity, whether they be black or white on the outside.

Col. Seybert turned and follered my look, and he see Victor, and he spoke out angrily:

"Why do you follow me, you dog you, tight to my heels? Can't I ever escape your watchfulness?"

(He had been on one of his sprees, so I hearn, and Victor had kep' watch on him, and his nerves wuz onstrung yet, and he felt hateful.)

"Mrs. Seybert sent me over for you."

"Why don't you say your mistress, you fool?"

Victor wuz perfectly respectful, but he did not change his words.

"General Lord and his son have come, and she wanted you told at once."

"Well, follow me immediately; don't dawdle now."

"Yes, sir," said Victor. And he turned at once to follow his brother (for I would keep on a callin' him so in my mind).

But I glanced down and see Col. Seybert a talkin' with Maggie down on the lawn (she and Thomas J. had been called down-stairs, and had been gone for some time entirely onbeknown to me, I had been so riz up and by the side of myself).

And I sez to Victor :

"You believe what I said?"

"Yes, God knows I do! It is true, and will be fulfilled in His own good time; but not in this land," sez he.

Genieve had come in with Boy, and she and Victor gin each other a silent greetin' of the eyes—a heart greetin', dear and sweet as earthly language cannot be.

And in her big, eloquent eyes I see too her belief in what I had said—I see that and more too. Them sweet eyes looked grand and prophetic. Sez she :

"The time is hastening. I have seen the glow of that to-morrow; its light is waking the sleepers.

"Africa has been asleep for ages. She has crouched down in her pain, her long stupor. But she is waking up. The dead form is beginning to move—to rise up. She will stand upon her feet among the nations of the earth. And when this warm-hearted, musical, beauty-loving people come to their own, who may paint their future?

"They will be leaders among the nations. Poesy, art, song, oratory will find in them their highest exponents. And after bending and cowering beneath its burdens for centuries, Africa will rise and tower up above the other nations of the earth."

Oh, how Genieve's eyes shone and glowed with inner light as she said these words, as if she wuz describin' sunthin' she see fur off.

And I declare it gin me such a feelin', sunthin' like a cold chill, only more riz up like, that I didn't know but she *did* see it.

And I don't know *now* but she did, and then agin I don't know *as* she did. But anon the illumination sort o' faded out of her eyes agin.

The old patient, brave look come over Victor's face, and he followed Col. Seybert home; and lo and behold! by the time Maggie come in to ask about Boy the rapt prophetess Genieve had changed agin into the faithful, quiet, patient nurse Genny.

Wall, Boy grew pretty every day—not a prettiness like Snow's, delicate and spiritual, but a sort of a healthy, happy boy pretty. Bold, bright blue eyes, rosy cheeks, and a mouth that seemed made for smiles and kisses, and cheeks that wuz perfect rose nests for dimples—short brown curls begun to lengthen on his round little head.

And he wuz altogether a very pretty boy, very.

But Snow, the darlin', wuz the very light of our eyes, the joy of our lives.

A sweeter child never lived, and that I know. She twined round our hearts as it seemed as if no other child ever had or ever could.

Her Pa and Ma watched her grow in beauty and goodness with love-glorified eyes; and as for her Grandpa, I should have said he acted fairly foolish if it wuz on any other subject than this that he wuz so carried away on.

But I could see plain that every word he said in

ROSY'S BABY.

commendation and praise of that child wuz Gospel truth.

There never wuz such a beautiful child before,

either in America, or Asia, or Africa, or the Islands of the Sea. And bein' entirely onprejudiced myself, of course I could see that he wuz in the right on't.

That man wuz jest led round by her like a lamb by the shearer, only the lamb might mebby be onwillin' and Josiah Allen went happy and smilin', the shearer wuz so awfully smart and pretty. (That metafor don't quite fit into my meanin', but I guess I will let it go. It is hard work sometimes to find metafors a layin' round handy all rounded off to suit round holes in your conversation, and square ones to fit the square places, etc.)

But as I wuz a sayin', I never see a man take more solid comfort than my pardner did a walkin' round, and a talkin', and a playin' with that beautiful, beautiful child.

And I too the same, and likewise.

And the help all jest about worshipped her, and they couldn't do enough for her, from Genieve down to Rosy and Rosy's baby.

That little ebony image would seem to laugh louder and show his white teeth and the whites of his little eyes like two pearl buttons sot in black beads, and babble his baby talk faster and faster, if she come in his sight.

Mebby it wuz her oncommon beauty and worth, and then, agin, mebby it wuz the little nice bits she always carried him—candy, and nuts, and cakes, and such, and lots of her toys that she had sort o' outgrown.

I want to be exact and truthful as a historian, and so I say, *mebby* it wuz this and *mebby* it wuz that.

URY.

Wall, now that they wuz all well agin and oncommon prosperous, Josiah and me begun to talk about goin' back to Jonesville and our duties there.

But our children wouldn't hear a word to it. They said nuthin' hendered us from stayin' and takin' a good rest, as Ury took good care of everything, and we had worked hard, and ort to rest off for a long time.

So we kep' on a stayin'. There wuzn't no reason why we shouldn't, to tell the truth—Ury wuz a doin' better with the farm than Josiah Allen could, or full as well anyway. And Philury took care of everything inside, and I knew I could trust her with ontold gold, if I had any ontold gold; so we stayed on.

SOME NEIGHBORS.

## CHAPTER XII.

IT wuz a dretful curiosity to me and a never-failin' source of interest to watch the ways and habits of the Southern people about Belle Fanchon, both white and colored.

The neighborhood wuzn't very thickly settled with white people. But still there wuz quite a number of neighbors, and they wuz about all of 'em kind-hearted, generous, hospitable people to their equals.

They seemed to like their own folks the best, the Southern folks; but still they wuz very kind to my son and his wife, and seemed willin' and glad to neighbor with 'em. While there wuz so much sickness in the house, they seemed anxious to help; and I see that they wuz warm-hearted, ready to take trouble for other folks, ready to give all the help they could.

And they wuz very polite to Josiah Allen and me,

and pleasant to talk with. But let the subject of the freedmen come up, or the Freedmen's Bureau, I could see in a minute that they hated that bureau—hated it like a dog.

I hit aginst that bureau quite a number of times in my talk with them neighbors, and I could see that it creaked awfully in their ears; its draws drawed mighty heavy to 'em, and the hull structure wuz hated by 'em worse than any gulontine wuz ever hated by Imperialists.

And colored schools, of course there wuz exceptions to it, but, as a rule, them neighbors despised the idee of schools for the " niggers," despised the teachers and the hull runnin' gear of the institution.

The colored men and wimmen they seemed to look upon about as Josiah and me looked onto our dairy, though mebby not quite so favorably, for there wuz one young yearlin' heifer and one three-year-old Jersey that I always said knew enough to vote.

They had wonderful minds, both on 'em, so I always said, and I petted 'em a sight and thought everything on 'em.

But the " niggers" in their eyes wuz nuthin' and never could be anything but slaves; in that capacity they wuz willin' to do anything for 'em—doctor 'em when they wuz sick, and clothe 'em and take care on 'em.

They wuz willin' to call 'em Uncle and Aunt and Mammy, but to call 'em Mr. or Mrs. wuz a abomination to 'em; and one woman rebuked me hard for callin' a old black preacher Mr. Peters.

Sez she, "I wouldn't think you would call a low-down nigger ' Mr.' "

But I sez, " I heard you call him Uncle, and that is goin' ahead of me; for much as I respect him for his good, Christian qualities, I wouldn't go so fur as to tell a wrong story in order to claim relationship with him. He hain't no kin to me, and so I am more distant to him and call him Mister."

But Mrs. Stanwood (that wuz her name) tosted her head, and I see my deep, powerful argument hadn't convinced her.

And most imegiatly after she begun to run down the white teachers in the colored schools and run the idee of their puttin' themselves down on a equality with niggers and bein' so intimate with 'em.

" But," sez I, " you have told me that your little girl always sleeps with her colored nurse, and you did with yours when you wuz a child. And,' sez I, " that seems to me about as intimate as anybody can get, to sleep in the same bed; and when both are a layin' down, they seem to be pretty much on a equality—that is," sez I, reasonable, " if their pillers are of the same height and bigness."

And I resoomed—" I never hearn of any white teacher bein' in that state of equality with the colored people," sez I; " they are a laborin' for their souls and minds mostly, and you can't seem to get on such intimate terms with them, if you try, as you can with bodies."

Miss Stanwood tosted her head fearful high at this, and didn't seem impressed by the depth and solidity of my argument no more than if it had been a whiff of wind from a alkelie desert. It wuz offensive to her. And she never seemed to care about conversin' with me on them topics agin.

But I wuz dretful polite to her, and shouldn't have said this if she hadn't opened the subject.

But from all my observations, I see the Southerners felt pretty much alike on this subject, they wuz about unanimous on it—though, as there always must be everywhere, there wuz a few that thought different.

There must be a little salt scattered everywhere, else how could the old earth get salted?

But I couldn't bear to hear too much skairful talk from Southerners about the two races bein' intimate with each other. I couldn't bear to hear too many forebodin's on the subject, for I know and everybody knows that ever sence slavery existed the two races had been about as intimate with each other as they could be—in some ways; and the white man to blame for it, in most every case.

And I couldn't seem to think the Bible and the spellin' book wuz a goin' to add any dangerous features to the case; no, indeed. I know it wuz goin' to be exactly the reverse and opposite.

But as interestin' as the white folks wuz to me to behold and observe down in them Southern States, the colored people themselves wuz still more of a curiosity to me.

To me, who had always lived up North and had never neighbored with anybody darker complexioned than myself (my complexion is good, only some tanned)—it wuz a constant source of interest and instruction to me " to look about and find out," as the poet has so well remarked.

And I see, as I took my notes, that Victor and Genieve wuz no more to be compared with the rest of the race about them than a eagle and a white dove wuz to be compared with ground birds.

These two seemed to be the very blossoms of the crushed vine of black humanity, pure high blossoms lifted up above the trompled stalks and tendrils of the bruised and bleeding vine that had so long run along the ground all over the South land, for any foot to stamp on, for every bad influence of earth and sky to centre on and debase.

(That hain't a over and above good metafor; but I'll let it go, bein' I am in some of a hurry.)

I spozed then, and I spoze still, that all over the land, wherever this thick, bleeding, tangled undergrowth lingered and suffered, there wuz, anon and even oftener, pure, fair posys lifted up to the sky.

I spozed there wuz hundreds and thousands of bright, intelligent lives reachin' up out of the darkness into the light, minds jest as bright as the white race could boast, lives jest as pure and consecrated. And I spozed then, and spoze now, that faster and faster as the days go by, and the means of culture and advancement are widening, will these souls be lifted up nigher and nigher to the heavens they aspire to.

A race that has given to the world a Fred Douglass, and that sublime figure of Toussaint L'Ouverture, that form that towers higher than any white saint or hero—and he risin' to that almost divine height by his own unaided powers, without culture or education—what may it not hope to aspire to, helped by these aids?

Truly the future is glorious with hope and promise for the negro.

But to resoom and continue the epistol I commenced.

The most of the colored people about Belle Fanchon wuz fur different from Victor and Genieve. But a close observer could trace back their faults and weaknesses to their source.

Maggie's cook wuz a old black woman who wuzn't over and above neat in her kitchen (it didn't look much like the kitchen of a certain person whose home wuz in Jonesville—no, indeed), but who got up awful good dinners and suppers and brekfusses.

She wuz tall and big-boned, and black as jet. Her hair, which wuz wool and partly white, wuz twisted up on top of her head and surmounted by a wonderful structure which she called a turben.

Sometimes this wuz constructed of a gorgeous red and yeller handkerchief, and sometimes it wuz white as snow; and when she wore this, she always wore a clean white neckerchief crossed on her breast, and a large white apron. She wore glasses too, which gave her a more dignified appearance. Evidently she wore these for effect, as she always looked over them, even when she took up a paper or book and pretended to be readin' it; she could not read or write.

Indeed, when she had heavy work on hand, such as washin', which made the situation of her best glasses perilous, I have seen her wear a heavy pair of bows, with no glasses in them whatever.

She evidently felt that these ornaments to her face added both grace and dignity.

AUNT MELA.

Her figure wuz a little bent with years, but the fire of youth seemed burnin' still in her black eyes.

She boasted of havin' lived in the best families in the South, and took great pride in relatin' instances of the grandeur and wealth of the family she wuz raised in.

The name she went by wuz Aunt Mela.

I spoze her name wuz or should have been Amelia, but there wuzn't no law violated, as I knows on, by her callin' herself " Mela." It wuz some easier to speak anyway.

I used to go down into the kitchen and talk quite a good deal with Aunt Mela.

At first she didn't seem to relish the idee of my meddlin' with her, but as days went on and she see that I wuz inclined to mind my own business, and to help her once in a while when she wuz in a bad place, she seemed to get easier in her mind, and would talk considerable free with me.

But she never thought anything of me compared to what she did of Maggie. She jest worshipped her; and Maggie wuz dretful good to her, gin her a sight besides her wages, and took care on her when she wuz sick, jest as faithful and good as she would of her own Ma or of me.

And Aunt Mela had sick spells often with what she called " misery in her back and misery in her head."

I spoze it wuz backache and headache, that is what I spoze.

Wall, Aunt Mela sot store by Maggie, for the reasons I have stated, and then she *liked* her. And you can't always parse that word and get the real true meanin' of the why and the wherefore, *why* we jest take to some folks and can't help it.

Wall, as I said, Aunt Mela wuz a wonderful good cook, a Baptist by persuasion, and I guess she meant to be as good as she could be, and honest. I believe she tried to be.

She had tried to keep the Commandments, or the biggest heft of 'em, ever sence she had jined the meetin' house; and then she loved Maggie so well that she hated to wrong her in any way. But old influences and habits wuz strong in her, and she had common sense enough and honesty enough to recognize their power.

One day Maggie and I went out into the vegetable garden back of the house, and she had stopped in the kitchen for sunthin', and she left the keys of the store-room in the lock.

And Aunt Mela come a hurryin' after us into the garden with the keys in her hand.

" Miss Maggie, chile, hain't I tole you not to lef' dem keys in de lock, an' now you've dun it agin."

She wuz fairly tremblin' with her earnestness, her white turben a flutterin' in the mornin' breeze and the air of her agitation.

" Why, Aunt Mela, you was there; what hurt would it do for me to leave them? You are honest, you wouldn't take anything."

" Miss Maggie, honey, chile, don' you leave dem keys dah no moah. You say I'm hones', an' so I hopes I am. But den agin I don' know. But when anybody can't do sumpin', den dey *don'* do it, an' don' you leave dem keys dah no moah."

" Why, Aunt Mela, I trust you," sez Maggie in

her sweet voice. " I know you wouldn't do anything to hurt me."

" To hurt you? No, honey. But den how can I tell when ole Mars Saten will jes' rise up an' try to hurt ole Mela? He may jes' make me do sumpin' mean jes' to spite me for turnin' my back on him. He jes' hates Massa Jesus, ole Saten duz, an' he's tried to spite me ebery way sense I jine him.

" So you jes' keep dem keys, Miss Maggie, and if ole Saten tells me to get sumpin' outen dat stow room to teck to my sister down to Eden Centre, I'll say :

" ' You jes' go 'long ! I can't do it nohow, for Miss Maggie done got de keys.' "

Maggie took the keys and tried to keep them after this.

But she told me that many times Aunt Mela had warned her in the same way.

One day she had been tellin' me a good deal about her trials and labors sence the War, and how she and her sister had worked to get them a little home, and how many times they had been cheated and imposed upon, and made to pay over bills time and agin, owin' to their ignorance of business.

And I asked her if she thought she wuz any better off now than when she wuz a slave.

She straightened up her tall figure, put her hands on her hips, and looked at me over the top of her glasses.

" Betteh off, you say ? You go lay down in de dahk, tied to de floah ; if dat floah is cahpeted wid velvet an' sahten, you'd feel betteh to get up an' go way out on de sand, or de ston'—you feel free—

you holt yur haid up—you breeve long brefs—you are free!"

"But," sez I, "the floor of slavery wuzn't covered with velvet, wuz it?"

"It wuz covered wid *blood* an' misery. De dungeon house wuz heavy wid groans, an' teahs, an' agonies.

"My missy wuz good to me, as good as she could be to a slave. But all my chillen, one aftah anoder, wuz stole away from me.

"Aftah havin' fo'teen chillen, lubbin' ebery one ob 'em, like I would die ef dey wuz tuck away from me—aftah holdin' dem fo'teen clost to my heart, so dey couldn't be tuck nohow, I foun' my ole ahms empty."

She stretched out her gaunt old arms with a indescribable gesture of loneliness and woe, and went on in a voice full of the tears and misery of that old time: "I wuz kep' jes' to raise chillen for de mahket, dat wuz my business. An' when I gin dem chillen my heart's lub, dat wuz goin' beyent my business.

"Slaves don' hab no call to be humans nohow; if dey had hearts dey wuz wrung clear outen der bodies; if dey had goodness dey los' it quick nuff.

"To try to be a good woman and true to your ole man wuz goin' beyent yur business.

"Dey sole him too, de fader ob leben ob my chillen. He lubbed dem chillen too, jes' as well Massy Allen lub little Missy Snow.

"He had to leab 'em—toah off, covered wid blood an' gashes, for he fit for us, fit to stay wid me —we had libbed togedder sense I wuz fo'teen.

"I neber see *him* agin. He wuz killed way down in ole Kaintuck. He turned ugly aftah bein' tuck from us, an' den he wuz whipped, an' he grew weak an' homesick for us an' his ole home. An' den dey whip him moah to meck him wuck.

"And he daid off one day right when dey wuz a lashin' him up. Didn't see he wuz daid, kep' on a whippin' his cole daid body."

Here Aunt Mela sunk down in a chair and covered her face in a corner of her apron, and rocked to and fro.

And I hain't ashamed to say that I took out my white linen handkerchief and cried with her.

But pretty soon Aunt Mela wiped her eyes, adjusted her glasses agin, and went about her preparations for dinner.

And I jest hurried out of the kitchen, for my heart wuz full, full and runnin' over.

And I gin her that very afternoon a bran new gingham apron, chocolate and white checks, all made up and trimmed acrost the bottom with as many as seven rows of white braid.

And I didn't give her that apron a thinkin' it would make up for the loss of her companion—no, indeed! What would store clothes be to me to take the place of my Josiah?

But I gin it to her to show my friendliness to her and to show her that I liked her, and to remind her that after she had been tosted and tore by the ragin' billows she had got into a good harbor now, and a well-meanin' one.

So I gin her the apron.

There wuz another family of colored folks who

lived pretty nigh to Belle Fanchon, and I got to know considerable about them because they used to come after so many things to my son's house.

Every day they came after milk or buttermilk—one little black face after another did I see there in the kitchen ; but they all belonged to the same family, so I wuz told, and seemed to be of all ages between six and twenty. I could see they must take after the Bible some, for all of the children had Skripter names—Silus, and Barnibas, and Elikum, and Jedediah, and St. Luke, and more'n a dozen others, so it seemed to me.

Aunt Mela didn't seem to think much on 'em. She said they wuz " lazy, no account, low-down niggers."

But still, when we hearn that the mother wuz sick (the father wuz always sick, or said he wuz), I went to see her, and see she needed a dress bad—why, Aunt Mela took holt and showed quite a interest in our makin' it.

We bought some good calico, chocolate ground with a red sot flower on it, and got her measure, and then we made it up as quick as we could, for she hadn't a dress to her back, only the old ragged one that she had on.

Wall, we made it the easiest way we could ; we started it for a sort of a blouse waist and a skirt, but Aunt Mela told us if we let 'em go that way she never would keep the skirt and waist together— there would always be a strip between 'em, for she wuz too lazy to keep 'em pinned together.

So we thought we would put some buttons on to fasten the skirt to the waist, and then we made a belt to go on over it of the same.

"DESPATCHED TO GET BUTTERMILK."

And as we wuz in a hurry, and knew the buttons wouldn't show under the belt, we used some odd buttons out of Maggie's button-bag, no two of a size or color, most of 'em pantaloons buttons, but some on 'em red ones, and one or two wuz white.

It looked like fury, but we knew the belt would cover it.

Wall, we made it, and I carried it down to her and explained the urgent necessity of the belt to her. And the very next day she wore it up to our house on a errant in the mornin'. I happened to be in the kitchen, and when she come in there I see the full row of pantaloons buttons a shinin' out all round her waist, from the size of a dollar down to a pea.

As I looked on it, I know I looked strange.

And she asked me anxiously "if I wuz sick?"

And sez I, "Yes, sick unto death."

She wuz too lazy and shiftless to put on that belt.

Sez I pretty severe like in axent, "Dinah, why didn't you put on that belt?"

"Foh Gord, Missy, I cleen don fo'get it.

"Wall, what good duz it do for us to work and make you a dress, if you are too shiftless to put it on?"

"Foh Gord, Missy, I dun no; spect nobody duz."

"No," sez I in a despairin' axent, "nobody duz."

The father could earn good wages at his trade, which wuz paintin' and whitewashin', and the mother wuz a good cook and laundress. And the boys wuz strong and healthy. But they would none of them work only jest enough to get a little something to eat and a few articles of clothin', and then they would stop all labor, and none of the family work another day's work till that wuz all used up.

Wall, she told me that day that her husband wuz sick agin, and they hadn't any provisions; so we sent them down a sack of flour and a few pounds of butter.

They wuz sent about the middle of the forenoon and St. Luke wuz imegiatly despatched to get buttermilk—he wanted to get a good deal, he said, for they wanted enough to make a good many messes of biscuit. And Barnabas wuz sent out to borry some soda.

I sez to St. Luke, "Why don't your Ma make riz bread? it would make the flour last as long agin, and then it would be fur more wholesome."

And he told me that they didn't love it so well.

Wall, we sent the buttermilk.

That night Thomas Jefferson wuz kep' out late on business, and he passed their cabin at twelve o'clock at night, and he see the family all up, seated round the table eatin'.

And I asked Barnaby the next day, when he come on his usual errant for milk, if they wuz sick in the night.

And he told me that they wuzn't sick, but his father got hungry in the night, and his mother got up and made some warm biscuit, and called 'em all up, and they had supper in the night—warm biscuit, and butter and preserves.

And I said to Maggie out to one side:

"They couldn't seem to eat up their provisions fast enough in the daytime, so they had to set up nights to do it."

And she said, " So it seemed."

Wall, the man's sickness wuz mostly in his stomach —pain in his stomach, so his wife told me.

And that wuz the reason she told me that she made warm biscuit so much.

And I told her it wuz the worst thing she could cook for him, for his health and his pocket.

But she said he loved 'em so well, and he wuz so kinder sick, she humored him dretfully; she said if anything should happen she shouldn't have reflexions.

She said she always made a five-gallon jar of strawberry preserves; she worked out to get the sugar and she picked the strawberries herself, and she said they wuzn't set on the table hardly any. When he didn't feel well in the night, he would get up and take a spoon and eat out of that jar. And she ended agin by sayin':

" I shouldn't hab no 'flexions to cast onto myself if anyting should happen to my ole man."

" Wall," sez I in deep earnest, " if you keep on in this way you'll find that sunthin' *will* happen, for no livin' stomach can stand such a strain cast onto it, unless it is," sez I reasonably, " a goat or a mule. I have hearn that they can digest stove-pipe and tin cans. But a human stomach must break down under it. And I'd advise you to feed him on good plain bread and toast till he gets well, and keep your preserves for meal-times and company. And I'd advise you to set them great boys of yourn to work stiddy, and not by fits and starts, and you'll have as much agin comfort in your house, and health too "

But, good land! I might jest as well have talked to the wind, or better. For the wind, even if it didn't pay no attention to my remarks—as it probably wouldn't, specially if it wuz blowin' hard—it wouldn't get mad. It would jest blow right on, and blow my remarks right away, and blow jest as friendly as ever.

But she got mad—mad as a hen. And she didn't send after milk for as much as three days. But it didn't hold out; she sent on the fourth day.

But it didn't change their course any. He kep' on a eatin' hot biscuit and butter and preserves, when they had 'em, night and day, and they all would. And when they hadn't anything to eat, and couldn't get anything in any other way, why, they would go without till they wuz most starved, and then they would sally out and work a day or two, and then the same scenes would be enacted right over agin.

Good land! there didn't seem to be no use of talkin', and still I sort o' kep' on.

There wuz one boy amongst 'em, and that wuz St. Luke, and mebby it wuz because he wuz named after that likely old apostel, and then, agin, mebby it wuzn't; but anyway, he did seem to have a little more pride and a little more sense and gumption than the rest.

And I kep' a naggin' at him, and his Pa and Ma, and Thomas J. and Maggie, and Josiah, till with a tremendus effort I did get that boy into a new suit of clothes and started him off to work for his board and go to school at a place about three miles off. And though he run away five times in as many weeks—twice to come home and three times to go a fishin'—I kep' on, and by argument, and persuasion, and a new jack-knife, and a coaxin' him up, and persuadin' the folks to try him a little longer, I got him quelled down, and he begun to go easier in the harness, and stiddier. And his teacher sez " he will make a smart boy yet."

So I see jest what I always knew wuz a fact, " that while the lamp holds out to burn the vilest sinner may return."

And if I wuz a goin' to sing that him, I would omit two words in the last stanza, and for the words " vilest sinner" I would sing " shiftless creeter."

For these two words are what will apply to his hull family, root and branch, specially the roots. Shiftless, ornary, no account, father and mother both ; and bein' full of shiftless, no account qualities, and bein' married, what could they do, or be expected to do, but bring into the world a lot of still shiftlesser, no accounter creeters?

Inheritin' shiftlessness, and lazyness, and improvidence on both sides, with their own individual lazyness and no accountness added, what can we expect of these offsprings?

But still I see in the case of St. Luke, as in the words of the him I quoted, that there is in education and the wholesome restraints of proper livin' and trainin' a hope for them—for the poor blacks and the poor whites, for the poor whites are jest as shiftless, jest as ignorant, and jest as no account.

"THE BIG PIAZZA."

## CHAPTER XIII.

ONE mornin' we wuz all a settin' out on the big piazza, for it wuz a cloudless day, and it wuz exceedingly pleasant out there.

Snow wuz a settin' to one side a playin' with her little dolly that I had carried down to her—a nice one, with real hair, and very round blue eyes and red cheeks.

I bought it at Loontown, at a expense of over seventy-five cents, and dressed it myself, with a little of Philury's help about the boddist waist.

Its dress wuz pink cambrick trimmed heavy with white linen lace—it wuz some I had on a nightcap, but it wuz so firm it had wore the nightcap out. It wuz a very good and amiable-lookin' doll when we had got it all trimmed off, and Snow thought her eyes on it.

She had named it to once Samantha Maggie Tirzah Ann.

"After the hull caboodle on us," as Josiah said; but at my request she called it Dolly.

Good land! I thought I never could hear her a goin' round a talkin' about Samantha Maggie Tirzah Ann. The idee! It would have been too much for her.

Wall, she wuz a settin' a playin' with Dolly, and anon sort o' lookin' up and talkin' to somebody she didn't see. Wuzn't it queer how she would always do this, and smile confidential at 'em, and wave her little white hand to 'em sometimes, as if in greetin' or good-bye?

Queer, but pretty in her, so I always thought.

I wish I knew who she had in her mind when she done it, or if she see anybody or hearn anybody. For once in a while she would sort o' lift up her little smilin' face and seem to listen—listen.

Wall, she wuz a beautiful child—and every child has its pretty ways and its dretful curius ones, its angel traits and its tuther ones. Bless their sweet hearts, wherever they be! I love the hull on 'em, and can't help it.

Boy wuz a layin' in his little crib, and Genieve wuz a settin' by it a mindin' the child. And my son and daughter, Thomas Jefferson and Maggie, wuz a settin' near each other (that is where they would always be if they had their own way).

Thomas J. was readin' a little to her out of a new book that come in a box of books the night before, and Maggie wuz a sewin' on a little white dress for Boy.

Cousin John Richard wuz partly a layin' down on a bamboo couch with a lot of pillows to his back—he

"A PERFECT DAGON."

had had a dretful backache for a day or two. But he wuz a lookin' some more comfortable than he had, and not quite so wan, but he wuz still fur wanner than I loved to see him. I myself wuz a knittin' and occasionally a liftin' my eyes to look over the path that led to the village, for my companion had walked down there to get a pair of new suspenders.

I knew it wuzn't time for him to get back yet; but such is woman's love, I kep' watch of the track on which I expected to see the beloved form approachin' bimeby.

That man is almost my idol.

It hain't right to worship a human creeter I know; and then agin, sometimes, when I would meditate on the wickedness of my bein' so completely wrapped up in him, I have tried to exonerate myself by this thought:

The children of Israel wuz commanded not to worship anything that wuz like anything else in heaven or on earth. And I have sometimes felt that I would get clear on that head if I knelt to him every day and burned incense under him, and made a perfect Dagon of him.

For my dear companion is truly onlike anything I ever see or hearn on; his demeaners is different, and his acts and his talk under excitement. And his linement looks fur different from any other folks'es linements.

But I am a digressin', and to resoom.

We sot there as happy as a nest full of turkle doves, when all of a sudden the girl come up with a card on a little silver server, and handed it to Maggie as if it wuz a cracker or a cup of tea, and Maggie took it and read out:

"Colonel Seybert."

And Thomas J. spoke up and told the girl to ask the Colonel out there where we wuz; and so she did, and sot him a chair by Thomas J., out amongst the rose-vines.

He come in as polite as ever, and accosted us all in a very genteel way. He had brought Maggie a great bunch of orchids, and said "the Madam had sent them to her with her compliments."

He meant his wife—he most always called her so.

The posys he brought wuz very rare. They grow on air mostly, and only have the very slightest soil to connect 'em with the earth.

And from all accounts (I thought to myself) that wuz the way that his angel of a wife lived herself. Almost all of the roots of her sweet nater wuz in heaven. Jest enough connection with this world so all could see the brightness and bloom and size of the divine flower of holiness that sprung up out of her lone, unhappy life.

Maggie took the flowers and thanked him, and told him to tell Mrs. Seybert how much she prized her kind thoughtfulness, and how sorry she wuz to hear of her continued ill health.

That woman, from all I hear, hain't long for this world.

Wall, they all passed the time of day in politeness and general conversation, till—for my life I can't hardly tell how it begun—but I believe Col. Seybert had had some trouble with his colored help —but anyway and tenny rate, Col. Seybert launched out into a perfect tirade of abuse of the black race.

He didn't notice Genieve a settin' there no more'n a ice-cold avalanche would stay its course for a idlewiss blossom—no; it would crunch right along down and crush the blossom without any pity or compunction.

Good land! you don't look for pity, or consideration, or any other of the soft, warm-souled graces in a avalanche of snow and ice, or the nater of a bad man.

But I jest think my eyes of Genieve, and so duz Maggie and all on us, and we every one on us tried to turn the conversation into more peaceful channels.

Why, I myself brung up religion, turnips, catnip, the tariff, the Dismal Swamp, and oranges, a tryin' to get his mind off.

And Maggie brung up as many, if not more'n I did, and Thomas J. the same, and etcetery.

And even little Snow, seemin' to understand what wuz incumbent on her to do as a little lady, brung up the doll and showed her to the Colonel, and called her by her hull name, Samantha Maggie Tirzah Ann.

As for Cousin John Richard, we didn't expect no outlay of strength from him, feelin', as he did, in pain all the time.

But Maggie, seein', I spoze, our efforts wuz futiler than we could hope, tried to make another diversion by orderin' in a pitcher of drink made from the juice of oranges and pineapples, very sweet and delicious. But he drinked it right off and went on; it seemed to jest refresh him and renew his strength to talk—we see he couldn't be stopped nohow.

And seein' he wuz a neighbor, and seein' that Genieve sot there jest as calm as a mornin' in June, and didn't seem to care a mite about his talk, why, we had to let him take his swing and talk his talk out.

But before several minutes had passed I jest found myself a soarin' up onbeknown to myself, and I felt that I must, if he went on much longer, jest wade in and give him a piece of my mind, and I felt that I shouldn't scrimp him in the piece nuther.

Why, his talk wuz scandalous.

He talked as if the blacks wuz of no more consequence than so many black ants on a ant-hill, and it seemed as if he would love to jest walk right over 'em and crush 'em all down under his heel.

Why, he showed such a deadly horstility, and contempt, and scorn to 'em and to everything connected with 'em, that at last I had to speak out.

And sez I, " If you feel like that, I shouldn't think you would oppose 'em in their skeme of colonization." (I knew jest how bitter he had been about his brother Victor goin', and the rest of his laborers.)

Sez I, " I should think, if you had such a opinion of 'em, the sooner you could get rid of the hull caboodle of 'em the better you would like it."

He fairly scowled, he looked so mad.

But the thought of Genieve sort o' boyed me up, and duty, and I didn't care for his black looks, not a mite.

And I felt that bein' a visitor myself, I could branch out and argue with him to a better advantage to the laws of horspitality than if I wuz master or mistress of the house. So, as I sez, seein' him determined to cut and slash, I jest boldly waded in.

But, good land! of all the talk, he did go on and talk about the deep and stupendous folly of colonization.

Why, he brung up every argument he could think on aginst the idee, and piled 'em up in front of me. But I jest sot there calmly a knittin', a seamin' two and one, and a not bein' skairt by any of 'em.

And pretty soon—I spoze it wuz seein' that I looked as calm as a summer day—he sort o' curbed himself in, as it were, and begun to talk some calmer and composeder.

And sez he, " If there wuz no other insurmountable objection, look at the expense, the enormous cost of taking the blacks to Africa and supporting 'em there till they could become self-supporting."

And I sez, " Will it make the conundrum any easier to get the answer to, to wait till the black people are twice as numerous? They obey the Bible strictly when it tells 'em to multiply and replenish the earth. In less than twenty years they will outnumber the white race here by a million or more. What will be done then?"

" Keep them under," sez he. " Let them keep their place, the place the Lord designed them for, as servants to the white man. And then," sez he, " one white man could control a hundred of the beasts."

But I sez, " To say nuthin' of the right or wrong of that matter, that day has gone by. They have tasted the air of freedom, and that sweet air always blows out the flower of liberty, not slavery. You can't put 'em back in their chains agin. Education and culture and the Emancipation Proclamation has forever done away with that.

"You can never make 'em slaves agin, but you can be their slaves. The white race, so long dominant, if it still cultivates the habits of tyranny, and cruelty, and injustice, it can be made slaves to the dominant black race; for it is, as you well know, only a question of a few years when they will outnumber the white people here.

"And which would you ruther have, the black shadow growin' deeper and deeper every year on this continent, and sectional hatred and race prejudice, and fear, and distrust, and jealousy, and alarm, and a constant variance all the time, onrest, and despair, and helplessness—which would you ruther have, them cruel spirits to camp down by you for good, and a growin' worse all the time, or to make a big effort and heave the load off for good, and clear the air of all the bad atmosphere of internal and inevitable war, and let Peace settle down on this onhappy land agin? For it would be jest as great a relief to the oppressor as to the oppressed. Lots of good folks South have all their life groaned under this problem of what to do with this burden laid upon their backs by their ancestors.

"They wanted to do right, but didn't see their way clear. They wanted to solve this problem, but it wuz too big for 'em."

Then Maggie, bless her sweet soul, spoke up, and sez she, "*I* believe in the great power of Christianity and education."

And Col. Seybert sez, "They have got too much

education now; that is what ails the brutish upstarts. In the old times, when they couldn't read nor write nor put on any of their cursed airs, you could get along as well again with them."

Cousin John Richard bent on him a look that held in each eye a hull Sermon on the Mount and the Ten Commandments, besides lots of Gospel, and pity, and a sort of contempt too.

It wuz a strange look.

But I wouldn't demean myself by even answerin' him, but replied to my daughter, and sez:

"I don't see how any one can help thinkin' that Christianity and education are the best solutions of this problem that can possibly be found if the black man remains here," or wherever he is, I added reasonably, in my own mind.

"These, with an educated sufferage, that includes the best of black and white, male and female, bond and free, is, in my opinion, the only hope of this Nation under these circumstances.

"But," sez I, "religion, though it can do almost anything, yet there are some things it hain't never done, and I don't spoze ever will do: it hain't never took the spots offen a leopard's back or made a jackal coo like a dove or a serpent walk upright, or a turkle dove mate with a tiger.

"The One who made all nater and true religion, who holds the heavens and earth and seas in His hands, has laid down certain laws ever sence the creation of the world. And it is perfectly impossible for us to break down them laws, or climb over 'em, or creep under 'em.

"There they are, firm, immutible, not to be stirred

one jot or tittle by all the strength that can be brought to bear aginst 'em. And Hypocrisy and Cant hain't a goin' to help any by sayin' that Religion is a doin' sunthin' that it can't do.

" So, what can we do? All we have got to do in this matter is to acknowledge them laws and submit to 'em; ignorin' 'em or walkin' by 'em with our heads up in the air a pretendin' we don't see 'em don't amount to anything at all, only we are liable to stumble and fall down ourselves.

"And one of these laws is the inherient difference between the black and the white races.

" There is no use a arguin' on it and a sayin' that it is onreasonable, and it ort to be overcome, etc.

" Who sez it is reasonable? I don't. It would be awful convenient sometimes if water would run up hill; but it won't. And I have to accept the plain fact and lug the water up hill in a pail. For me to stand on top of the hill and holler for it to come up would be foolish. I might yell all my life, and couldn't start a drop up hill, and my lungs would be tired out for nuthin'. And you might think sometimes that a good old childless cat might adopt a mouse; but she won't, only in one way. Mebby it hain't Christian in her, but she wuz made that way. If she accepts it at all, it will be inside of her. I can't help it, and she can't. She wuz made that way before the mountains wuz formed, like as not.

" Religion can do much, but it never has made black white or put the nater of a eagle into a snail, or the virtues of a angel under the hide of a bear.

"And the spellin' book is extremely desirable and good, and highly worthy, and to be praised. But then there are things too strong for education to overcome. For instance, to draw up the simely that I have drawed before—it hain't poetick, but one which is familiar to men or wimmen: Education can't put a number seven foot into a number three shoe.

" No, it can't be did, and education may orate to them big toes in Greek or Latin, and it may read essays to 'em in words of seven or eight syllables, and quote all the poets to 'em, livin' or dead, but it hain't a goin' to quell 'em down, and make 'em any smaller. It hain't a goin' to get 'em into that shoe.

"And when folks talk too much about the sudden miracles that education and Christian teachin' is going to do to the black race, and seem to expect 'em to become perfect all to once, I want to ask 'em why it hain't made our own race perfect?

" The white race has had the benefit of Christianity and Education for hundreds of years, and all the means of culture, and it hain't hendered 'em from bein' as mean as the Old Harry to the black man, and they despise and wrong the negro jest as much to-day as if St. Paul had never preached or Jesus had not died for the world."

(I meant some on 'em—I didn't mean all; but I wuz kinder carried away by my own eloquence.)

" Now," sez I, " it is a settled thing, and can't be got round, this inherient, instinctive difference between the black and white races—if they would, they never *can* amalgamate and be a united people.

" I have said it and repeated it time and agin, and it is true every time, and will keep on bein' true 'after my poor, feeble, falterin' tongue lies silent in the grave.' "

I sez this in a kinder him axent, very strikin' and touchin', but Col. Seybert wuzn't touched nor struck by it, as I could see ; but I kep' on all the same.

"As I have said, time and agin, this law has stood ever sence creation ; and so what is the use of thinkin' it can be broke up by writin' on a little slip of paper at Washington, D. C. ?

"Good land! angels and principalities, and powers, and things present and things to come, nor height, nor depth, nor any other creeter has never made any difference in that law, nor never will.

"And then how silly to think a little mite of paper, made out of old rags and straw, mebby, and wrote over with a few man-made words by a steel pen, is a goin' to overcome this law and vanquish it! Why, it can't be done. And your talk, and my talk, and talk from all the pulpits and legislators in the world is only a few whiffs of air a blowin' over this law—a refreshin' of it, so to speak.

"Now, this is a settled thing, and it only remains for us to deal with it the best way we can."

Col. Seybert, I believe, wuz fairly browbeat and stunted to hear such remarkable eloquence from a female ; but he wouldn't demean himself by ownin' it—in fact, he wanted to give me a rebuke for venturin' out of what he considered a woman's spear.

He did not dain a reply to me, but he kinder wheeled round in his chair and accosted Cousin John Richard. He hadn't said a word to him—only when he wuz introduced to him he passed the usual compliments. But he had hearn about him a sight, I know, and his labors amongst the freedmen, and I spoze mebby half of his mean talk had been aimed at that good creeter a layin' there on the lounge with a rug over his feet and three plasters onto his dear achin' back.

And then he didn't want to hear me talk any more—I could see that, and he branched right off onto another branch of the subject, and sez he to John Richard:

"I should think your preaching would have some effect if you are a preacher of Christ. You ought to teach the niggers to depend on the consolation of the Gospel, and you ought to preach the Gospel of Peace; and that means, I should think, to have the niggers obey their masters, and so save war and bloodshed, instead of inciting them to rebellion and putting absurd ideas into their heads about colonization and a country of their own." He spoke in a dretful sneerin', disagreeable tone, that madded me more'n considerable; but John Richard's face wuz as serene as new milk, and he answered calmly, in a voice kinder low from sickness, but clear as a silver bell:

"The Book says, 'There is a time for peace and a time to resist oppression.'"

And I spoke up agin, bein' bound to take John Richard's part, and keep him from talkin' all I could, sick as he wuz, and them plasters all a drawin'.

I sez, "No doubt the colonies wuz preached to to set down in chains and enjoy religion, and give up all idees of independence; but our old 4 fathers couldn't be made to feel so. They seemed to feel that the time had come when the Lord wuz a goin' to lead 'em out into freedom. And they felt they wuz a preachin' the Gospel of Liberty and Freedom, the backbones of Christianity, when they struck out for Independence."

A KU-KLUXER.

Cousin John Richard looked real satisfied to me, though wan, as I went on, and sez he:

"Yes, to resist intolerable and unjust laws has always been considered lawful and right."

"But," sez Col. Seybert, "the Bible commands you, if you are smitten on one cheek to turn the other also."

"Then why don't you do it?" sez I, all wrought up. "Your race has had centuries of Christianity to civilize and Christianize it, and why don't you set a example to the ignorant ones? Mark out a sampler that they can foller on and copy. Why don't your Regulators and your Ku-Kluxers turn their right cheeks? I'd love to have 'em turn 'em to me a spell," sez I darkly.

Col. Seybert kinder snorted out sunthin' that I didn't quite hear. I believe, and always shall, that there wuz a cuss word in it; but I didn't care, and before I could speak agin, Cousin John Richard's calm voice riz up a sayin':

"You say this race is totally ignorant and brutish, and yet you expect high qualities from them—extraordinary virtues. You expect patience more perfect than long years of training has given the white race. You expect endurance, nobility, forbearance, forgiveness of injuries and wrongs—in fact, you expect the goodness of angels and the wisdom of Solomon, and expect an insolvable problem to be solved by those you rank with your cattle.

"It is a strange thing," sez Cousin John Richard, as he lay back agin on his cushions. But I went up and gin him a spoonful of spignut before I let him speak agin.

Col. Seybert waved off John Richard's noble rebuke, and went on on his old ground:

"Your teachers and preachers have overrun the South ever since the War, with your carpet-bags full of Bibles and hymn-books, and tracts, and spelling-books. Why don't you sit down now and wait and see the fruit of your labors ripen about you instead of encouraging them in this preposterous idea of colonization?"

But Cousin John Richard sez gently but strongly :

"Perhaps this is the fruit that the Lord of the harvest is causing to spring up from the seeds planted in the hearts of this people. Perhaps the full ripening of this fruit depends upon the sunshine of another and a calmer sky."

"Yes," sez I, " who knows but this race, who stood harmless and patient durin' the War, while the first half of their chains wuz bein' struck offen 'em, who showed such a spectacle of remarkable magnanimity and wisdom that the hull world admired and wondered, and who used their first weak strength to fight for the safety of the race that had held them in bondage—the race that could do this," sez I, " has got the strength and the divine nobility and wisdom to get their full liberty in a nation of their own without the sound of a gun or the liftin' of an arm in warfare.

"They will do it, too," sez I, carried away and enthused by the thought of how this people had stood still and see the salvation of the Lord.

Sez I, " They will not turn into a brutal, bloodthirsty mob now, after ' Thus far the Lord hath led them on.' "

I repeated these last words in my melodius him axents ; but Col. Seybert wuzn't melted by it—no, indeed.

He went on in witherin' axents aginst the idee of colonization ; sez he in conclusion :

"If there was not any other insurmountable objection to the project, the expense would be so enormous that the Government never would nor never could undertake it."

"As to the never could, we might leave that out," sez I, "and deal with the never would. For the never could hain't true. If a war should break out to-morrow between this country and England, do you believe that this country never could furnish the means to carry it on? Why, it would seem the easiest thing in the world to raise millions on millions of dollars.

"It would seem the only thing and the right thing to do to imegiatly and to once raise ten times the amount that would be necessary to take the hull black race to the Congo Valley and support 'em there for a year.

"They would do this because public safety demanded it; and I can tell 'em plain that they will most probable see the day, and pretty soon too, that the public safety demands 'em to do as they'd ort to in this case.

"Who got the black race here? They didn't want to come—no, fur from it. This nation got 'em here; and now, as the two races can't live together in peace, and the land is gettin' too small for both of 'em, if the white race don't want to leave the country themselves, let 'em carry this people back to the land they stole 'em from.

"They wouldn't all go; it hain't probable nor possible to suppose such a thing.

"There are many who would be perfectly willin' to remain here, and who would perhaps be better off by doin' so—many aged ones who would choose to stay here and go to heaven from the land of their adoption, many who have a flourishin' business, and are doin' well here, and who do not wish an immediate change.

"But the Race Problem would be solved if the main body of the host passed over into the New Republic. The few that remained would not endanger the commonwealth, and would most likely, in the fulness of time, and as the glowin' story of the New Republic reached their ears, be gathered into the Land of Promise, to become leaders there, and helpers of the weak."

Sez Col. Seybert, "They would starve there. They are a low, degraded, helpless, lazy set. They had rather lay in the sun and do nothing than to work."

As Col. Seybert said this he lay back in his chair in a still more lazy and luxurious manner, and stretched out his long legs in the sun.

(What wuz he doin' himself, I'd like to know? Talk about laziness! the idee!)

And I sez, "Wall, it's easier for most folks to rest than it is for 'em to work. As to their entire helplessness and ignorance, twenty-five years ago there wuz never an escapin' Union prisoner who found a negro so low and ignorant that he could not help him to escape; or so destitute of resources and influence that he could not command the help of other black men.

"In fact, there wuz a great silent army kep' up under the surface, a systematic underground railroad, maintained and controlled in the most efficient and prudent manner by this despised people all through the War. Twenty-five years of partial

"PILOT A HELPLESS UNIONIST."

education and partial freedom has not weakened this foresight and caution.

"If they could carry on this secret and most dangerous enterprise right under the eyes of their enemies without violence or bloodshed, if they could, under peril of detection and death, pilot a helpless Unionist through a network of dangers—Confederate soldiers, spies, pickets, false friends, and foes—out into safety, it seems as if they might conduct their own selves through the environing camps of ignorance and need, out into safety and prosperity.

"Specially, as they would be out from under the paralyzin' gaze of enemies, out where they wuz breathin' free air, and amongst friends.

"I have been spozin'," sez I, "that the Nation should do as it ort to, and when it borrys a thing take it back home agin, jest as I would do if I borryed a cat of Miss Gowdey, or Josiah would do if he borryed a horse.

"We should carry 'em back when we got through with 'em, specially if we stole 'em (though you wouldn't ketch us at it).

"I have been spozin' that Uncle Sam should rig out a few ships and put some money in his pockets, and take back a few shiploads of this people, and start 'em to livin' in the beautiful Congo Valley.

"I should think as much agin of him if he would. And he would think more of himself, I would bet.

"He would stand riz up in the eyes of the other admirin' nations of the world as a man that wuz honest and laid out to do as he had ort to do, and as he would be done by.

"Why, if Uncle Sam had been stole away from

his home and his faithful Columbia, and had been worked to death, and whipped, and abused every way, wouldn't he be glad to be took back to his own home agin, and wouldn't he expect the ones that stole him to do it?

" Yes, indeed.

" Then why hain't he willin' to do as he would be done by?

" But as I say, I have been spozin' this, that Uncle Sam should turn honest and do this; but some think the colored people would do it themselves.

" They have amassed millions of dollars sence the War, in the face of the almost intolerable drawbacks put upon 'em. You will find thousands of 'em ownin' their houses and lands; you will find thousands and thousands of wealthy ones; you will find a hundred thousand graduates of schools and colleges, and fillin' every station—lawyers, clergymen, senators, and every place where merit can win, and the law couldn't keep them down—they have found their way. That don't look like entire helplessness and ignorance, duz it? for they have done all this with the tide settin' full aginst 'em, right in the face of class prejudice, and unjust laws, and customs, and rivalry, and hatred."

" Well, of course," sez Col. Seybert, " there are some intelligent niggers, and industrious ones; but look at the mass, the ignorant, depraved, totally incompetent ones."

And I sez, " There has been a few in our own race, ignorant, shiftless, lazy, and depraved, who has learnt the colored men to be vicious for 200 years.

And as for laziness, it seems as if there *had* to be some drones amongst the hive of busy workers. Nater has seemed to plan it so for some reason, I can't tell why, nor Josiah can't.

"Now, with our bees, there are sights of drones that don't do nuthin'—only steal and eat up what the workers work so hard for.

"I don't see why it is so; it is one of Nater's mysterys.

"And in all communities there has got to be some lazy, shiftless hangers-on. And the strong will have to do till the end of time, so far as I can see, what the Bible tells 'em to: 'Bear the burdens of the weak.'

"I don't know as there will ever be any change," sez I, lookin' dreamily off beyend Col. Seybert into the everlastin' strangeness of things present and things to come—"I don't know as there will ever be any change in that particiler, for the Bible sez expressly:

"'The poor you always have with you.'

"And always means always, I spoze; and poor means poor in every sense of the word, I have calculated.

"And that text applies to black and white folks alike.

"But as I have said prior and heretofore, if the colored people have done so well in the last twenty-five years, in spite of all the burdens and hindrances of race prejudice and the weights that unjust laws impose on 'em, by the hatred and envy of them that can't bear to see their prosperity—if they have done so well in the chill and the dark, as you may say, what can't they do when they come out in the light and the warmth of a place where sure rewards wait upon honest labor—where the atmosphere is helpful, and inspirin', and hopeful, instead of icy, and draggin' down, and chokin', and stiflin'.

"Where their color is fashionable, and not a badge of disgrace.

"Where their rulers will be them that love 'em and seek their best good, their own people, their peers, only wiser and more helpful than they be—as the Declaration of Independence sez free men must be, in a free land, judged by their peers, their equals.

"Where there will not be dishonest members of an alien and dominant race to step in and steal their first poor earnings in the name of law or might, or both.

"Where their daughters, if beautiful, will be free from their ruler's lust, and their small possessions safe from his avarice.

"If in the last quarter of a century in this persecuted, hampered state they have been able to accumulate, in one of the worst States of the Union for them, six million dollars' worth of property, what can they do in the next twenty years, when their labor and their persons will be protected by the law, and they will be encouraged by wise advice, and their intellects and reason enriched and broadened by education and means of culture?"

Genieve's dark, beautiful eyes jest brightened and glowed as I talked; she fairly hung onto my words, as I could see.

"But," sez Col. Seybert, "they don't want to go."

Thomas J. leaned back in his chair in deep enjoyment of his Ma's talk, as I could see plain; and he says to Col. Seybert:

"How do you know they don't want to go?"

"SET DOWN IN OUR SWAMP."

"Because I do know it," sez he. "They say they are not Africans now, but Americans; they have a right here; they have just as good right here now as we have."

"Wall, I don't dispute that idee," sez I.

"I have got a right to go and set down in our

swamp and set there ; but I should be dretful apt to get all covered with mud and mire, I couldn't see nuthin' but dirt and slosh ; the bad, nasty air would make me deathly sick, to say nuthin' of my bein' bit to death by muskeeters and run over by snakes and toads, etc.

"It hain't a question of right—nobody could dispute that I would have a right to stay there if I wuz a minter ; but the question is, would it be as well for me as it would to move up on the higher ground out of the filth, and darkness, and sickly, deathly air and influences, etc., etc., etc. ?"

Col. Seybert waved off these noble and convincin' remarks of mine, and kep' on a sayin' his former say. And he spoke the words in the axent of one who has settled the matter and put on the final argument.

"They don't *want* to go, that is a reason nobody can get round."

He looked triumphant, as if he had settled the hull matter ; but he hadn't.

I sez, "I d'no whether they do or not ; you say they don't, somebody else may say they do. But anyway, I don't know as that is much of a reason," sez I ; for my mind is such that as I hearn Col. Seybert's big, swellin' talk, my mind seemed to look at the matter from Genieve's and Victor's eyes more and more—I am made so, jest so sort o' curius.

But I am all made now, and can't help it ; I have got to take myself as I am.

And I sez, "I don't know as that is very much of a reason about their not wantin' to go. I don't believe there has ever been any blows struck for freedom and liberty sence the world begun but what there has been some that the blows wuz a bein' dealt for, to hang onto the axe-helve and beg the choppers to stop.

"There has always been them who had, as Mr. Shakespeare sez, 'Ruther endure the ills they have than fly round to others that they don't know so much about,' sort o' oncertain.

"Strikin' blows for freedom hain't like cuttin' down a tree. You know what you are a strikin' when you hit into a maple or a ellum. The axe hits aginst sunthin' solid, and the chips fly.

"But strikin' out for freedom is sometimes a hittin' out aginst emptiness in the dark. You know your cause is good, you know you are a fightin' for the most precious thing in the world, but you can't exactly see before you, and you don't feel anything solid, and you don't see the chips fly—it is sort o' oncertain and resky.

"You can't seem to see the immediate result of your blows. And so it hain't no wonder to me that lots of weak ones, and skairt ones, and so-called prudent ones, cry out and hang onto the axe and try to stop the noble chopper's hands. They don't want a change. The old Torys in the Revolution didn't want a change. It wuz strikin' out in the darkness and bringin' dangers and war onto their heads. They didn't want to go away from English rule.

"But the noble band of choppers kep' on a hackin' the tree of tyranny till it crashed down and they walked over its prostrate trunk into freedom; and the weak ones wuz glad enough when the dangers wuz all past, and they sot down under the joy bells of 1776 and leaned their backs up aginst Bunker Hill, and enjoyed themselves first rate.

"The Israelites didn't want a change. They didn't want to go out of the land of bondage. Lots of livin' ties united 'em to the land of their birth, and lots of onseen ones too. The graves of their ancestors, and memories, and loves, and joys, and sorrows all hung onto their heart-strings, and they didn't want to go.

"But Moses wuz in the right on't. And they come out at last into a land flowin' with milk and honey.

"And they wuz glad they went.

"The Unbelievers didn't want Jesus for a King and a Ruler—they didn't want a change. They fit aginst God's plan for 'em, and conquered, so they thought. But they didn't, and now the world is glad on't, as it stands under the glow a fallin' from the glorious twentieth century.

"Ask the United Christian Nations of the World if it hain't a blessed change. Ask 'em if they hain't glad they went out of the superstitions and bondage of the old dispensation, out into the glorious liberty of the Gospel, out under the blessed rule of the Prince of Peace.

"No, Col. Seybert, I don't think it is much of a reason, even if it is true, to say that the negroes don't want to go. In all these cases I have brung up—and I might go on a bringin' 'em up and a layin' 'em down in front of you for hours and hours if it would do any good—but in all on 'em, as in these supreme cases I have mentioned, what difference did it make in the end whether the majority wuz willin' or not to be saved, only in the discouragement and trouble it made the noble few who see clear from the beginnin' to the end?

"What difference did their onwillingness make? The best, the right wuz done. The minority wuz

"HE HASTENED OFF."

wise and the majority wrong, as is dretful apt to be the case in this world. And the people wuz led through darkness, and sorrow, and onwillingness out into the broad sunshine. Led through Jordan's stormy waves, out into 'Canaan's fair and happy land, where their possessions lay.'"

I had fell into that kinder melodius axent of mine almost entirely onbeknown to me, for it wuz from a him that I wuz quotin'. But it didn't seem to impress Col. Seybert as I wanted it to.

He looked at his watch, and sez he:

"I have got a pressing engagement in just five minutes by my watch; I will bid you good-day."

And he hastened off, and Thomas Jefferson laughed, and sez he:

"You talked him out, mother; but," sez he, "I didn't know as you believed so strongly in colonization; I never heard you talk just in this way before."

"Wall," sez I, "the Race Problem is such a enormous conundrum that it is hard to know jest how to get the right answer to it. But," sez I, "I wuz a talkin' jest now from Genieve's platform, I wuz a viewin' the subject from her standpoint, and from Victor's, and also," sez I, glancin' to where that dear man lay, lookin' pleasant as ever, "from Cousin John Richard'ses;" and I added, "considerable from my own." And sez I, a turnin' to Genieve where she sot quietly with Boy in her arms, "You don't feel any oncertainty as to this conundrum, do you? You see your way clear to a right answer?"

"Yes," sez she. And her eyes wuz as clear as two wells of pure water on which the stars wuz a shinin'.

"Yes, I *know* what is best and what *will* take place in God's own time."

There it wuz, no more doubt in her mind about the negroes havin' a country and a nation of their own some time than there wuz to Moses as he stood on the mountain-top and looked over Jordan's stormy banks into the land that should be the home of his weary and sorrowful people.

Genieve stood upon some invisible mountain-top; we couldn't see this rise of ground, our eyes wuz too weak, but her feet wuz placed there. And she see over the rollin' billows of turbulent factions, and swellin' hatred, and mistaken zeal, and perils from friends, and perils from foes, and perils from high places, and perils from low ones, and the black waters of ignorance, and laziness, and discontent, and old habits and customs a breakin' up and a dashin' their spray here and there, and all the horror and woe and danger of an uprisin' and a exodus —she see over all these swellin' waves into the fair country that lay beyond.

We couldn't see the calm sunshine that lit the Promised Land, but we could see a faint glow from its radiance in Genieve's inspired eyes.

She didn't say much, but her look spoke volumes and volumes.

"TO KISS SNOW AND BOY GOOD NIGHT."

## CHAPTER XIV.

THAT very night I went into Genieve's room to kiss Snow and Boy goodnight.

But both the darlin's wuz fast asleep, Snow in her little white bed and Boy in his crib. Their faces looked like fresh roses aginst their white pillers, and I did kiss 'em both, but light, so as not to wake 'em up.

Sweet little creeters, I think my eyes on 'em.

Genieve, I see, when I went in wuz a readin' some book, and as I looked closter at it I see it wuz the Bible. I see she wuz a readin' about her favorite topick, the old prophets and their doin's and their sayin's.

And as I sot down a few minutes by the side of my sweet darlin's she begun to talk to me about Daniel, and St. John, and some of the rest of them good, faithful old prophets.

Why, she wuz brung up with 'em, as you may say.

She had sot under them old prophets ever sence she had sot at all.

And why shouldn't she went on about 'em and love 'em when she had fairly drinked in their weird, fascinatin' influence with her mother's milk?

She wuz a readin' about Daniel jest as I went in—about how Daniel stood by the deep waters and heard a voice sayin' to him:

"Understand."

And sez she, with her great, beautiful eyes all aglow, "Don't you think that we who stand by deep waters to-day can hear the voice if we listen?"

"Yes," sez I, "I believe it from the bottom of my heart; if we do as Daniel did, 'set our hearts to understand,' we can be kep' from perils as he wuz, and we can hear that Divine Voice a biddin' us to understand and to be strong."

Sez I, "I believe that Voice almost always comes to us in the supreme moments of our greatest need. When we have been mournin' as Daniel had, and 'eaten no pleasant bread,' and lay with our faces on the ground by the deep waters, then comes One to us, onseen by them about us, and touches our bowed heads and sez:

"'Beloved, fear not. Peace be unto thee. Be strong. Yea, be strong.'"

And then we went on and talked considerable, and she told me how her mother had read to her, as soon as she wuz able to understand anything, all about the prophets, and how she had always loved to think about 'em and their divine work.

And I told her I felt jest so; I thought they wuz likely old creeters, them and their wives too.

And Genieve looked up dretful startled and surprised, and said she had never thought about their wives, not at all.

And I sez, "Like enough, nobody duz. Nobody ever did think anything about old Miss Daniel, or Miss Zekiel, or any of 'em. Nobody ever thought of givin' the wimmen any credit, but they deserve it," sez I. "I believe they wuz likely old females, every one of 'em."

Genieve still looked dretful wonderin', and as if I had put a bran new idee into her head. As much as she had pondered and studied them prophets, she never had gin a thought to them good old females— faithful, hard-workin' creeters, I believe they wuz.

And she sez, sez she, "I never thought anything about them, whether they had any troubles or not."

"No," sez I, "I spoze not, but I believe they had 'em, and I believe they had a tuckerin' time on't more'n half the time.

"Why," sez I, "it stands to reason they had. While their husbands wuz a sallyin' out a prophesyin', somebody had to stay to home and work, split kindlin' wood, etc."

Genieve looked kinder shocked, and I sez warmly:

"Not but what I think a sight of them old prophets, sights of 'em. My soul burns within me, or almost burns, a thinkin' of them old men of whom the world wuz not worthy, who *had* to tell the secret things that the Lord had revealed to 'em to the ears of a blasphemin' and gainsayin' world. I jest about worship 'em when I think of their trials, their persecutions, their death for duty's sake.

"But while I honor them old men up to the very

highest pint honor can go in a human breast, still I have feelin's for their wives—I can't help feelin' sorry for them poor old creeters.

"Not a word do we hear about them, and it makes me feel bad to see my sect so overlooked and brought down to nort.

"And I'll bet (or would bet if it wuzn't for principle) that old Miss Daniel, and Miss Zekiel, and Miss Hosey, and Miss Maleky, and all the rest of them old female wimmen had a tough time on't.

"Why, if there wuzn't anything else to trouble 'em, it wuz enough to kill any woman to see the torment and persecutions that follered on after the man she loved. To see 'em wanderin' about in sheepskin and goatskin, and bein' afflicted, and destitute, and tormented.

"That wuz enough to break down any woman's happiness; but they had to buckle to and work head work most likely to take care of themselves and their children.

"'Destitute' means privation and starvation for old Miss Prophet and the children, as well as for the husband and father.

"And I'll bet that old Miss Hosey and Miss Maleky jest put to it and worked and made perfect slaves of themselves.

"And with all this work, and care, and privation on their minds and hearts, they couldn't have got such a dretful sight of sympathy and companionship out of their husbands, to say nuthin' of help and out-door chores.

"For though the old prophets wuz jest as likely as likely could be and did what wuz perfectly necessary and right, still while they wuz out in the streets a hollerin' ' Woe! woe! to this wicked city!' etc., etc., they couldn't at the same time be to home a talkin' affectionate to their pardners or a sawin'

"AND KILLED HER HENS."

wood. I'll bet old Miss Maleky picked up more than half she burned, and split pretty nigh all her own kindlin' wood, and killed her hens, and sot 'em, etc., etc.

"Them days seem a good ways off to us, and things seen through the misty, hazy atmosphere of so many years seem sort o' easy to us.

"But I don't spoze water would bile then without a fire no more than it would now. And I spoze the dishes, or whatever they kep' their vittles in then, had to be washed.

"And I spoze the goatskins and sheepskins that them good old men wandered round in had to be cleaned every now and then—it stands to reason they did. And I don't believe them prophets did it; no, I don't believe they had the time to, even if they thought on't.

"No; I dare presume to say that every time you found a prophet you would find some woman a takin' care on him, so he could have the freedom of mind and the absence of domestic cares necessary to keep his soul the calm medium through which divine truth could pour down upon a sinful world.

"The sieve must be held right end up or you can't sift through it; hold it sideways or bottom end up, and where be you?

"No; old Miss Hosey and Miss Maleky, I dare presume to say, jest wrastled round with household cares and left them old men as free as they could.

"I'll bet the minds of them good old prophets wuzn't opset with pickin' geese and ketchin' gobblers, or makin' hens set, or fastenin' down the tent stakes if the wind come up sudden in the night.

"No; I'll bet Miss Hosey, that good old creeter, got up herself and hung onto them flappin' ends and drove down the stakes herself, so's Mr. Hosey could get a little sleep. Or if little Isaac, or Lemuel, or Rebeckah Hosey wuz took sudden with the croup or infantum, I'll bet it wuzn't old Mr. Hosey that got up and hunted round for the goose oil, or groped his way round and started up a fire, and steeped catnip, and heat cloths, and applied 'em.

"No; it wuz that good old female creeter every time, I wouldn't be afraid to say it wuz.

"And ten to one if her pardner didn't wake up and ask her 'what she wuz makin' such a noise for in the middle of the night, and tell her she wuz jest spilin' them children a indulgin' 'em so, and if she had kep' their sandals on, they wouldn't have took cold,' etc., etc., etc.

"And then if she got into bed agin with cold feet he complained bitterly of that.

"And so, I dare presume to say Miss Hosey or Miss Maleky, as the case might be, sot up with them children, pulled one way by her devoted affection for 'em, and the other way by her wifely love, and tried to keep 'em as still as she could, and shet up them babies if they went to cry, for her husband's sake, and tried to doctor 'em up for their own sake, and felt meachin' through it all, borne down by the weight of her husband's onmerited blame and fault-findin'.

"And the next mornin', I dare presume to say, she went round with a headache, and got as good a breakfast as she could with what she had to do with; and if her husband waked up feelin' kind o' chirk and said a kind word to her, or kissed her, I dare say she forgot all her troubles and thought she had the best husband in the world, and she wouldn't change places with anybody on earth.

"For female human nater is about the same from Eve down to she that wuz Samantha Smith.

"And then I dare presume to say that as bad as she felt, and as much as she needed a nap, she jest helped him off on his prophesying trip, did everything she could for his comfort before he went, brushed his goatskin, and mebby cleaned it, and took care of the children till he come back, fed the camels, and watered the goats, and I dare presume to say got kicked by 'em, as bad as she felt.

"Made her butter—like as not she had a big churnin'—or a baggin' I don't know but it ort to be called—I spoze they used a bag instead of a churn.

"And then mebby she had lots of little young goats and camels to bring up by hand. I shouldn't wonder if she had a camel corset that took lots of care.

"And then mebby she had a lot of onexpected company come onto her—old Miss Aminidab and her daughter-in-law, and old Miss Jethro, and Miss Lemuel and her children, a perfect tent full, and she had to buckle to and get dinner for 'em, and mebby dinner and supper; and it would be jest like 'em to stay all night, the hull caboodle of 'em, and mebby she had to pound every mite of corn herself before she cooked for 'em.

"And she all the while with a splittin' headache, and her back a achin' as if it would break in two.

"And then jest as they got onto their camels and sot out home agin, then like as not old Mr. Hosey would come home all wore out and onstrung from

"ONEXPECTED COMPANY."

the persecutions he had had to contend with, and that good old female, as beat out as she wuz, would have to go to work to string him up agin, and soothe him, and encourage him to go on with his prophesyin' agin.

"But who thinks anything of these old female wimmen's labors and sufferin's? Nobody.

"Who thinks of their martyrdom, their efforts in the good cause, and the help they gin the old male prophets? Nobody, not one.

"I spoze the account of these things bein' writ down by males and translated by 'em makes a difference; it's sort o' naterel to stand up for your own sect.

"But folks ort to own up, male or female; and them old females ort to have justice done 'em.

"And though it is pretty late in the day—thousands of years have flown by, and the dust of the desert lays deep over their modest, unassumin' graves, where they have lain unnoticed and overlooked by everybody—

"But here is one in Jonesville that is goin' to brush away the thick dust that has drifted down over their memory, and tell my opinion of 'em.

"It is too late now to tell them old Miss Prophets what I think of 'em, thousands of years too late to chirk 'em up, and lighten their achin' hearts, and brighten their sad eyes by lettin' 'em know the deep sympathy and affection I feel for 'em.

"I can't make 'em hear my words, the dust lays too thick over their ears.

"But yet I am a goin' to say them words jest out of a love for justice.

"Justice has stood for ages with the bandage on tight over her eyes on one side, on the side of wimmen, and her scales held out, blind as a bat to what them old females done and suffered.

"But she has got a little corner lifted now on the side of wimmen; Justice is a beginnin' to peek out and notice that 'male and female created He them.'

"Bein' so blind, and believin' jest what wuz told her, Justice had got it into her head that it read:

"'Male created He them.'

"Justice never so much as hearn the name of wimmen mentioned, so we spoze.

"But she is a liftin' up her bandage and lookin' out; and it stands to reason she can weigh as well agin when she can see how the notches stand.

"Jest even, so I figger it out, jest even, men and wimmen, one weighin' jest as much as the other.

"If there are some ingregiencies in one of 'em that are a little better, that weigh a few ounces more, lo and behold! in the other one's nater and soul are a few ounces of different goodness that even it up, that weigh enough more to make it even.

"If Justice takes my advice—and I spoze mebby she will, knowin' I am a female that always wished her well, even in her blind days—if Justice takes my advice she won't put on her bandages agin, she will look out calm and keen and try to weigh things right by the notch, try to hold her steelyards stiddy.

"And no matter what is put into 'em—men, wimmen, colored folks or white ones—get the right weight to 'em, the hull caboodle of 'em, black or white, rich or poor, bond or free.

"She will get along as well agin, and take more comfort herself.

"It must have been a tejus job for her to be a standin' up there a weighin' things as blind as a bat."

But sez I, as I kinder come to myself, and glanced up at the little clock over the bureau:

"I am a eppisodin', a eppisodin' out loud, and to

a greater extent than I ort to, and it is bedtime," sez I.

Genieve looked sort o' bewildered and strange, and said "she had enjoyed my talk," and I dare presume to say she had, for she hain't one to lie.

But it wuz bedtime, and I went to my own peaceful room. My beloved pardner wuz fast asleep and a dreamin' most likely about the farm and Ury; and if he dreamed some about Philury, I didn't care, I hain't one of the jealous kind. And I knew his dreams would be perfectly moral and well-behaved ones anyway.

"MISERY."

## CHAPTER XV.

ABOUT five months after Rosy's marriage her old grandmother's "misery" become greater than she could endure, or ruther a sudden cold which she took proved fatal to her, and she took to her bed, and after a week's illness passed away.

She wuz stayin' with Rosy when she wuz took sick, and Maggie and I did everything we could do to relieve her wants and help her; but I see the first time I put my eyes on her face after her seizure that we could not help her—it wuz pneumonia; it carried her off after a few days of sufferin'.

The night before her death I went down to her cabin with a basket of jelly and broth and fruit, but she wuz beyond takin' any nourishment.

She wuz propped up on pillows, her black face in marked contrast to the snowy linen that Maggie had furnished for her bed.

Genieve, patient nurse, wuz settin' by her, her beautiful face wearin' its usual look of triumphant sorrow, joyful ignominy, or—I don't know as I can describe the look in words, but, anyway, she had the look she always had, different from anybody else's, more sorrowful, more riz up, more inspired.

The Book of books wuz in her hand; she had been readin' to her till she had fallen asleep.

At last Aunt Clo opened her eyes and looked up long and thoughtfully into the beautiful and pityin' face bent above her, and finally she said to Genieve:

"Honey, did you come down out'n de Belovéd City dat you read me about?"

"Oh, no, Aunt Clo. Don't you know me? I am Genieve, your old friend Genieve."

"I done thought I see a light round your forehead, honey. It seems like I *did* see de light; sure you hain't one of dem angels?"

"Oh, no, Aunt Clo; you know me, don't you?"

And Genieve lifted her head and gave her a spoonful of the hot broth I had brought.

She sunk back on the pillow, and after a minute said, with the old persistency that Aunt Dinah wuz wont to cling to any idee she had formed:

"It jess seems as if I did see de light a shinin' down out of your eyes, honey, into my ole heart."

A more peaceful look settled down upon the face that had been drawn and seamed with "the misery." And when she fell into her last sleep the same expression remained.

And I wondered if indeed Genieve's sweet soul did not by some magnetism of attraction draw down a band of bright spirits whose heavenly looks wuz

"WHEREFOAH, BREDREN, LET US PRAY."

reflected upon her own, and if indeed a glow from the heavens she tried to picture to the old black woman might not be reflected dimly into her poor old heart.

But we see through a glass darkly; we may not see clearly into the beauties and wonders of the Belovéd City.

Genieve stayed and rendered all the assistance she could.  She stayed as long as she wuz needed.

But as soon as the news got out that Aunt Clo wuz dead, a crowd of her relations, near and distant, come in and took possession of the cottage and begun preparations for an elaborate funeral.

A colored minister wuz sent for, and he preached a long sermon in which her virtues wuz held up as a pattern, and her sudden death as a warnin' for 'em all to be ready for " de Master's call, which might come in de night time, or in de heat and burden of de day, but wuz shuah to come.  Shuah, young, careless girl ; shuah, gay, happefyin' young man, for de trumpet must sound, and de dead must go at de bugle call of de Reapeh.

" He reaps de flowehs of de gahden," sez he, pintin' to the grave of Belle Fanchon, which wuz not fur from the cabin-door.

" He reaps de flowehs in all deir beauty, an' de ripe grain an' de wheat.  Dis wheat we lay in de grave to-day, knowin' dat de incorruption will rise up incorruptible, an' de glory will come up glorious, an' we shall all see it in de twinklin' of de eye—an' wherefoah, bredren, let us pray."

And he knelt down and offered up a prayer full of faith, and pathos, and the wise ignorance of his childlike race.

Rising up from his knees, he directed the mourners to pass in front of the coffin and view the remains, which they did with loud groanings and many tears and exclamations of grief.

Then the coffin wuz closed, and the minister stood up in front of it and sez :

"Christians, fall into line."

And the church-members silently fell into line two by two till they wuz all in their places.

Then he sez, "Sinners, fall into line."

And the irreligious came forward jest as calmly and took their places, and the procession moved off, and Aunt Clo wuz carried away to her last sleep, in a little colored graveyard some mile and a half away.

I told Josiah about it after I got home; I sez:

"The good and the bad always foller on after every departed friend; but I never see 'em sorted out so careful before, and I never see such a calm willingness to be put amongst the goats as I see there."

"Wall," sez he, "they knew they wuz goats, so what wuz the use of kickin'?"

"Wall," sez I, "I have seen white folks lots of times that must have known they wuz goats, but they didn't love to be sorted out on the left side, and no money could have made 'em walk up and fall into a sinner's line."

Sez he, "If they be sinners, why can't they own up to it? I would if I wuz a sinner."

But I felt that it wuz ofttimes hard work to tell the difference; and I sez:

"I am glad it hain't me that has to do the separatin' between the good and the bad, for I shouldn't know where to lay holt, appearances are so deceitful sometimes. Sheepskins are wore often over goats, and anon a sheep puts on the skin and horns of a goat to face the world in and fight with it. I shouldn't know where to begin or leggo."

"Wall, that is because you are a woman," sez Josiah. "Wimmen *never* know where or how to lay holt of any hard work or head work. I could do it in a minute, and any man could that wuz used to horned cattle."

I sithed and thought to myself the thought I had entertained more or less ever sence I stood up with Josiah Allen at the altar. How different, how different my pardner and I looked on some things, and how impossible it wuz seemingly for us to ever get the same view on 'em.

But I didn't multiply any more words with him, knowin' it wouldn't be of any use; and then agin, as I looked clost at him, I see a shade of serious pensiveness, and even sadness, as it were, a shadin' down onto his eyebrow.

And my talk didn't seem to lighten it any as I went on and told him that they said that this custom of dividin', as it were, the sheep and the goats wuz practised a good deal in different parts of the South.

But I still see the shadowy shade on his foretop, and went on more cheerful, and told him that the little boy Abe wuz goin' to be took into the family of the good colored preacher, so he wuz sure of a good home and good treatment.

But in vain wuz all my cheerful perambulations of conversation. I see that he looked demute, and broodin' over some idee; and finally he spoke out:

"Samantha, goin' to funerals, or hearin' about 'em, puts folks to thinkin'."

"Yes, it duz, Josiah;" and sez I, in quite a solemn axent, "it stands us all in hand to be prepared."

ABE.

Sez he, "I wuzn't thinkin' of that side of the subject, Samantha; but it brings back to me that old thought and fear that has been growin' on me for years more or less. Samantha," sez he, "I worry, and have worried for years, for fear that you will some time be left a relict with nuthin' to lean on."

I glanced up at him, and the thought come to me instinctively that it would be the ondoin' of us both if I should try to lean heavy on him now, for my weight is great, and he is small-boned, and I knew that he would crumple right down under the weight of 200 pounds heft.

But I didn't speak my thoughts—oh, no; I merely looked at him real affectionate, and I took up a sock I wuz mendin' for him (we wuz in our own room), and I attackted it as socks should be attackted if you lay out to make 'em good and sound. And he went on still more confidential and confidin', and told me several things he thought I had ort to do if I wuz ever left a relict of him.

It wuz real touchin', and I wuz considerable affected by it—not to tears—no; I thought I wouldn't shed any tears if I could help it, for darnin' is close work, and it calls for all the eyesight you have got; and then I had on a new gray lawn dress that I felt would spot easy; so I restrained my emotions with a almost marble composure, and anon I sez to him as he wuz a goin' on in that affectin' way, and sez I:

"I may be took first, Josiah Allen."

And he admitted that that might be the case, though he couldn't bear to think on't, he said, it gin him such awful feelin's.

He said he had never been able to think on't with any composure. But after a while he talked more diffuse on the subject, and owned up that he had thought on't; and sez he, in a still more confidin' and affectionate way:

"For years, Samantha, I have had it in my head what I would put on your tombstun if I should live to stand up under the hard, hard blow of havin' to rare one up over you.

"I have thought I should have it read as follers, and to wit, namely:

"'Here lies Samantha, wife of Deacon Josiah Allen, Esquire, of Jonesville. Deacon in the Methodist Church, salesman in the Jonesville cheese factory, and a man beloved and respected by every one who knows him but to love him, and names him but to praise.'

"Its endin' in poetry, Samantha, wuz jest what I knew wuz touchin', dumb touchin', and would be apt to please you; and it is always a man's aim to write the obituarys of his former deceased pardner in a way that would suit her and be pleasin' to her."

Sez I calmly, "Yes, I should know a man wrote that if I read it in the darkest night that ever rolled, and I wuz blindfolded."

"Wall," sez he anxiously, "don't it suit you? Don't you think it is uneek, sunthin' new and strikin'?"

"Oh, no," sez I, "no, it hain't nuthin' new at all; but mebby it is strikin'—or that is," sez I, "it depends on who is struck."

"Wall," sez he, "it is dumb discouragin', after a man racks his brains to try to get up sunthin' strong and beautiful, to think a woman can't be tickled and animated with it."

Sez I calmly, "I hain't said that I wuzn't suited with it." And sez I with still more severe axents, for I see he looked disappointed, "I will say further, Josiah, that it meets my expectations fully ; it is jest what I should expect a male pardner to write."

"Wall," sez he, lookin' pleaseder and more satisfieder, "I thought you would appreciate it after you thought it over for a spell."

"I do, Josiah," sez I, turnin' over the sock I wuz a mendin' and attacktin' a new weak spot in the heel, "I do appreciate it fully."

Josiah looked real tickled and sort o' proud, and I kep' on in calm axents and a darnin' too, for the hole wuz big, and night wuz a descendin' down onto us. And I could hear Aunt Mela's preparations for supper down below, and I wanted to get the sock done before I went down-stairs. So I sez, sez I :

"I have thought about it sometimes too, Josiah, and I have got it kinder fixed out in my mind what I would have on your tombstun—if I lived through it," sez I with a deep sithe.

"What wuz it?" sez he in a contented tone, for he knows I love him. "It is poetry, hain't it?"

"Yes," sez I calmly, "I laid out to end it with a verse of poetry ; it wuz to run as follers : 'Here lies Josiah Allen, husband of Samantha Allen, and—'"

"Hold on!" sez Josiah, gettin' right up and lookin' threatenin'. "Hold on right there where you be ; no such words as them is a goin' on my tombstun while I have a breath left in my body. Husband of— Josiah, husband of— I won't have no such truck as that, and I can tell you that I won't."

"Be calm, Josiah," sez I, "be calm and set down," for he looked so bad and voyalent that I feared apperplexy or some other fit. Sez I, "Be calm, or you will bring sunthin' onto yourself."

"I won't be calm, and I don't care what I bring on, and I tell you I ruther bring it on than not, a good deal ruther. The idee! Josiah Allen, husband of— It has got to a great pass if a man has got down to that—to be a husband of—"

"Why," sez I, lookin' up into his face stiddily, as he stood over me in a wild and threatenin' attitude —and some wimmen would have been skairt and showed it out; but I wuzn't. Good land! don't I know Josiah Allen, and through him the hull race of mankind? I knew he wouldn't hurt a hair of my foretop, but he would like to skair me out of the idee, that I knew.

But sez I in a reasonable axent, "You had got it all fixed out 'Samantha, wife of Josiah—'"

"Wall, that is the way!" sez he, hollerin' enough almost to crack my ear-pan—"that is the way every man has it on his pardner's headstun. Go through the hull land and see if it hain't; you can look on every stun."

Oh, how that "stun" rolled through my head! And sez I, "I am not deef, Josiah Allen, neither am I in Shackville, or Loontown, or the barn. Do you want to raise a panick in your son's household? Moderate your voice or you will harm your own insides. I know it is the way every man has wrote

"HE WUZ A WALKIN' UP AND DOWN."

it about their pardners, and it seemed so popular amongst men I thought I would try it."

"Wall, you won't try it on me!" he hollered as loud as ever. "You won't try it on me, and don't you undertake it. Why, ruther than to have them words rared up over me I would—I would ruther not die at all. 'Josiah Allen, husband of—' No, mom, you don't come no such game over me; you don't demean me down into a 'husband of—'!"

"Why," sez I, lookin' calmly into his face (for I see I must be calm), "don't you know how I have wrote my name for years and years, 'Josiah Allen's Wife'?"

"Wall, that wuz the way to write it; it wuz stylish," he yelled. Oh, how he yelled! Why, that "stylish" almost broke a hole through my ear-pan; the pan jest jarred, it wuz so voyalent.

Sez I, "Set down, Josiah, and less argue on it."

"I won't argue on it, it is too dumb foolish; I am goin' out to walk in the back garden before supper."

And he ketched down his hat and drawed it down over his ears enough to break 'em off if they hadn't been well sot on, and slammed the door so one of them panels is weak to this day—it wuz a little loose to start with.

And I went and stood in the winder with my hand over my eyes, and watched him all the while he wuz a walkin' up and down them walks, for I wuz most afraid he would totter and fall over, or mebby he would start off a bee-line for the crick and drown himself, he wuz so rousted up and agitated. And I hain't dasted to open my head sence on the subject—I don't dast to, not knowin' what it would bring onto him. At the table they noticed my pardner's excited and riz up mean—they couldn't help it.

And Maggie asked him " if he wuzn't feelin' well."

And I spoke right up, such is a female's devoted love for her companion—I spoke right up and sez:

" We have been a talkin' over funerals and such, and your Pa got agitated."

I spoze I told the truth—I spoze I did ; I didn't tell what the " such" wuz that he had been a talkin' about ; I don't know as 1 wuz obleeged to.

"THIS DARK EARTH VALLEY."

## CHAPTER XVI.

IT wuz dretful sudden, as we count suddenness. But then we don't know down here in this dark Earth Valley, with high mountains a towerin' up on each side on us that we can't see through—we can't really tell what to call the onexpected, or the expected.

I spoze if we wuz high enough up to see the light and beauty of the Divine Plan, we shouldn't call anything the onexpected.

But it seemed dretful sudden to us that Miss Seybert should be took down voyalent with a fever that wuz a prevailin' round Eden Centre, and should die off the second day after the attack.

And for all the world it would seem as if havin' waited on her through all time, and she laid out to go on a doin' it through all eternity, old Phyllis, Victor's mother, jest follered right on after her the next day.

Some say she took the disease a hangin' over her bed and a waitin' on her. .

But anyway, she passed away the very next day, and wuz buried right at the feet of her beloved "Miss Alice."

Col. Seybert wuz away on one of his annual wildcat excursions, so her wishes wuz carried out. And she had her old friend nigh her through the long sleep, jest as she always had had her durin' her fitful sleep for years. But they both slept well now, and wuzn't no more to be disturbed by drunken abuse nor mournful forebodings. No, they slept sound and sweet.

Victor mourned deep, deep for 'em both—it would be hard to tell which he mourned for most.

But after the first shock of his heart-felt grief had passed away, he felt that the last ties had been broke now that bound him to this land.

He felt that God had showed him more plain by this dispensation what He wanted him to do.

And as everything wuz ripe for the exodus, and he felt that he could not remain an hour under Col. Seybert's roof, now that the necessity for his remainin' had been removed, everything pointed to an immediate departure for Africa.

The party who wuz to go with him wuz all ready, eager, resolute, prepared, only waitin' for the word of their leader.

And he wuz ready to go. But first he must be married to the light of his eyes, the desire of his heart. And under the circumstances of the case we could not counsel any great delay.

And though, as I said, Victor wuz a mourner, and a deep mourner for his mother and sister mistress, still it wuz mebby partly for that reason that he wuz so happy in the thought of havin' a sweet wife and a sweet home of his own.

And it wuz a pretty sight to witness the love of Victor and Genieve. And though we all hated to lose her, we wuz happy in the thought of her happiness and her approachin' marriage.

As for me, though mebby I didn't say so much, I did the more. I wuz a knittin' some of the very finest linen edgin' out of number ninety thread to trim a hull suit of underclothes for her. And if any one would examine close the fineness of the thread, they could see the delicacy and tenderness of my feelin's for her, and the strength.

I had bought some of the very finest muslin I could get to make the garments of. So, as I say, if I didn't say so much, mebby I did the more, and acted.

Maggie and Thomas J. wuz goin' to get her a bedroom set in pretty light wood, and Maggie wuz embroiderin' some beautiful covers for the bureau, and washstand, and table.

It wuz a pattern of pink and pale blue mornin' glories on a sort of a cream-colored ground.

They wuz goin' to be lovely.

Little Snow wanted to do sunthin', and I told her she should.

So I, myself, cut her out some little linen napkins, and let her fringe out the edges, and I laid out to orniment 'em myself for her in cat stitch. Cat is a very handsome stitch.

And as I sez, we wuz all happy in witnessin' Genieve's happiness, which wuz glowin' and radiant, and Victor's calm, deep bliss. For he could not undo the past. And the Bible sez a man shall leave all and cleave to his wife. And he wuz only a followin' the Skripter.

He had been a good son, no better could be found —a good, faithful helper and friend to his mistress; and I felt that he could leave 'em in their peaceful graves and walk off into the Eden road of his happy love with no reflections, and with the desire of his heart.

Col. Seybert wuz ragin', as we knew, at the thought that his trusty servant wuz goin' to leave him. He wuz invaluable to him in so many ways. He had no other man in his employ so trustworthy; no one else who would take care of his business durin' the frequent intervals when he wuz incapable of it; no one else who wuz so honest, so reliable, so intelligent; for Victor wuz one who would do his duty, and do a good day's work, if he wuz workin' for Nero or the Old Harry himself, though you wouldn't ketch him a workin' for this last-named personage—no, indeed.

Col. Seybert raged over the idee of Victor's leavin' him; he had always ruled everything about him, bent everything to his wishes.

And now "this black dog," as he named Victor in his scornful wrath, had dared to defy him. And worse still, the very best and most intelligent of his hands, nearly all the younger ones, had been influenced by Victor's purpose and teachin's, and wuz makin' preparations to leave this sin-cursed South, that had held only misery and humiliation for them, and join him in his colony in Africa.

Col. Seybert knew, through his spy Burley, that

they wuz secretly and quietly makin' preparations to leave him and go to the New Republic—some of them to go with Victor and his party, some of them to go with the next party fitted out.

HIRAM WIGGINS'S TWO DAUGHTERS.

Deep in his heart and loudly to his chosen friends did Col. Seybert curse Victor—his long-sufferin' brother, as I would and did call him in my mind—I *would*.

Why, good land! if Victor had been translated to the court of some mighty kingdom and been proclaimed king, wouldn't Col. Seybert have claimed relationship with him pretty quick?

Yes, cupidity and ambition would have propped him up on both sides, and he would have proclaimed the fact through his brother's kingdom that he wuz brother to the king.

Wall, if he wuz his brother under one set of circumstances, I say he wuz under any other.

He wuz his half-brother; if every other evidence had failed to assure the relationship, the portrait of old Gen. Seybert down in the long drawin' room of Seybert Court would have proclaimed the fact to a gainsaying world. He wuz a fur truer son to Gen. Seybert than Reginald wuz. For by all the ties of congenial tastes, mind, and spirit, he wuz the courtly old Southerner's true son and heir.

Reginald had always been and always would be true son and heir of Hiram Wiggins, the manufacturin' tailor. Although as relationships go in this world, he wuz only his grandnephew.

But he had laid claim, and wuz the only possessor of all his crafty, cruel, brutal, aggressive nature, his low habits and tastes, his insolent, half bold, half meachin' manners.

Hiram Wiggins'es own children wuz two old maid daughters, so meek they could hardly say their souls wuz their own.

They worked samplers, copied from their mothers, and regulated their behavior on this model, which wuz a eminently Christian one, and did much good in a modest, unassumin' way with the wealth their father had heaped up. They wuz the children of their mother, and their cousin Reginald, true son of their father.

But I am a eppisodin', and to resoom.

Col. Seybert, like all men of his class, had some choice spirits that copied his manners and carried out his plans. And among them all who toadied to him and carried out his base plans, the foremost one wuz Nick Burley, as we have said prior and before this.

He hated Victor as much as Col. Seybert did. One of the causes of Burley's dislike was what feeds enmity so often in base natures—Victor wuz so superior to him that Burley wuz always oncomfortable in his presence.

To be with a young man who neither drank, swore, nor tore the characters of women to tatters, and boasted of great deeds in love and valor, wuz to Burley incomprehensible. What wuz mysterious must be wrong.

And then Victor evidently shunned the society of Burley, and avoided him whenever he could. And as Burley wuz a white man and Victor " a damned nigger," such a state of things wuz not to be borne.

Col. Seybert had, we may be sure, fanned the coals of hatred to a still greater heat, till at last they wuz at a white glow, and Nick Burley wuz ready to do any act that Col. Seybert recommended, anything for vengeance and " to show that cussed black dog not to feel above a gentleman and a white man."

And Col. Seybert and Burley had subtly played upon the ignorance and superstition of the lower black element about them, so they had come to look upon Victor as their enemy and the enemy of his people.

He who had all his life long sought only the good of his race, planned through long, wakeful nights for their advancement, and had labored early and late for an education, mainly for the reason that he could help them better—so ignorant wuz they that they could see nothin' of this, and looked at him through the hate-prejudiced eyes of his enemies.

His preachin' to his people to be patient under their wrongs and to return good for evil; his warnings to them aginst their habits of lawlessness, and laziness, and theft; his pleadings with them to turn in their evil ways and try to become decent citizens; his admonitions that their future lay in their own hands, and they could become, by the grace of God and by hard work and education, whatever they chose to be, had been mistaken by these more ignorant ones. And subtly wrought upon by Col. Seybert and Burley, they looked upon Victor as one who, while he taught them lessons of patience, and meekness, and unselfishness, wuz himself carryin' on a secret plan for their humiliation and his own personal wealth and ambition.

Victor knew something of this secret antagonism towards him from the lower black element and his revengeful white enemies, but he hardly knew how strong it wuz.

And so the mills of the gods wuz turnin' slowly but surely, and slavery, and oppression, and class hatred, and personal spite, and bitterness, and social contempt, and ignorance wuz gettin' ready to be ground out into the food whereby Vengeance and Horror should be sated.

Very quickly but very surely wuz the preparations goin' on for Victor's departure for the colony. Nearly all of them who wuz goin' with him had been able to get a little money ahead.

On an average, they had about five hundred dollars each.

Some had more than this, and wuz takin' out wife, or children, or parents, who had less; so that the actual amount each member of the colony would have would be about five hundred dollars.

Victor had planned that, with careful and prudent management in that warm climate, where no extra amount wuz needed for fuel or heavy clothin', where food of a certain kind could be obtained almost by pickin' it off the trees about them, where a very simple and cheap cabin would be all the shelter and protection they might need—

He thought that this money, in the hands of intelligent and prudent managers, would keep the colony fed and clothed, buy necessary tools and stock, and keep them in comfort till they could raise crops in their own home.

Father Gasperin, the good missionary who had labored all his life amongst the black people, wuz goin' with them, and he, havin' the love and confidence of them all, Victor had made chief adviser and treasurer of the company.

Father Gasperin had a good deal of influence with them high in authority (he had renounced a high name and estate to dwell amongst and labor for the poor and lowly). He had made all the necessary arrangements with parties in Africa, and the site of the location wuz already chosen.

When Cousin John Henry decided to cast in his lot with the colonists, Victor wuz overjoyed, for he felt that the good he would accomplish could hardly be estimated in teachin', and preachin', and helpin' the colony in every way.

Their future home wuz a beautiful valley lyin' between two low, heavily wooded mountain ranges, and a clear river runnin' through it to the sea.

A sheltered, lovely spot, but with pure air flowin' in from the east and the west along the course of the sparklin' river.

This river they looked to as bein' for the present

"A CLEAR RIVER RUNNING THROUGH."

their highway out to the nearest town, some twenty miles away.

And already in his mind Victor saw the white sails of their boats bearin' away the fruit of their hands to be exchanged for articles of necessity and comfort.

He could see the little wharf where these boats should come back laden with comforts for his people and news from the great world.

He imagined Genieve and himself standin' at the door of their tiny cottage, in the golden sunset or the golden dawn, lookin' down this sparklin' highway fringed with glistenin' palm-trees.

He could almost hear the song of the gayly hued birds as they called out to their mates in the glossy foliage overhead.

Here wuz home, here wuz peace, here wuz independence for a long-enslaved and tortured people.

Hard work he knew there must be, and perhaps hard fare for a time ; but the reward would be so sweet that it would sweeten toil. It would not be like the hopeless, onthanked-for, onrewarded drudgery for them who returned insults and curses for patient labor, and too often blows and stingin' lashes.

Felix and Hester wuz makin' all preparations to go with Victor. On him Victor counted as one who could be relied upon to help the weaker ones, to be a guide and an example of what the black man could do and be.

For Felix, so far as he knew, had not a drop of white blood in his veins, and he wuz faithful, honest, hard-workin' and intelligent.

Three times he had had his home broken up and his earnings stolen from him by this cursed, unslain spirit of slavery.

But he had agin, by his industry and frugality and by Hester's help, earned and laid by the sum Victor thought necessary for each colonist to possess, and he and Hester wuz ready to make another start in the New Republic.

He had decided not to build another home in the soil guarded by the American eagle.

He knew the fowl to be largely boasted about as bein' the first and noblest bird beneath the skies.

But he felt that he had been pecked by its too sharp bill, he had been clawed by its talons, he had been wearied by its loud, boastin', resonant voice.

No, he would make no more homes under the skies where that eagle built its nest.

He wuz ready for a newer republic.

He felt that he would ruther dare the soft embraces of the biggest African serpents than be enfolded about by our beneficent civilization.

He wuz embittered, that wuz a fact. But when we see what he had gone through, I don't know as anybody could blame him.

But anyway, he wuz ready to go.

And so the days rolled by one after another, as they always will, whether you are gay or sorrowful, whether the hours seem weighted down with lead or tipped with fleet sunbeams.

And to Genieve and Victor all sadness and shadows lay fur away like a faint cloud in the horizon, almost unseen and forgotten in the clear sunshine of their happiness. For true love will make happiness everywhere. Everything looked prosperous, and I had got my edgin' done, and Maggie and I had made the nice linen garments and ornimented 'em with the lace.

They looked beautiful.

Little Snow's work on the napkins wuz done, and the cat stitch almost completed—a few stitches only of the cat remained to do, then they would be done.

Maggie had completed her pretty embroidered covers, and they lay folded up on top of a pretty sashay-bag of sweet perfumery in the bureau-draws of the handsome chamber set, and that wuz all packed away in a strong box ready for the voyage.

The weddin' dress had come home all fini hed, even to the pretty lace in the neck and sleeves.

It wuz white mull, and I knew Genieve would look like a picture in it.

"EVERYTHING WUZ READY."

## CHAPTER XVII.

AT last the time come, as every time will come if you wait long enough for it—the time had come when the colony wuz to embark for their new home.

Victor and Genieve wuz to be married the mornin' they started, Cousin John Richard a performin' the ceremony in the parlor at Belle Fanchon, and Father Gasperin a layin' out to make a good prayer on the occasion.

And the evenin' before everything wuz ready.

In Genieve's room, acrost the white bed lay the simple grey travellin' dress and wrap she wuz a goin' to wear on her journey, with a little grey velvet turban by the side of it, and the heavy travellin' cloak she would most probable need on her long sea voyage.

The little grey gloves and the handkerchief and

the well-filled travellin' bag lay all ready to take up at a minute's notice, for we knew there wouldn't be any too much time in the mornin'.

The pretty plain white dress she wuz a goin' to wear to enter her new life in, and which would be a good dress for years, and handy where she wuz a goin', lay acrost two chairs, ready for her to put on the first thing in the mornin'.

Yes, everything wuz ready in Genieve's room. And in the kitchen, though I am fur, fur from bein' the one to speak on't (as I had done the most of the cookin'), wuz as good vittles as I ever see in my hull life.

Aunt Mela done well and done considerable; but I wanted Victor and Genieve and Cousin John Richard to have some of my own particular Jonesville cookin', and everything had turned out jest right.

Every cake had riz up in good form, ready for the icing; not one lop-sided or heavy cake wuz there in the hull collection.

And the roast fowls wuz jest the right brown, not a speck of scorch on one of 'em.

The jellys wuz firm and clear as so many moulds of rose and amber ice. And the posys had all been picked, and Maggie had arranged 'em in great crystal bowls and vases of sweetness and beauty.

The table wuz all sot. We thought we would arrange it the night before, when we had plenty of time, so it would suit us.

And we had got everything ready, and though I dare presume to say I ortn't to say it, it looked good enough to eat, vittles, table-cloth, posys, and all.

(Though it is fur from me to propose eatin' stun china and table-cloths; but I use this simely to let you know the exceedin' loveliness of the spectacle.)

Genieve went in to see it after it wuz all ready. We wouldn't let her do much, knowin' what a journey wuz ahead on her.

But when she went in to look at it she looked as if she wuz in a dream, a happy dream. And she wuz pleased with every single thing we had done for her. Snow, the dear little lamb, follered Genieve round tight to her all the time; she knew she wuz a goin' away from us, and she couldn't bear the thought; but we had tried to reason with her and tell her how happy Genieve wuz a goin' to be, and she, havin' such a deep mind, seemed to be middlin' reconciled.

Boy wuz of course too small to realize anything. And it wuz on Genieve's heart that the tug of partin' with him come hardest. She wanted him in her arms all the time, a most. And as happy as she wuz, I see more than one tear drop down on his little short brown curls and dimpled cheeks and on Snow's golden locks.

But I looked forward to the time when Genieve, sweet, tender heart, would hold a child of her own in her arms, and give it some of the love she lavished on everything round her.

Wall, as evenin' drew on and the mockin' birds begun singin' to their mates down under the magnolias, we see Victor's tall figure a comin' along the well-known path, and Genieve went out to meet him for the last time as a maiden.

The next time she went out to meet him it would

be as his wife. And I spoze they both thought of that with a sort of a sad rapture, for they both loved Belle Fanchon and the folks that lived there.

And they knew it would be on the soil of a strange land when she next sot out to meet him in the starry dusk of the evenin' shadows.

And the birds that would be a singin' over their heads would not be the mockin' birds of old Georgia. And different stars would be a shinin' down on 'em, and it would be in a new world.

I spoze they thought of all this, I spoze so, as they slowly wended their way up to the house in the soft glow of the semi-twilight amidst the odor and bloom of the blossomin' flowers, and the melancholy, sweet notes of the mockin' birds.

They come into the settin' room, and Victor sot down as usual and took Boy up in his arms—he loved the child.

Genieve went up into her room to tend to some last thing she wanted done, and we sot there in the settin' room, and visited for a spell back and forth.

Josiah and Cousin John Richard had walked down to the village, and Thomas Jefferson hadn't come home yet.

Genieve found a letter from Hester a layin' on her table, and she opened it and read it in the last faint rosy glow of the daylight. Hester and Felix wuz to meet them where they embarked. Hester's letter wuz full of joyful anticipation about the new home to which she wuz a goin'. Poor thing! bein' so tosted about and misused as she had been, it is no wonder.

She and Felix wuz lookin' forward with such delight and happiness towards the new home that their fervor thrilled Genieve's heart anew, and she sot there after she had read the letter and looked off into the rosy light of the sunset, and she dreamed a dream.

It wuz a still twilight. The flowers about her window stood sweet and motionless against the glowin' light.

The last golden rays come through the vine-wreathed casement and fell on the letter lyin' open in her lap, and as she sot there with her beautiful head leanin' back against the old carved chair-back, the shinin' rays seemed to move and get mixed with the shadows of the vine leaves.

They moved, they shone, they took form, and as she sot there Genieve saw—whether in the body or out of the body I cannot tell, God knoweth—but she saw her future home in the New Republic.

She saw a fair land lyin' under a clearer, softer sky, but it bent down on strange foliage—giant palm-trees cleaved the blue sky, and birds, like great crimson and golden blossoms, were flyin' back and forth in and out of the green, shinin' branches.

Crystal rivers wuz flowin' through that land, whose clear waves wuz dotted with the sails of a busy commerce.

She looked on these heavily freighted ships and see that the commanders and officers, as well as crews, wuz her own dark-skinned race.

By the side of these blue crystal highways for the Republic's wealth wuz flourishin' towns in which stood great manufactories and workshops for all useful and valuable purposes. She looked into these busy places, and she saw at the loom, and the forge, and the work-bench her own people, and also in the countin' rooms, and offices, and the superintendent's rooms—all wore the dark livery of the sun. And she saw that none wuz very rich and none wuz poor, for the work wuz co-operative, and all wuz paid livin' wages, and all owned a share, even if a small one, in these large undertakings; and she saw that none of the toilers looked haggard and overworked, for their hours of labor wuz short enough to give them all a chance for bodily rest and recreation.

She looked into the pulpits of the beautiful churches whose spires rose from the glitterin' foliage, and wuz scattered over this new land.

Colored men and colored wimmen stood in the pulpits and sot in the pews.

Large, noble universities and a multitude of public schools dotted the land of this New Republic; colored men and colored wimmen wuz presidents, professors, teachers. The old lessons learned by their ancestors with many a heartache in the Old World wuz bearin' its rich fruit in the new.

She saw great museums, lecture rooms, art galleries, all filled with the glowin' imagery of the race that tried to orniment and wreathe the chains of servitude with some pitiful blossoms of crude beauty; she beheld these gorgeous fancies trained into magnificent results. The walls wuz glowin' with beauty and bold magnificence that the tamer, colder-blooded races never dreamed of.

She entered the halls of song, free for all, rich or poor, and heard melodious sounds such as she had

"IN THE CHAIR OF THE RULER."

never dreamed of hearin' this side of heaven. And the musicians wuz all of her own music-lovin' race, and the melody almost seemed to have the secret of Paradise in it, so heavenly sweet it wuz.

All through this favored land out in the rich country wuz immense co-operative farms stocked with sleek herds, and worked with new and wonderful machinery invented by her own people.

And in the Capitol, in the chair of the ruler, sot one of her own race, wise and beneficent. And all the offices and chairs of State wuz filled by the colored people.

Over all the land wuz prosperity, over all the land wuz peace, for there wuz no conflictin' elements of diverse and alien races and interests mixed up in it; and purified by past sufferings, grown wise by the direct teachings of God, the rulers ruled wisely, the people listened gladly, and the teachings of the Christ who more than two thousand years before come upon earth wuz fulfilled to His chosen people, whom He had brought up out of the depths to show His glory to the heathens.

She saw—for her vision wuz ontrammelled by time or space—she saw the wise and kind influences of the Republic stretching out like the rays from a star into the darkest corners and deepest jungles of this great Eastern Hemisphere—she saw the light slowly dawning in these depths.

She saw missionaries ever goin' into these places from this New Republic with the Bible in their hands and its sweet wisdom in their lives, and then ever goin' back with some new recruits gathered from the lowest places, to be in time educated in all good things, and then sent back as missionaries to their own tribes.

And the sunlight lay lovingly on this land like the love of God long hidden under the cloud of His judgments, but now seeming the sweeter from what had gone before.

And from all these cozy homes in city and in country she heard the steady tread, tread of the children walkin' along to the music of the future, the future of accomplishment, of education, of promise. She saw them forever learnin' new things, the newer things that wuz forever displacin' the old—newer, grander, broader views and aims. For heaven and earth wuz drawin' nearer to each other, and the era of peace on earth, good-will to man had come.

Long did Genieve set there wrapped in the glory of what she saw—whether in the body or out of the body I do not know. God knoweth.

At last the voice of little Snow aroused her, and she took her up in her arms.

But the light remained in her face.

Little Snow come into our room in a few minutes, and she sez, " Genny took me up in her lap, and her face shined."

And I sez, " Like enough, darlin'. She is one of the Lord's anointed, anyway."

And Josiah sez—he had come back, and wuz a layin' on the lounge—" Probable the sun wuz a shinin' into her face."

And Snow sez, " The sun had gone down; it wasn't shinin' into her room."

" Wall," sez Josiah, " it wuz most probable the lamp."

"She hadn't lighted one," sez Snow.

"Wall, it wuz most probable sunthin'," sez Josiah.

And I sez, "I presume so."

And I felt that it wuz.

Wall, while this happy glow wuz still a shinin' in Genieve's eyes, Victor wuz a settin' down below. Genieve had gone across the garden to bid baby Tommy good-bye.

When I went down agin Victor wuz a settin' by the open window of the settin' room.

It wuz a lovely night, as I could see plain, for the big windows wuz wide open and the moon shone bright in the east, while yet the rosy glow had not faded out of the western sky.

I sot down with my knittin' work, and as I sot there a peacefully seamin' three and one on Josiah's sock, I see a little white bird come a flyin' along from towards the clump of roses and magnolias that riz up over little Belle Fanchon's grave.

It flew along most to the window, and settled down on a wavin' rose branch, and there it swung back and forth and sung a sweet sort of a invitin' song. And into its liquid notes seemed to be blent sunthin' sad and sort o' comfortin', and sunthin' high, and inspirin', and glad.

I thought I had seen and hearn most every kind of song bird sence I had been South; but thinkses I to myself, I don't believe I ever see a bird that looked exactly like that, or heard a song that wuz quite so sweet, so sad.

It sot there for all the world as if it wuz a waitin' for sunthin'.

I didn't say nuthin', but I couldn't help watchin' it I felt queer.

Bimeby Victor came up the steps and come in—he had been down on the lawn for a flower for Genieve—and bein' startled by him, I spoze, the bird flew up a little ways onto a branch that hung over the porch, and kep' on with that same plaintive, sweet song, and it had that same air as if it wuz a waitin', waitin' for somebody or sunthin'.

But pretty soon Maggie come in, and Victor begun to tell us how all his preparations wuz completed, and about his plans, and his hopes, etc., and I got all took up with 'em, and then I had to set my heel—or ruther Josiah's heel, and that takes up sights of mind and intellect to do it jest right.

And jest as I got it set, in come Snow, the precious darlin', with her youngest dolly in her arms.

She made me kiss it good-night. I didn't really want to, its face wuz pasty and bare in patches, but I done it, and got two kisses from Snow's sweet little lips to take the taste out of my mouth.

And as I had kissed the doll affectionate and accordin' to her wishes, she put up her little hand to my face in that sweet caress she always gin me when she wuz real satisfied and happy with what I had done, or when I felt bad about anything.

And as I bent my head for that lovin' and tender caress, oh, how joyful and clear that bird's song did sound through the twilight; it rung out as if whatever it wuz waitin' for had come nigh it, and its little lonesome heart wuz full of content and joy.

And after she left my side, Snow kissed her mamma and then went up to bid Victor good-night. She loved Victor, and he loved her dearly. And knowin' it would be the last time he would ever have the chance agin most likely, he felt agitated and sorry, and took the dear little creeter up in his arms, dolly and all.

As he did so I thought I heard the sound of steps in the garden, but I glanced out past Victor and couldn't hear anything more, only that plaintive bird song, low, and strange, and thrillin'.

And I kep' on with my work. But agin we all thought we heard steps, and we listened for a minute, but everything wuz still. But sunthin' drawed my eyes to look up at little Snow, and even as I looked a ball come crashin' through the window and went right through that baby's breast.

Victor sprung to his feet and sez:

"That wuz meant for me!"

And as he looked down on Snow he cried out:

"My God! has it killed the child?"

But he laid her down on the lounge right by him, and, bold as a lion, and as if to shield us all from further harm, he sprang out on the piazza and from there to the ground, and faced the gang of masked men we could see surroundin' him.

But we couldn't foller him with any of our thoughts; all of our hearts wuz centred on our little lamb.

She lay there white as death where Victor put her. She lay there still, with her big blue eyes lookin' up—up—and what did they see? Wuz the Form a bendin' over her? We thought so, from her face— such a look of content, and understandin', and comprehension of sunthin' that wuz beyend our poor knowledge.

For a minute she looked up with that rapt look on her face, and then she tried to lift her little white hand in that pretty gesture of greetin' somebody we couldn't see.

And then she slowly turned her look onto all of us, full of love—love and pity; and then she wuz gone from us; we had only the beautiful little body left.

We couldn't believe it; we wuz stunned and almost killed with the suddenness of it, the terribleness, the onheard-of agony and pity of it.

But it wuz so. When we had come to ourselves a little, and sent for the doctor, and worked over her, and wept over her till fur into the night, we had to believe it—dear little Snow had gone.

Victor, full of thought for Genieve, for us all, led the gang away under a clump of magnolias in a distant part of the grounds, nigh to the little tomb of Belle Fanchon.

They faced him, their faces full of brutal anger, and low envy, and all bad passions. Led on by the cruel lies and influence of Col. Seybert, and their own low distrust and dislike of superiority in one of their own class, their own besotted ideas of their personal freedom—

They told Victor they would give him a chance for life. Let him give up his ideas of colonization, let him give up his plans of enrichin' himself on the earnings of the poor, let him show he wuz one of his own people by goin' back to his work again to Col. Seybert's—they would give him this one chance.

"FACED THE GANG OF MASKED MEN."

Victor turned his deep, pitiful eyes on the imbruted forms before him, some black and some white, but all covered with the blackness of ignorance, and superstition, and causeless anger, and brutality—

And he sez to them, "My friends and brothers, I have only wanted to do you good. Heaven is my witness I have only sought out a better way for you. And I have been willing to spend my life and strength to help you. This country is no place for us."

"It wuz good nuff for our faders and muders, and, 'fore Gawd, it is good nuff for us," shouted out some one in the crowd.

"I have wanted to help you all—to help myself to a better way of living. The evils we have about us are not of our own making nor of this generation—they are old and heavy with sorrow and iniquity. This land is burdened, and cries out under this load of woe, and perplexity, and sin. I have tried the old way—we all have—we have been burdened more than we could bear in the old paths. I have only sought to lead my people out into a safer, broader place, where we could be free from some of the worst evils that beset us here, and where there is a chance for us to have a home and a country of our own."

"Curse you! shet up your jaw!" sung out one burly ruffian, in the thick tones of semi-intoxication. For Col. Seybert had not failed to prime up their courage with bad whiskey. "We have heard enough of your yawp! Will you give up your plans or not?"

"Never!" said Victor. "I will never give up this hope, this work while I live."

"Then you may die, curse you!" said one voice.

And another voice rose up in venomous, brutal tones:

"You have preached your damned sermons about patience, and forgiveness, and all that bosh, and you have been all the time a carryin' on your underhanded stealin', and featherin' your own nest out of the hard-earned wages of the black men. And they say," went on this voice, which wuz evidently the voice of a white man, "they say that you are a goin' to sell the hull crew you take over for slaves and line your own pockets with the blood-money of your brothers—you traitor you!"

Victor raised his arms mutely to the heavens as if to plead aginst the injustice of men.

And as his clasped hands wuz raised, a bullet struck that noble heart, and he fell, breathin' out that old prayer:

"Lord, lay not this sin to their charge."

"WHEN THE MOON HAD RISEN."

## CHAPTER XVIII.

HEN the moon had risen a little higher and its direct rays fell down through the glossy leaves onto that white, kingly face, another shadow fell on the green, blossomin' sward, and a pale face looked through the branches, and Genieve stood there by the dead form of the man she worshipped.

It wuz all over. She could do nothin'—wimmen seldom can in tragedys arisin' from grave political difficulties.

But there is one thing she can do—she is used to it—she can suffer. Genieve could throw herself down upon the silent, cold body of her lover, while like a confused dream the whole past rushed through her mind. Her glowing hopes cut short, her life's happiness all slain by the enemies of truth. She could lie there and try to think of the years between her and death. How could she live them?

As she lies there prone in her helpless and hopeless wretchedness, she is not a bad symbol of her race.

Heart-broken, agonized through the ages, helpless to avenge her wrongs, too hopeless and heart-broken to attempt it if she could.

Her life ruin brought about by the foolishness of preachin' what is wrong.

The happiness or the wretchedness of one colored woman is of too little account to make it a factor in the settlement of grave political affairs.

The tragedy in the magnolia shadows is nothin' unusual; such things must occur in such environment—statesmen expect it.

And after all, they may reason, it is only the takin' off of one of the surplus inhabitants. Indeed, some contend that the speedy extinction of all newly made citizens, colored, and troublesome, either South or West, is the surest and safest solution of the vexed problem.

And this is only one the less of an inferior race.

And yet as he lays there, his wide-open eyes look up into the bending heaven as if demanding justice and pity from Him who left thrones and divine glory to dwell with the poor and despised, who wept with them over their dead, and who is now gone into the heavens to plead their cause aginst their oppressors.

As he lays there his face is wet with tears of a very human anguish.

Somehow this easy answer is not workin' well in this case.

And up in the mansion house grief wails for the eternal losses caused by this same blunder.

There are the innocent sufferin' for the guilty. The old puzzle unfoldin' itself anew—of the close links bindin' human brotherhood. And how the rough breakin' of one link is hazardous to all the golden rings of the chain that binds humanity together.

Poor Josiah Allen! the doctrine he preached so long—that if you let an evil alone it will do you no harm—wuz all broke down and crushed to pieces. Poor old man! mournin' over the sweet bud that too ontimely perished in its first bloom.

Poor man! poor, broken-hearted old Grandpa—with the silver voice that used to make a music of that name stilled forever.

How can any pen, no matter how touched with flame from the altar, how can it picture that night? Maggie layin' like death, passin' from one faintin' fit into another.

Thomas Jefferson, poor, poor boy, lookin' up into my face with dumb pleadin' for the comfort he could not find there.

No, I couldn't comfort him at that time, for what wuz I a thinkin' of, in the impatience of my agony, the onreasonableness of my bewildered, rebellious pain?

I said in them first hours, and I turned my face away from the light as I said it, "Darkness and despair is over the hull world. Snow is dead!"

And I thought to myself bitterly, what if the South duz rise up out of its dark dreams into a glorious awakenin', a peaceful, prosperous future—what of it? Our darlin', the light of our eyes, has gone forever. What can any sunshine do, no matter how bright, only to pour down vainly upon the sweet blue eyes that will never open again? And fur in the East a grand republic may rise holdin' in its newer life the completed knowledge of the older civilizations. But Snow is dead!

Yes, I sez to myself, as did another, "If they want a new song for their Africa free, let none look to me," I sez, "my old heart cannot raise to anthems of joy and glory."

No; my heart is bendin' over a little cold form. Between the sun-bright glory of that new and free land stands a little tender form with a bleedin' stain on its bosom.

Or is it beckonin'? Was it the glow from them shinin' curls that lightened the eastern sky? Duz she speak in the pathos and beauty of our hearts' desire for a race's freedom? Dear little soul, so pitiful of all sufferin', duz she help them who loved her to be patient with ignorance, and intolerance, squalor, and power? Patient with all and every form of error and woe?

She lays under a flowery mound in the summer grounds of Belle Fanchon, close to the grave of the other little sleeper that slept so long there alone. The rivulet wraps its warm, lovin' arms close about both little graves.

Near by, just across the valley, reposes the form of Victor the king. Victor over ignorance, over wickedness, victor over his enemies, for he died blessin' them. How else could he get the victory over his murderers?

Ah! the flowers from these graves risin' up together, will they not sweeten and purify the soil that nourishes them—subtle perfume risin' out of the black soil and darkness, sweet and priceless aroma risin' to the heavens?

Upon the ancient altars the ripe fruit wuz laid, and the flowers.

God knows best! Oh, achin' heart, where the silken head rested, and which will be empty and achin' forevermore; oh, streamin' eyes, tear-blinded and anguished, that will never again see the sweetest form, the loveliest face that earth ever held, what can they say but this—God knows best!

And they can think through the long days and nights of hopelessness and emptiness, that her sweet, prophetic eyes have found the Realities made visible to her onknown to the coarser minds about her.

The Form that bent over her cradle and whispered to her has taken her now to a close and guardin' embrace.

Wuz it some fair, sweet messenger, some gentle angel guide, or wuz there in the hands held out to her the mark of the nails?

The glow that lit up her shinin' hair from some radiant realm onbeknown to us wraps her round in its pure radiance.

Little Snow has gone into the Belovéd City; but alas for the hearts that strive to follow her and cannot!

But her sweet little body is a layin' close by the side of the little girl who went to sleep there thirty years ago.

Over her is a small headstone bearin' this inscription: "Little Snow," and under it are the only words that can give any comfort when they are cut in the marble over a child's grave : " He carries the lambs in His bosom."

And so as the years go on the leaves and blossoms will rustle in the soft mornin' breeze over the two little girls sleepin' in peace side by side in the old garden.

I wonder if they have found each other up in the other garden that our faith looks up to—if they have made garlands of the sweet flowers that have no earthly taint on 'em and don't fade away, and crowned each other's pretty heads. I wonder if they ever lean over the battlements of Heaven and drop any of them sweet posies on the bare, hard pathways their friends that they left below have to walk in.

Mebby so ; mebby, when in our hard, toilsome day marches, a hint of some strange brightness and glory touches our poor tired spirits, when some strange comfort and warmth seem to come sudden and sweet onto us, comin' from we know not where —mebby, who knows, but it is from the glowin' warmth and beauty of them sweet invisible flowers that we cannot see, but yet are a lyin' in our pathway, droppin' on our poor tired heads and hearts.

I don't know as it *is* so, and then, agin, I don't know as it hain't so.

"EXILED BIRDS."

## CHAPTER XIX.

WHEN a long flight of exiled birds stand ready to leave the South land for their old home again, whence they fled before the stormy blasts—

As they are drawn up in a line, high in the mornin' sky waitin' for the leader's signal to raise their wings and strike out northward through the pathless fields of blue—

If some cruel shot strikes down that gallant leader, the hull flock is bewildered and full of panic and distress for a time.

But a new leader takes his place, and the solid phalanx rises up and takes wing for their old home, which is again to them the new.

The flight goes on just the same, and perhaps no one but his mate feels the loneliness and emptiness of the clear blue sky.

Though mebby, if she is so blesséd, she may feel the waftin' of shadow wings beside her, and a nearer presence than the livin'.

Felix took the place of leader in the enterprise, and though it wuz delayed for a little time, it went on to success. Though the great heart that planned it lay silent in death.

Perhaps Genieve felt that his influence wuz still guidin' her, that he wuz helpin' the colony still; that bowin' down in the presence of the Crucified, he brought gifts of surer success to his people than he could if he wuz still with them in the mortal body.

Felix wuz a favorite with the company, and though he had not Victor's genius nor the native gifts of prudence and foresight that he had possessed, his long apprenticeship to sorrow and peril had made him wise and patient.

He wuz helped, too, greatly by the calm fortitude and Christian principle of Cousin John Richard and the fervid devotion of Father Gasperin.

There wuz a rumor that the Government wuz bein' importuned by one in high authority, and wuz only waitin' to learn the success of this venture, to send Government vessels over with the freedmen, with help to maintain the poorer ones for a year and get them started in their new life. But it might have been only a rumor. As I said, Victor's death made a delay in the exodus, and it wuz durin' those weeks of delay that Genieve received a large packet of law letters.

Her father had died in France, and Genieve had been left his heiress. A goodly sum had been left to this lawyer if he wuz successful in findin' his child. Perhaps by reason of this the search had proved successful.

Genieve wuz a great heiress, for Monseur De Chasseny had no children by his French marriage—his lawful wife wuz dead. And the memory of the great love of his life wuz with him to the last. In a will made on his death-bed, he left all his large fortune to Genieve, "the child of the only woman he had ever loved."

So said a letter left in the same package with the will.

This wealth enabled her to do much for the colony, helpin' them to good schools, good books, good food and clothin', and the teachin' and the trainin' that would make them self-supportin'.

Genieve studied harder than ever, worked harder than ever for the good of her people, after the livin' Victor passed from her life. The immortal Victor, the saint, the hero Victor, always stood beside her. He would not let her sink into the gloom and inactivity of hopeless sorrow. He nerved her to new activities. He held her hand that wrote stirrin' appeals, and helpful, encouragin' words for the New Republic. He inspired the vision that saw it risin' fair and proud from the ashes of a dead past.

She studied history that she might help make a noble history for the new land; she studied law, and literature, and music, all with this sole ambition of helpin' her mother's race.

The children of the colony almost idolized her, and in their love and constant companionship she found her greatest earthly comfort.

She taught them all that she learned herself, taught them with the present love of all her lovin' heart, and with the fur-seein' eye of one who sees in this new generation the future blessing and regeneration of her people.

And above all other lessons she taught them the Bible with the childlike faith of one who sits at the feet of the Christ.

She studied it and taught it with the rapt vision and earnestness of a prophet who saw that the best future of her beloved New Land rested upon the victories of the bloodless armies of the cross.

She had the faith that Paul had when he gave utterance to these incomparable words, and she saw through faith that her race should "subdue kingdoms, work righteousness, stop the mouth of lions, out of weakness be made strong."

Her people needed her; she wuz in no hurry to lay down her life-work. She wuz willin' to stay in the vineyard and work as long as the Master willed.

But she felt that when the starry nightfall come and the workers wuz dismissed, the rest would be sweet. And oh! how wistfully she looked forward to that land that lay beyond the New Republic, where she should receive " her dead raised to life again." When on the threshold of the new life Victor would meet her and lead her forward to Him that wuz slain. Where she would dwell with him forever in that continuin' city which by faith she saw while yet in the body.

VICTOR.

## CHAPTER XX.

THE relation on Maggie's side is dead. Some said of heart failure, others said of a broken heart caused by disappointed ambition.

Yes, somebody else got higher than he wuz, and he fit too hard. Goin' round electioneerin', makin' speeches by night, travellin' by day, pullin' wires here and pullin' wires there, bamboozlin' this man, hirin' that man, bribin' the other man, and talkin', talkin', talkin' to every one on 'em. Climbin' hard every minute to get up the high mount of his ambition, slippin' back agin anon, or oftener, and mad and bitter all the time to see his hated rival a gettin' nearer the prize than he wuz.

No wonder his heart failed. I should have thought it would.

So little Raymond Fairfax Coleman wuz left a orphan. And in his father's will, made jest after that visit to my son Thomas Jefferson, he left directions that Raymond should live with his Cousin Maggie and her husband till he wuz old enough to be sent to college, and Thomas J. wuz to be his gardeen, with a big, handsome salary for takin' care of him.

There wuzn't nuthin' little and clost about the relation on Maggie's side, and as near as I could make out from what I hearn he kep' his promise to me. And I respected him for that and for some other things about him. And we all loved little Raymond; and though he mourned his Pa, that child had a happier home than he ever had, in my opinion.

And I believe he will grow up a good, noble man—mebby in answer to the prayers of sweet Kate Fairfax, his pretty young mother.

She wuz a Christian, I have been told, in full communion with the Episcopal Church. And though the ministers in that meetin' house wear longer clothes than ourn duz, and fur lighter colored ones, and though they chant considerable and get up and down more'n I see any need of, specially when I am stiff with rheumatiz, still I believe they are a religious sect, and I respect 'em.

Wall, little Raymond looked like a different creeter before he had been with us a month. We made him stay out-doors all we could; he had a little garden of his own that he took care of, and Thomas J. got him a little pony. And he cantered out on't every pleasant day, sometimes with Boy in front of him—he thinks his eyes of Boy. And before long his little pale cheeks begun to fill out and grow rosy, and his dull eyes to have some light in 'em.

"MAKIN' SPEECHES."

He is used well, there hain't a doubt of that. And he and Babe are the greatest friends that ever wuz. They are jest the same age—born the same day. Hain't it queer? And they are both very handsome and smart. They are a good deal alike anyway; the same good dispositions, and their two little tastes seem to be congenial.

And Josiah sez I look ahead! But, good land! I don't. It hain't no such thing! The *idee!* when they are both of 'em under eight.

But they like to be together, and I am willin' they should; they are both on 'em as good as gold.

And on Babe's next birthday, which comes in September, I am goin' to get, or ruther have my companion get her a little pony jest like Raymond's. I have got my plans laid deep to extort the money out of him. Good vittles is some of the plan, but more added to it.

I shall *get* the pony, or ruther it will be *got*. And if them two blessed little creeters can take comfort a ridin' round the presinks of Jonesville on their own two little ponys, they are goin' to take it.

Life is short, and if you don't begin early to take some comfort you won't take much.

But to resoom. The relation on Maggie's side has passed away, but the relation on Josiah's side is still in this world, if it can be called bein' in this world when your heart and spirit are a soarin' up to the land that lays beyond.

But I guess it would be called bein' in this world, sence his labor is a bein' spent here, and his hull time and strength all ready to be gin to them who are in need.

He is doin' a blessed good work in Victor, for so their colony is named, after the noble hero who laid down his life for it.

And the place is prosperin' beyond any tellin'. All that Genieve dreamed about it is a comin' true.

And she is a helpin' it on; she spends her money like water for the best good of her people.

She didn't raise no stun monument to Victor; no, the monument she raised up to his memory wuz built up in the grateful hearts of his people.

Upon them, his greatest care and thought when here, she spends all her life and her wealth.

She felt that she would ruther and he would ruther she would carve in these livin' lives the words Love and Duty than to dig out stun flowers on a monument.

And she felt that if she wuz enabled to cleanse these poor souls so the rays of a divine life could stream down into 'em, it wuz more comfort to her than all the colors that wuz ever made in stained glass.

She might have done what so many do—and they have a right to do it, there hain't a mite of harm in it, and the law bears 'em out—

She might have had lofty memorial winders wrought out of stained glass, with gorgeous designs representin' Moses leadin' his brethren through the Red Sea, or our Saviour helpin' sinners to better lives—

And white glass angels a bendin' down over red glass mourners, and rays of glass light a brightenin' and warmin' glass children below 'em.

There hain't a mite of harm in this; and if it is a

comfort to mourners, Genieve hadn't no objection, and I hain't. And the more beauty there is, natural or boughten, the better it is for this sad old world anyway.

But for her part, Genieve felt that she had ruther spend the wealth of her love and her help upon them that suffered for it.

Upon little children, who, though mebby they didn't shine so much as the glass ones did, but who

FATHER GASPERIN.

wuz human, and sorrowful, and needy. Little hearts that knew how to ache, and to aspire; innocent, ignorant souls whose destiny lay to a great extent in the ones about 'em; little blunderin' footsteps that she could help step heavenward.

By the side of the plain but large and comfortable church in the colony there wuz a low white cross bearin' Victor's name.

But within the church, in the hundreds of souls

who met there to worship God, his name and influence wuz carved in deeper lines than any that wuz ever carved in stun.

It wuz engraved deep in the aspirin' lives of them who come here to be taught, and then went out to teach the savage tribes about them.

Many, many learned to live, helped by his memory and his influence; many learned how to die, helped by his memory and his example.

Good Father Gasperin, who went with the colony, has passed away. He preached the word in season and out of season. And his death wuz only like the steppin' out of the vestibule of a church into the warm and lighted radiance of the interior.

He knew whom he had believed. He had seen the good seed he had sown spring up an hundred fold, and ripenin' to the harvest, that sown agin and agin might yield blessed sheaves to the Lord of the harvest.

And when the summons come he wuz glad to lay down his prunin' knife and his sickle and rest.

The same sunset that gilds the mound under which he sleeps looks down upon a low cottage not very fur away.

It stands under the droopin', graceful boughs of a group of palm-trees that rise about it, its low bamboo walls shinin' out from the dark green screen of leaves.

An open veranda runs round it half shaded with gorgeous creepin' vines glowin' and odorous, more beautiful than our colder climate ever saw.

Inside it is simple but neat. The bare floors have a few rugs spread upon them, a few pictures are on

"FELIX, HIS WIFE AND LITTLE NED."

the walls. A round table stands spread in a small dinin' room, with a snowy cloth woven of the flax of old Georgia upon it.

Round the table are grouped Felix, his wife and little Ned. In a cradle near by lies a baby boy born in the New Republic; his name is Victor, and he is the pet of Genieve, whose cottage, much like this, stands not fur away.

Through the open lattice Felix sits and looks out upon his fields. It is a small farm, but it yields him a bountiful support.

He and Hester have all they want to eat, drink, and wear, and their children are bein' educated, and they are *free*.

The vision that Genieve saw in the sunset light at Belle Fanchon has not fully come yet, but it is comin', it is comin' fast. Little Victor may see it.

Genieve and Felix and Hester write to us often, and specially to Thomas Jefferson, who has been able to help the colony in many ways, and wuz glad to do it.

For Thomas Jefferson, poor boy, though I say it that mebby shouldn't, grows better and better every day; but then I hain't the only one that sez it. He found poured out into his achin' heart the baptism of anguish that in such naters as hisen is changed into a fountain of love and helpfulness towards the world.

His poor, big, achin' heart longed to help other fathers and mothers from feelin' the arrow that rankled in his own.

His bright wit become sanctified into more divine uses. His fur-seein' eyes tried to solve the problems of sad lives, and found many a answer in peace and blessedness for others that reflected back into his own.

More and more every day did the memory of little Snow, so heart-breakin' at first, become a benediction to him, and a inspiration to a godlier livin'. He could not entertain a wilful sin in the depths of the heart where he felt them pure, soul-searchin' eyes wuz lookin' now.

He couldn't turn his back onto the Belovéd City, where he felt that she wuz waitin' for him. No, he would make himself worthy of bein' the father of an angel. He must make his life helpful to all who needed help.

And to them that she felt so pitiful towards, most of all the dark lives full of sin and pain, he must help to light up and sweeten by all means in his power. And Maggie felt jest like him, only less intenser and more mejum, as her nater wuz.

Thomas Jefferson and Maggie jined the Methodist meetin' house on probation, the very summer after little Snow left them.

And, what wuz fur better, they entered into such a sweet, helpful Christian life that they are blessin's and inspirations to everybody that looks on and sees 'em.

To Raymond and Robbie they give the wisest and tenderest care. The poor all over Jonesville, and out as fur as Loontown and Shackville, bless their names.

And at Belle Fanchon, where they always lay out to spend their winters, their comin' is hailed as the comin' of the spring sun is by the waitin' earth.

The errin' ones, them from whom the robes of Pharisees are drawed away, and at whom noses are upturned, these find in my boy Thomas Jefferson and his wife true helpers and friends. They find somebody that meets 'em on their own ground—not a reachin' down a finger to 'em from a steeple or a platform, but a standin' on the ground with 'em, a reachin' out their hands in brotherly and sisterly helpfulness, pity, and affection.

Dear little Snow, do you see it? As the tears of gratitude moisten your Pa's and Ma's hands, do you bend down and see it all? Is it your sweet little voice that whispers to 'em to do thus and so? Blessed baby, I sometimes think it is.

Mebby you turn away from all the ineffable glories that surround the pathway of the ransomed throng, to hover near the sad old earth you dwelt in once and the hearts that held you nearer than their own lives. Mebby it is so; I can't help thinkin' it is sometimes.

I said that the relation on Josiah's side is still in the world, and I believe it, because we had a letter from him no longer ago than last night. I got it jest before sundown, and after Josiah handed it to me he went to the barn to onharness—he had been to Jonesville.

I sot out on the stoop under the clear, soft twilight sky of June, and the last red rays of the sinkin' sun lay on the letter like a benediction. And under that golden and rosy light I read these words:

"My dear Cousin: Here in this distant land, where my last days will be spent, my human heart yearns over my far-off kindred.

"And I send you this greeting and memorial to testify that the Lord has been gracious to me. He has permitted me to see the desire of my heart. He has blessed my failing vision with the blessed light of this Land of Promise.

"I SOT OUT ON THE STOOP."

"I sit here as I write on the banks of a clear river that runs towards the South land.

"My little cabin stands on its banks, and I sit literally under my own vine and fig-tree, and I can say of my home as the prophet of old said of a fair city: 'It is planted in a pleasant place.'

"As my eyes grow dim to earthly things I catch

more vividly the meaning of immortal things hidden from me in my more eager and impetuous days.

"I am now willing to abide God's will.

"I see, in looking back to those old days, that I was impatient, trying to mould humanity according to my poor crude conception.

"I am now willing to wait God's will.

"I see it plainly working out the great problem which vexed me so sorely.

"How slowly, how surely has this plan been unfolding, even in those long days of slavery, when the eager and impetuous ones distrusted God's mercy and scouted at His wisdom.

"But how else was it possible to have taken these ignorant ones from the jungles of Africa and made of them teachers and missionaries of Christianity and civilization to their own people?

"How else could the story of Christ's life and Christ's sufferings and risen glory have been so clearly revealed to them as when they were passing through deep waters and coming up out of great tribulations?

"Out of the wrath of men He made his will known. While they suffered they learned the fellowship of suffering as they could not by any tongue of missionary or teacher.

"While they were in bonds they learned something of the patience and long suffering of Him who endured.

"While the war was raging on each side of them and they passed unharmed out through the Red Sea, while the contending hosts fell about them on every side, they learned of the strength of the Lord, the sureness of His protecting care.

"While they were encamped in the dark wilderness between the house of bondage and the Promised Land, they learned to wait on the Lord.

"And in that long waiting they brightened up the sword of wisdom and the spirit so they could vanquish the hosts of ignorance surrounding the land from whence they were taken in their black ignorance, and to which they returned rejoicing, ready to work for Him who had redeemed them.

"I look into the future and I see the hosts of ignorance, and superstition, and idolatry falling before the peaceful warfare of these soldiers of the cross.

"I see the idols of superstition and bestial ignorance falling and the white cross lifted up and shedding its pure, awakening light over the hordes of savage men and savage women brought in, washed and made clean, to the marriage supper of the Lord.

"As for myself, I truly care not how long I may wait my Master's call  For whatever pathway I may tread, in this world or the other, I know that He that is risen will go before me ; so I fear not the way by land, however long, nor the swelling of Jordan.

"And either in the body or out of the body, God knoweth best. I shall see the fulfilment of His promises, I shall see the working out of His plan as it draws nearer and nearer to its perfect fulfilment."

I dropped the hands that held that letter into my lap, and sot there in silence.

The sun had gone down, but the west wuz a glowin' sea of pale golden light, and above it a large clear star shone like a soul lookin' down into this world, a soul that had got above its troubles and perplexities, but yet one that took a near and dear interest in the old world yet.

Fur off, away over the peaceful green fields, I could hear the cow-bells a tinklin' and a soundin' low and sweet, as the herds wended their way home through the starry dusk.

Everything wuz quiet and serene.

And as I sot there my heart sort o' waked up, and memories heavenly sweet, heavenly sad, come to thrill my soul as they must always do while I stay here below, till my day of pilgrimage is over.

But as I sot there with tears on my cheeks and a smile on my lips—for I wuzn't onhappy, not at all, though the tears wuz in my eyes through thinkin' of such a number of things—all at once a light low breeze swept up gently from the south or down from the glowin' heavens—anyway it come—and swept lovingly and kind o' lingeringly, as if with some old lovin' memory, over the posies in the door-yard, and sort o' waved the sweet bells of the mornin' glories, and fell on my forehead and cheek like a soft, consolin' little hand.

It sort o' stayed there and caressed me, and brushed my hair back, and then touched my cheek, and then—wuz gone.

www.ingramcontent.com/pod-product-compliance
Lightning Source LLC
Chambersburg PA
CBHW032023220426
43664CB00006B/348